611058

D1338470

WITHDRAWN FROM LIBRARY STOCK

Maritime Transport Security

COMPARATIVE PERSPECTIVES ON TRANSPORTATION SECURITY

Series Editors: Joseph S. Szyliowicz, *University of Denver, USA* and Luca Zamparini, *University of Salento, Italy*

Focus on security has dramatically sharpened at all levels of government following the terrorist attacks experienced in several regions of the world in the last decade. Improvement in transport security now represents one of the key topics on the agendas of counter terrorist agencies worldwide. The Comparative Perspectives on Transportation Security series provides a much-needed platform for international and comparative analysis of transport security policies and practices. Looking at different modes of transport in turn, each book in the series offers a comprehensive and multi-disciplinary analysis of security issues for a particular transport mode, incorporating case studies of several key countries.

Maritime Transport Security

Issues, Challenges and National Policies

Edited by

Khalid Bichou

Imperial College London, UK

Joseph S. Szyliowicz

University of Denver, USA

Luca Zamparini

University of Salento, Italy

COMPARATIVE PERSPECTIVES ON TRANSPORTATION SECURITY

Edward Elgar

Cheltenham, UK • Northampton, MA, USA

© Khalid Bichou, Joseph S. Szyliowicz and Luca Zamparini 2013

All rights reserved. No part of this publication may be reproduced, stored in a retrieval system or transmitted in any form or by any means, electronic, mechanical or photocopying, recording, or otherwise without the prior permission of the publisher.

Published by
Edward Elgar Publishing Limited
The Lypiatts
15 Lansdown Road
Cheltenham
Glos GL50 2JA
UK

Edward Elgar Publishing, Inc.
William Pratt House
9 Dewey Court
Northampton
Massachusetts 01060
USA

A catalogue record for this book
is available from the British Library

Library of Congress Control Number: 2013949819

This book is available electronically in the ElgarOnline.com Social and Political Science Subject Collection, E-ISBN 978 1 78195 497 3

ISBN 978 1 78195 496 6

Typeset by Servis Filmsetting Ltd, Stockport, Cheshire
Printed and bound in Great Britain by T.J. International Ltd, Padstow

Contents

Contributors

Khalid Bichou, Imperial College London, UK

Mary R. Brooks, Dalhousie University, Canada

Shakeel B. Burthoo-Barah, Mauritius Ports Authority and University of Mauritius, Mauritius

Alec D. Coutroubis, University of Greenwich, UK

Girish Gujar, Hong Kong Polytechnic University, Hong Kong

Nazery Khalid, Malaysia Maritime Institute, Malaysia

George Kiourktsoglou, University of Greenwich, UK

David Menachof, Hull University, UK

Sigurd Neubauer, Independent Editor and Security Specialist

Adolf K. Y. Ng, University of Manitoba, Canada

Frank Ojadi, Lagos Business School, Nigeria

Verena Tandrayen-Raghoobur, University of Mauritius, Mauritius

Mark Rowbotham, Port Cullis and Liverpool John Moores University, UK

Joseph S. Szyliowicz, University of Denver, USA

Risto Talas, Hull University, UK

Hong Yan, Hong Kong Polytechnic University, Hong Kong

Zaili Yang, Liverpool John Moores University, UK

Luca Zamparini, University of Salento, Italy

Preface

The last decade has witnessed an increasing worldwide concern for security-related issues. Terrorist and piracy attacks hitting several regions of the world have raised the interest towards security in a dramatic way at all levels of government (local, national and international). The improvement of security in transport represents one of the key topics in the agendas of counter terrorist agencies worldwide. Moreover, the policy concern with transportation security has been matched by researchers in various disciplines (among them economics, law, engineering, political science) who have analysed security systems and devices and the transport networks to propose viable alternatives to strengthen the security procedures. This book aims to discuss key issues in maritime security and provide a comparative analysis of maritime security policies and practices in several key countries.

Part I provides a general introduction on the policy, regulatory, risk and economic frameworks for maritime security.

Part II provides a series of country case studies related to several geographic regions (North America, Europe, Asia, Africa and Small Islands Developing States). In order to ensure that meaningful comparisons can be made and relevant lessons drawn accurately, a structure for the chapters related to all country studies have been provided to all contributors along the following lines:

> Discussion of the structure and functioning of the maritime security system should consider its evolution, organization and relation to the national security structure. This section should include a discussion of the various domestic and external factors that have influenced its organization and functioning. Relevant domestic factors include the role of security related events in the country of reference as well as the impact of cultural, political and economic factors. Relevant external factors include external events, the role of international organizations, rules and regulations and the policies and actions of other states. The goal of this section is to identify how maritime security issues are defined, agendas established, decisions made, policy formulated and resources allocated. The strengths and weaknesses of this structure and its functioning should also be identified. The second element involves a description and analysis of the policy outputs. Here the focus is on the policies that have been adopted in regards to port security, container security etc. Contributors should discuss the content and substance and how it has evolved. Equally important is the analysis

of the effectiveness and shortcomings of the measures that have been adopted over time and the gaps that remain.

The last chapter of the book is explicitly comparative in orientation. It analytically compares the policies introduced and discussed in the previous chapters as well as the structures and constraints.

1. Introduction

Khalid Bichou, Joseph S. Szyliowicz and Luca Zamparini

The security of maritime transport and ports has long been a concern to governments, traders and industry, especially at times of wars and crises. However, it was not until the hijacking of the cruise ship *Achille Lauro* in 1985 that the international shipping community formally recognized maritime security as an issue for inclusion in the international legal and regulatory frameworks that govern shipping and port operations. Until then, maritime security essentially involved state actions against piracy, an activity with a long and often romanticized history, and traditional naval warfare though the issue of maritime safety that had emerged as a matter of international concern.

The first Safety of Life at Sea Convention (SOLAS) was adopted in 1914 following the sinking of the *RMS Titanic* in April 1912 on her maiden voyage to New York and was modified on various occasions. With the establishment of the United Nations in 1948, it became possible to achieve a long-standing goal, the creation of an international organization devoted to ensuring maritime safety and the International Maritime Organization (IMO) convention was finally ratified in 1958, ten years after its formal establishment. Various international rules and regulations were subsequently adopted in order to enhance the safety of ships and their crews.

The issue of maritime security, however, did not receive the same level of attention because the *Achille Lauro* incident did not mark the beginning of a series of sustained attacks against ships, perhaps because the terrorists' favourite target remained aviation. Only in 2000 was a suicide boat attack launched, and though this one failed, a similar technique was successfully used against the *USS Cole* later that year.

The events and aftermaths of the terrorist attacks of 9/11 marked an important turning point. Though the number of actual attacks against maritime transport had been limited, the potential threat was readily recognized so that maritime security, which had not featured at the forefront of the agenda of market players nor of that of policy makers, began to receive increased attention. They not only implemented a series of new policy, regulatory and operational measures targeted at the security of maritime transport, ports and the wider supply chain operations but these measures also triggered a fundamental shift in the perception and definition of security risks and fostered the addition of further dimensions to maritime and port security.

The USA, for obvious reasons, has taken the lead in the effort to ensure the security of the global supply chain. It adopted the Maritime Transport Security Act (MTSA) in 2002 and other security measures, most notably the Container Security Initiative (CSI), the Customs-Trade Partnership against Terrorism (C-TPAT) and the 24-hour advance vessel manifest rule, commonly known as the '24-hour rule'. Many other countries primarily in the Western hemisphere have followed the US lead and introduced a wide range of maritime security regulations that often adapted or incorporated US security provisions.

Globally, the International Ship and Port Facility Security (ISPS) code, a set of security measures and procedures that were drafted and developed by the IMO, entered into force on 1 July 2004. Since then, the ISPS code has been the most important global maritime security initiative, with its impacts affecting the international shipping and port community and beyond. Other global initiatives have also been adopted including the World Customs Organization (WCO) SAFE programme and the IMO/ International Labour Organization (ILO) code of practice on security in ports. Parallel initiatives have been introduced at regional levels, for instance, the European Community (EC) Regulation 725/2004 on enhancing ship and port facility security, the Association of South East Asian Nations (ASEAN)/Japan Maritime Transport Security and the Secure Trade in the Asia Pacific Economic Cooperation (APEC) Region (STAR). Elsewhere, a number of industry-led and voluntary programmes have been introduced to strengthen and streamline maritime and supply chain security. Examples include but are not limited to the Smart and Secure Trade-lanes (SST) and the ISO/PAS 28000: 2005 standard (specification for security management systems for the supply chain).

The growing concern with maritime security and the implementation of such a plethora of programmes and policies designed to safeguard ports and shipping has, not surprisingly, been accompanied by a rapidly growing body of scholarly and policy work. Much of the literature has focused on the prescriptive details of the measures being put in place, the computation of their costs of compliance and their *ex ante* economic evaluation, and the analysis of their scope and impacts either on location-specific or industry-specific operations. Other researchers have addressed risk aspects of maritime security including the threats and vulnerabilities and the systems and procedures for ensuring security resilience, mitigation and recovery. Nevertheless, the global scope and wider impacts of maritime security still remain under-researched and fragmented and only a very limited number of comparative analyses have been carried out.

Moreover, since the attack on the *MS Limburg* in 2002 very few terrorist incidents have involved the maritime sector. The most notable was the Abu Sayaf Group's bombing of a ferry in the Philippines in 2004 that killed 116 persons. Thus, since the years following the introduction and adoption of the ISPS code and the numerous policy measures implemented by individual countries have been marked by the absence of a major terrorism-led security accidents in international shipping and ports, the danger of complacency is very real and questions can readily be raised concerning the wisdom, especially since most countries often confront financial difficulties, of continuing to spend billions of dollars on securing this sector. Many researchers and practitioners may well share this perspective and be of the view that since the current policy and regulatory framework of maritime security has proved its fitness of purpose and robustness against maritime security threats and vulnerabilities, it is appropriate to reduce such expenditures.

In this book, we aim to challenge several assertions, normally used as justifications for the scope and the shape of the current body of research on the subject, that maritime security has now achieved maturity in both theory and practice and thus attention should be drawn to other or new areas of research. Consequently, the chapters highlight the prevalent issues and challenges of maritime transport security and examine their policy frameworks and applications within and across national, regional and global contexts. We consider the likelihood and consequences of a successful attack since there is general agreement that terrorist organizations, especially Al-Qaeda, have developed the capability to wreak havoc with the global economy as well as consider techniques for developing more effective and efficient policies and the ways in which different nations have defined and attempted to deal with the many issues subsumed under the general label of maritime security.

1.1 THE STRUCTURE OF THE BOOK AND ITS CONTENT

The book is divided into two parts, the first identifies critical themes, issues and frameworks related to maritime security. The second part presents analyses of how countries in several regions of the world (North America, Europe, Africa, Middle East and Asia) are dealing with issues

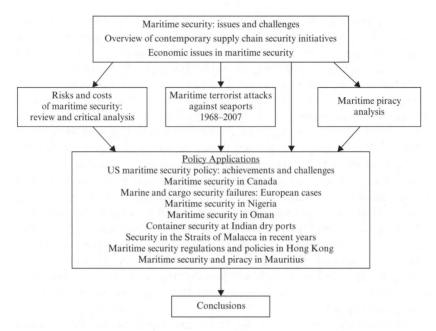

Figure 1.1   Structure of the book

of maritime security and thus providing data to draw generalizations concerning the nature and dimensions of maritime security, best practices, unresolved issues and areas for further research.

Figure 1.1 displays the structure of the book. Chapters 2, 3, and 4 ('Maritime security: issues and challenges', 'Overview of contemporary supply chain security initiatives' and 'Economic issues in maritime security') provide a preliminary analysis of the main themes of the book.

This introductory analysis is complemented by the discussions developed in Chapters 5, 6 and 7 of three major issues, the risks and costs of maritime security, the degree to which seaports have presented attractive targets and the problems posed by maritime piracy.

Chapter 2, 'Maritime security: issues and challenges' by Joseph Szyliowicz and Luca Zamparini, provides a general overview of the main issues that have had a determinant impact on maritime security in the last decades. It first considers the ways in which technological developments have impacted security through increased globalization, the development of container-based transport, the increasing destructiveness of weapons available to terrorists and the elimination of physical distance. It then discusses how piracy has evolved from crime organizations mainly oriented to obtain the highest possible ransoms to syndicates who use the financial resources obtained through ransoms as founding sources for large-scale criminal activities, sometimes in collaboration with other criminal and ideological groups. It then considers ports as the most relevant targets for terrorist actions related to the maritime sector. These are difficult to secure because of their physical layouts and the need for coordinated interactions by numerous public and private agencies and actors. Lastly, the chapter considers the efforts that have been made by the USA and the key international organizations to safeguard ports and global trade routes.

In Chapter 3, 'Overview of contemporary supply chain security initiatives', Khalid Bichou and Risto Talas discuss the main initiatives that have been related to supply chain security. These can be divided into the following categories: (1) mandatory; (2) voluntary; (2a) voluntary location-specific; and (2b) voluntary business-specific. The first set (mandatory initiatives) includes the IMO ISPS code, whose objective is to establish an international framework for cooperation among governments, agencies, local administrations and port and shipping industries, and by the 24-hour rule, which obliges sea carriers to provide US customs with a detailed description of the containers bound for the USA. The second set (voluntary supply chain security initiatives) is constituted of the efforts by the Business Alliance for Secure Commerce to reduce the risks of legitimate cargo used by illegal organizations for narcotics trade, cargo theft and contaminated cargo, by the CSI, which addresses the threat to border security and global trade by attempts to minimize the potential for terrorist use of a maritime container to deliver a weapon, by the European Union Authorized Economic Operator, which grants customs simplifications to reliable traders, and by the WCO framework of security standards to secure and facilitate global trade. The most important voluntary location-specific supply chain security initiative is the C-TPAT, whose core principle is to strengthen and improve overall supply chain and US border security by incorporating sound security practices and procedures into existing logistical activities. The Partners in Protection initiative also enlists the cooperation of private industry in the effort to enhance border security, combat organized crime and terrorism, increase awareness of customs compliance issues and help detect and prevent contraband smuggling. The StairSec initiative, originated by Swedish customs, is based on higher inspection rates of uncertified cargo in order to increase early warning and prevention. Lastly, the Secure Export Partnership is designed to protect cargo against tampering, sabotage, smuggling of terrorists or terrorist-related goods. The last section of the chapter deals with the Technology Asset Protection Association, a voluntary business-specific initiative related to emerging threats to the technology industry and high-tech businesses.

Chapter 4, 'Economic issues in maritime transport security' by Luca Zamparini, provides an overview of the main economic issues that are related to maritime transport security, highlighting the possible trade-offs and synergies. It first considers the economic costs of an attack to a port by surveying three studies that focused on Los Angeles and Long Beach ports, ports which play an important role in global trade. The chapter then takes into account the economic costs of another aspect of maritime security, piracy. These are divided into nine different components (ransoms, military operations, security equipments and guards, re-routing, increased speed, cost to labour, prosecutions and imprisonment, insurance and counter piracy organizations). The enormous costs of terrorist acts and piracy highlight the need for security regulations whose costs and benefits are analysed in the last section of the chapter, which concludes by presenting a general framework, based on marginal costs and benefits, that can be used to assess the worth of security plans at country and international levels.

The kinds of risk assessment and management models that have been developed and that are applicable to maritime and port security and their adequacy is discussed by Khalid Bichou in Chapter 5, 'Risks and costs of maritime security: review and critical analysis'. He first considers safety risk-based models and discusses the limitations in extending these models to security issues given the difficulty of estimating the probability of malicious acts. He then considers a layered approach to security systems that emphasizes the interconnections among three channels (logistics, trade and supply) and three flows (payment, information and physical). The interplay between supply chain security and supply chain risk is then discussed, with the importance of considering network-related vulnerabilities highlighted. Lastly, the author proposes an economic evaluation of the maritime security regulations contained in the ISPS code.

Risto Talas and David Menachof in Chapter 6, 'Maritime terrorist attacks against seaports 1968–2007' utilize the RAND Database of Worldwide Terrorism Incidents (http://www.rand.org/nsrd/projects/terrorism-incidents.html) in order to validate the hypothesis that these attacks have followed a Poisson distribution. The chapter first proposes a review of several alternative definitions of port security risk and merges them into a new one that considers the probability of an attack, the vulnerability of the target and the financial consequences of the terrorist act. The analysis of the database leads the authors to identify a series of recurrent patterns that are then used to quantify the risks and, consequently, to estimate a reasonable insurance premium against terrorist acts.

In the last chapter in Part I, 'Maritime piracy analysis', George Kiourktsoglou and Alec Coutroubis focus on this important aspect of maritime security. They begin by considering how piracy is currently defined. They then evaluate the business models of pirates, which they find to vary on a geographical basis (West Africa, East Africa, Caribbean/Latin America and South East Asia). The authors then focus on the current counter piracy policies and stress the importance of such key factors as intelligence and information (especially with respect to the Djibouti code of conduct, the satellite automated information system and unmanned underwater vehicles), of reporting and of operational responses on land. They note that the activities and interests of the major groups of stakeholders (national governments, supranational organizations and business firms) are tightly interwoven and, hence, that cooperation and coordination are essential prerequisites to tackle piracy in an effective way.

Essentially, these chapters provide the general framework for Part II, which consists of analyses of how a number of countries selected in order to reflect a variety of approaches are defining and dealing with issues of maritime security.

This part of the book opens with an analysis of the policies implemented by a key actor in efforts to enhance global maritime security, the USA. In Chapter 8, 'US maritime security policy: achievements and challenges', Joseph Szyliowicz discusses the limits on maritime security policies created by the fact that international organizations cannot impose effective policies upon nation states and by the continuing focus on single modes of transportation while international trade is inherently multimodal. In this context, the chapter considers the policies that the USA has adopted to counter the challenges posed by ports and by containers, discussing their strengths and weaknesses. The chapter concludes by discussing the challenges that the USA confronts in policies towards maritime security including the problems that arise when attempting to coordinate policy with foreign countries possessing unique cultural, political, social, economic and environmental attributes.

In Chapter 9, 'Maritime security in Canada', Mary Brooks deals with another North American country. She reviews recent Canadian maritime regulations and comments on the fact that, until recently, security was not mentioned in legislative Acts. She then stresses the importance of trade with the USA as one of the main driving forces that has led Canada to consider security issues in a different way. A description of recent regulations of marine and port security in Canada is then provided along with a discussion of the maritime security function. Lastly, the chapter evaluates the current maritime security activities in Canada, stressing that integrated security arrangements have made considerable progress, although the sheer size of the US Department of Homeland Security (DHS) creates major difficulties in coordinating and implementing policy.

Chapter 10, 'Maritime and cargo security failures: European cases' by Mark Rowbotham, shifts the attention to Europe and critically discusses the ISPS code and the Entry Summary Declaration (ENS) system and the way in which they are used by the European Union to maximize the degree of cargo security. Moreover, the chapter presents and discusses the most relevant security-related episodes in Europe. A particular emphasis is placed on the *Hyundai Fortune* case in 2006, the *MSC Napoli* and the container feeder vessel *Annabella* in 2007, the *Husky Racer* episode in 2009 and the *Genoa-Voltri* container that developed between 2010 and 2011. The chapter concludes by proposing some recommendations on the basis of the analysed cases.

The very different issues and challenges faced by an African nation are discussed by Frank Ojadi in Chapter 11, 'Maritime security in Nigeria'. He begins by outlining the political structure and the policy-making organizations of the country and then provides a historical profile of the maritime security institutions. The first was the Nigerian Maritime Department, created by the British in 1914, which evolved into the Nigerian Ports Authority, the Inland Waterways Department and the Naval Defence Force in 1955. Maritime security problems faced by Nigeria are discussed, highlighting the most important one connected with energy (oil) security in the Gulf of Guinea, requiring country-level but, above all, regional initiatives. The lack of regional coordination appears to be the most relevant issue limiting maritime security in the area. Lastly, funding issues are considered as well as the strategies pursued by the Nigerian government in this sector.

Another area where maritime security poses a complex challenge is the region around the Arabian Sea. This is clearly explained in Chapter 12, 'Maritime security in Oman' by Sigurd Neubauer. The chapter first describes how Oman has pursued a policy of independent internationalism and then concentrates on the sea threats faced by Oman, especially Somali piracy and the tensions between the international community and Iran. It notes that maritime security is a national priority that is managed by the Royal Oman Navy, the coast guard and the Royal Air Force. Large efforts are devoted to international cooperation and bilateral and multilateral security exercises with various countries. Oman's strategy to use diplomacy to mitigate the tensions in the Hormuz Strait and its port security practices and anti-terrorism procedures are also discussed.

We then turn to the Asian continent. Chapter 13, 'Container security at Indian dry ports' by Girish Gujar and Hong Yan discusses container security initiatives and instruments at global and country levels. It discusses Indian dry ports as key hubs in the global trading system and classifies them with respect to size, primary mode of connectivity to gateway sea ports and distance from sea ports. The chapter then considers three possible types of security failures. The least damaging involves the non-matching of containerized cargo to that declared in the manifest by quantity/value. The intermediate one is related to the fact that the entire container does not match what was declared. The most dangerous type is related to undeclared dangerous goods transported with a criminal or terrorist intent. An analysis of the occurrence of these problems indicates that the majority of events are related to the first type of security failure. The chapter concludes by analysing the possible tools that can be used to minimize security failures.

Another type of maritime security is discussed by Nazery Khalid in Chapter 14, 'Security in the Straits of Malacca in recent years'. The chapter begins by noting the importance of the Straits as a 'choke point' and discusses the important improvements with regards to piracy since the declaration of the Straits of Malacca as a war risk area by the Joint War Committee of Lloyd's Market Association in 2005 and the related increase in insurance risk premiums for ship transiting the area. This led to protests by Malaysia, Singapore and Indonesia. However, security initiatives were put in place that have resulted in a drop in the number of piracy events since 2009. The chapter describes how these countries have handled an actual maritime security alert and concludes by discussing the relationships between piracy and terrorism.

The last chapter dealing with a port on the Asian continent, 'Maritime security regulations and policies in Hong Kong: a critical review and the development of a risk-based security assessment model' by Adolf Ng and Zaili Yang, considers the maritime regulations and policies issued by the Hong Kong maritime department and their actual implementation. The chapter emphasizes the efforts to involve all important stakeholders in an advisory committee and in a working group. The chapter describes the strengths (that is, compliance with international regulations and guidelines) and weaknesses (that is, rather ambiguous implementation of the security assessment process). A risk-based model for port security assessment and management on the basis of the earlier analysis is proposed that could be a basis for decisions and procedures in maritime security.

The final chapter in Part II deals with the maritime security issues that small island nations confront. In Chapter 16, 'Maritime security and piracy in Mauritius', Shakeel B. Burthoo-Barah and Verena Tandrayen-Raghoobur note that Mauritius and similar states have to sometimes deal with a geographical challenge – they have to patrol maritime areas that are thousand times bigger than the island itself. After presenting an overview of Mauritius's economy and the role of the maritime sector therein, the way in which maritime security is organized and deployed are considered

– by complying with international regulations, by enacting idiosyncratic policies and by collaborating with international organizations in order to tackle the piracy threat.

The last chapter in the book carries out a comparative analysis of the case studies and draws general conclusions regarding the state of maritime security in both practice and theory. It seeks to integrate the diverse country studies by analytically comparing the security policies that have been adopted, their achievements and the issues that remain. It concludes with a discussion of best practices and proposing possible future directions of research.

PART I

Themes and frameworks

2. Maritime security: issues and challenges

Joseph S. Szyliowicz and Luca Zamparini

2.1 INTRODUCTION

The concept of maritime security has changed dramatically over the years. For centuries it was limited to the ability of a state to project naval power to protect its interests, usually during times of inter-state conflict with occasional forays against pirates and smugglers. In recent decades, however, maritime security has expanded to encompass a new threat – terrorism – as well as enhanced traditional threats such as smuggling and piracy. Thus, maritime security now involves the protection of a state's land and maritime territory and assets from all potentially harmful acts that can emanate from the seas. These may be the outcome of illegal fishing, people smuggling, illicit trafficking in drugs and weapons, piracy, terrorism and intentional and unlawful environmental damage. The damage caused by such acts may not only be economic but also environmental and/or societal (implying the loss of several or many lives). And, modern terrorists and pirates have at their disposal deadlier weapons than ever before.[1]

The present chapter aims to provide a general overview of the main phenomena that have had a momentous impact on maritime security in the last decades. Section 2.2 discusses the various facets of the relationships between technology and security; the increased globalization, container-based transport, destructiveness and (social and physical) distance. In Section 2.3 an analysis of piracy, in its various forms, is developed. Moreover, the impact of a terrorist attack on a port as a main hub of international trade is discussed. Section 2.4 introduces the main policies that have been adopted by the United States and by international organizations such as the International Maritime Organization (IMO) and the World Customs Organization (WCO) to tackle the security of ports and container transport. Section 2.5 concludes.

2.2 TECHNOLOGY AND SECURITY

Nowadays, the impact and the scale of maritime security have drastically changed (increased). This is mainly due to several factors that are, to different extents, rooted in the advancements of technology; globalization, container-based transport, destructiveness and (social and physical) distance. Globalization and security are intertwined in various respects. On the one hand, the last decades have witnessed the emergence and consolidation of global supply chains. This process has been fostered by the new and uprising information and communications technologies and by the establishment of hub and spoke maritime transport activities. Significant investments in infrastructure facilities have allowed several ports (that is, Singapore, Hong Kong, Rotterdam, Antwerp, Los Angeles, to name a few) to become the main hubs of international maritime transport. In 2006, this modality moved 70 percent by value and 90 percent by volume of traded goods (Rodrigue, 2010). Apart from the above-mentioned hubs, the maritime network is made up of about 4700 ports (World Port Source) that serve an estimated 35,000 large ships carrying cargo valued at $7.4 billion ('Ship,' Wikipedia). The network being international, the terrorist acts perpetrated locally in one of the main hubs can cause major disruptions that severely impact on the global economy. The consequences of these events may be catastrophic, ranging from a sharp rise in the price of energy and other goods due to a temporary or prolonged shortage of supply and the worsening of social and economic conditions in some countries that suffer from lack of food and medical products. Moreover, terrorist attacks can determine major environmental disasters in cases in which the attacks are directed towards heavily loaded oil tankers.

Another factor that has drastically changed maritime transport and has had an important impact on the security requirements is the container technology. Invented in the second half of the 1950s, it was soon recognized as a very valuable device to minimize the cost and time of terminal operations and the rate of damage to the transported goods. A further thrust to the adoption of the container technology has been given by the definition of specific dimensions by the International Organization for Standardization. The impact of containers on the world economy has been momentous. The decreased shipping and logistics costs have probably been the main reason for the setting up of the above-mentioned supply chains and of leaner and more efficient warehousing procedures. Moreover, new ports specializing in this specific form of maritime transport have emerged (for example, Gioia Tauro in Italy) and the productive processes have been outsourced to take advantage of heterogeneous labor costs in the various regions of the world. Manufacturing activities are thus no longer close to docks. Between 1990 and 2008, the number of twenty-foot equivalent unit (TEU) containers climbed from 28.7 million to 152 million, accounting for a large percentage of total world cargo (Rodrigue, 2010). These move by sea through an integrated and international system that involves many actors, each making its own decisions for a specific part of the supply chain. However, containers can also represent a security threat for maritime transport given that dirty bombs, explosives, radioactive materials or weapons of mass destruction (WMD) may be hidden inside and shipped to a port where they may then be detonated. A recent example in this respect is represented by the discovery of a highly radioactive container at the Voltri Terminal of the port of Genoa in 2010. This container was supposed to carry 18 tons of copper for an Italian customer. It was exported through the Red Sea port of Jeddah and trans-shipped via Gioia Tauro to Genoa. The container had first been isolated by using other containers filled with stones and water. Subsequently, several alternative ways to deal with this dangerous container have been considered. The container was handled by a specially designed robot that ascertained the presence of Cobalt 60 inside it. This situation generated remarkable distress among the citizens that lived in the vicinity of the port and who urged for the removal of this container from the area. The entire operation was successfully performed during 2011 (after the container had been stored for almost one entire year at the Voltri port for a total cost of €800,000[2]).

In order to minimize the risks connected to container-based trade, countermeasures have been studied and proposed in the last decades. The Container Security Initiative (CSI) was launched in 2002 by the US Bureau of Customs and Border Protection (CBP) in order to try and minimize the probability that a container may be used to smuggle WMD to the United States. As stated by the CBP, the core elements of CSI are the use of intelligence and automated advance targeting information to identify and target containers that pose a risk for terrorism and the pre-screening of those containers that pose a risk at the port of departure with the use of state of the art detection technology. CSI operates in 58 ports in the American continent, the Caribbean, Europe, Africa, the Middle East and throughout Asia.

The third element related to technology having an important impact on security and risk is the increased destructiveness of weapons that may be used for one of the several possible forms of terrorist attack. Historically, the most common form of terrorist attack has been deployed by using some kind of explosives, with different degrees of destructive power. Nowadays, the threats come from other, more sophisticated sources. First, terrorists may make use of a cyber attack, originated anywhere (that is, in the case of STUXNET) and whose consequences are immediate and widespread.

Table 2.1   Value losses from security incidents

Description	Cost ($)
Estimated cost on the entire supply chain of a WMD shipped via container	1 trillion
Cost of the 9/11 attacks on the two World Trade Center buildings (direct and indirect)	83 billion
Cost of cyber attacks against companies worldwide in 2003	12.5 billion
Cost to the Canadian beef industry of a case of mad cow disease found in Alberta in 2003	2.5 billion
Drop in the European Market (FTSE) immediately following the Madrid bombings	55 billion

Source: Eggers (2005).

The attack may come from a dirty bomb (nuclear or radiological) with devastating consequences, at the local level at first but on a country or global scale in the subsequent weeks or months (see Chapter 5 on three different studies related to the consequences of a dirty bomb in the harbor compound of Los Angeles and Long Beach). Lastly, the threat may be of a biochemical nature. Several instances may be mentioned in this respect; plague, botulism, sarin, anthrax. Eggers's (2005) study has tried to estimate the various economic costs that may be associated with some of these different forms of attack and the outcomes are listed in Table 2.1.

It can be seen that the most relevant form of attack is the one related to a dirty bomb/WMD shipped via container and detonated in a harbor. However, cyber attacks may also have relevant consequences.

The last security-related domain that the advances in technology have contributed to modify is the social and physical distance. The majority of violent acts that have widespread consequences require interaction among people. Historically, the social distance, either in terms of cultural heterogeneity, lack of equality or integration, has been coupled by physical distance that means many terrorist acts are very hard to complete. In the words of Black (2004, p. 20): 'For most of human history, social geometry largely corresponded to physical geometry . . . Terrorism has mostly been impossible . . . the aggrieved civilians have had little or no physical access to enemy civilians. At the same time, those physically close enough were not socially distant enough. Although both the social and physical geometry of terrorism are necessary conditions for its occurrence, then neither alone is a sufficient condition.' In the last decades, the situation has totally changed and generated the need to consider the modified geometry of terrorism and pose the necessary countermeasures, including for the case of maritime transport. In the following section, we shall discuss how this last issue of physical and social distance can be applied to the terrorist organizations that determine the major risks for this mode of transport.

2.3   ANCIENT THREATS, NEW CHALLENGES: CRIME AND PIRACY

The phenomena of crime and piracy and the consequent and related issues are not novel ones. However, the current dimension of these phenomena has reached proportions that cannot be compared to previous times. Crime organizations have now a transnational or international feature based on the most lucrative activities in which they are engaged. These include human, drugs and arms trafficking, theft and smuggling of cultural artifacts. The new international order that has emerged after the end of the Cold War at the beginning of the 1990s has also fostered the international exposure of the criminal syndicates. From the threat of a global conflict, the world is currently experiencing a series of local wars that normally generate political instability and pave the way for the implementation of criminal activity. In some cases, criminal cartels are used for the provision of arms and weapons to the various conflicting groups. In other instances, lack of government and security controls is used for illicit trafficking, as in the case of Somalia. Since 1991, when its government collapsed, the country has been the target and final destination of illicit waste trafficking, mainly by European and Asian firms. The polluting wastes have ranged from uranium radioactive waste to industrial, hospital, chemical leather treatment and other toxic waste (see Papa and Zamparini, 2012). For nearly 20 years, these foreign firms have used the breach in maritime security and control to dump their nuclear and toxic wastes in Somali waters, or even on the beaches, with no regard to the high damaging impacts on the environment and the health of the local population.

Somalia is also at the core of the other above-mentioned phenomenon; maritime piracy. At the general level, it is important to acknowledge that the attacks have decreased, as jointly stated by the IMO, the International Chamber of Shipping, the Oil Companies International Marine Forum, the International Association of Independent Tanker Owners, the International Association of Dry Cargo Shipowners, the International Parcel Tankers Association and the International Shipping Federation (ISF).[3] This has mainly been due to effective international efforts and cooperation (that is, the Cutlass Express) to try and minimize the number of occurrences and the costs of piracy (see Chapter 5). However, even though several security measures have been implemented (such as the increase in speed of ships passing through dangerous areas such as the Strait of Malacca or the Horn of Africa and the military escort of ships) maritime piracy is still an established criminal activity with a relevant cost in economic terms and in human lives.

In a general perspective, maritime piracy had historically represented a non-destructive threat as pirates were mainly interested in the ransom that they could obtain for a hijacked vessel and for the sailors working therein. In the last decades, pirates have increasingly become ideologically oriented. Therefore, in some cases, the ransoms obtained for the captured ships have become one of the founding sources for large-scale criminal activities that are then perpetrated by associated terrorist groups. In this context, maritime security is converted into a component of wider-scale security strategy that also encompasses a land side and a more general country security policy.

2.3.1 The Terrorist Threat and Port Security

The terrorist threat has historically been considered a relatively minor issue apart from the diffusion of piracy that has been discussed in the previous section. Only ten terrorist attacks that have been committed between 1977 and 2007 have been related to maritime facilities or ships (RAND Database of Worldwide Terrorism Incidents, n.d.). However, some episodes have generated an important alert both for politicians and practitioners. Among the several episodes that have been related to maritime security, the following ones are particularly worthy of discussion. Recently, German intelligence uncovered an Al-Qaeda plan to highjack a cruise ship and then start killing passengers while demanding the release of prisoners (Robertson et al., 2012). Though this plan has not been implemented, the Italian cruise ship, *Achille Lauro*, carrying 400 passengers was hijacked by Palestinian terrorists in 1985. The terrorists murdered a 69-year-old disabled American tourist, Leon Klinghoffer, tossing his body and wheelchair overboard. Other attacks on ships included boats loaded with explosives hitting the *USS Cole* in 2000 in Yemeni port of Aden and a French tanker in the Gulf of Aden in 2002. The most sophisticated and devastating attack occurred in 2008 when terrorists hijacked a boat and landed in Mumbai where they attacked several locations, killing 174 people.

The main ports in the world are definitely the most relevant targets for terrorist actions related to the maritime sector. They represent the main hubs of the entire maritime network and of the economic system. A successful attack on a major port can determine economic losses to the large number of supply chains insisting on that infrastructure that can be as high as one trillion dollars (see Section 2.2). A particular consideration of the need to strengthen port security is due to the fact that these infrastructures can be 'soft targets.' First, they are normally accessible by both land and water with several different transport means (passenger ships, cargo and container ships, trains, cars, trucks) by a large number of workers and visitors. Moreover, an attack to a port may also be carried out from the air. Moreover, they normally cover very large areas in the vicinity of crowded metropolitan centers. In some cases, they also host the storage and processing facilities of a large number of chemical firms (as in the cases of Houston, Antwerp and Rotterdam) or of other dangerous goods. As mentioned above, ports are also important intermodal nodes that are necessary to provide ready access to a large number of other transport and production infrastructures and facilities, which are reliant on these nodes for the development of their activities. Therefore, compromised port facilities may represent a bottleneck for the development of the productive processes of many sectors of an economic system. Moreover, ports are normally used for the temporary storage of a large number of containers; each representing a potential threat for the port and the adjoining metropolitan centers. Lastly, harbors are dependent on a number of other critical infrastructures, such as information technology and energy, to operate. Consequently, in order to attack a port, it is not always necessary to reach it physically. It is sufficient to target it from a remote location with the appropriate technology/means.

The security of a port then requires the interaction of several agencies and actors. For example, the port of Long Beach employs more than 30,000 workers who in 2011 handled more than six million containers (TEUs) aboard about 5000 vessels with cargo valued at more than $155 billion[4].

The security of this infrastructure depends on the joint activity of ship owners, insurance agents, port and facility operators, naval forces, non-governmental, local, national and international organizations, local police, fire and harbor commissioners and intelligence (US CBP and US Coast Guard). The presence of such a large number of different stakeholders raises a series of issues that have to be taken into account in order to maximize the level of security of the infrastructure. It is first relevant to consider that the various actors may have very heterogeneous security postures, each one depending on idiosyncratic interests. The previous point is tightly linked to the issue of funding of the various security initiatives in terms both of the amount and matching of funds and administration. It is uncertain who should have the leading role and what the mechanisms to foster coordination for the implementation of policies should be. In this respect, the role of port owners and operators is not very clear. All the above-mentioned issues determine a lack of resiliency of the port infrastructure. For effective port resilience, a wide array of (organizational, structural, planning and operational) activities and strategies have to be implemented in terms both of resistance to adverse phenomena and swift return to regular operations. All these issues clarify that port and maritime security is a complex subject that has stimulated the planning and implementation of policies at country and international levels. In the next section we shall discuss the most relevant US policy initiatives alongside the main international programs.

2.4   THE POLICIES FOR PORTS AND CONTAINERS' SECURITY

The three most relevant policies enacted by the United States in order to increase the security of ports and containers' logistics are the 24-hour advance vessel manifest rule, the Customs-Trade Partnership Against Terrorism (C-TPAT) and the CSI. The first one began to operate in February 2003 and obliges carriers to present cargo declaration documentation 24 hours before the cargo is loaded onboard a vessel from a place of departure outside the United States and having a US port as destination. Not complying with this requirement results in denial for the ship departure and also fines and civil penalties. The C-TPAT initiative represents a cooperative attempt of the US Customs and Border Protection with the international trade community in order to plan, develop and ameliorate efficient and effective security processes along entire supply chains for the various traded goods. The benefit of such protocols for the shipping operators are related to a significant reduction of customs clearing times (Papa, 2013). At the beginning, the plan was only open to importers but it was then extended to all other supply chain actors, subject to the eligibility criteria mentioned in the C-TPAT initiative website.[5] The CSI (see Section 2.2) initiative aims to identify the high risk containers by making use of automated information and screening them before their arrival in the US port. In order to accomplish this goal, the United States have signed a series of bilateral agreements to assign US customs inspectors in 58 foreign ports. The advantage for foreign operators would be the possibility to benefit from accelerated clearing times. An issue with overseas inspections is that they rely on the integrity, reliability and honesty of the operators and US officials and also on a sound intelligence and analysis of the likelihood of a container to be a risky one. The proposed goal was a 100 percent screening of inbound containers that could not be met and was subsequently abandoned.[6]

Analysis of the 24-hour rule, of C-TPAT and of CSI initiatives has shown that the cooperation of foreign governments is a critical point in order to achieve the desired improvements in security. Janet Napolitano, head of the Departement of Homeland Security, has publicly stated that the achieved degree of cooperation is not adequate (Reuters, 2011). Moreover, liquefied natural gas (LNG) ports cannot be considered sufficiently protected against attack. As a specific case, the Drug and Crime office (an institution of the United Nations) has stated that lack of resources results in ineffective control of the arrival of narcotics at ports. Moreover, two important weaknesses are inter-agency mistrust and the complex port processes and systems.

Various international programs have been implemented by the IMO to enhance maritime security. The *Achille Lauro* hijacking led to the IMO's adoption of various resolutions including, in March 1988, the Convention for the Suppression of Unlawful Acts against the Safety of Maritime Navigation (SUA) and, following the 9/11 terrorist attacks, it amended the International Convention for the Safety of Life at Sea (SOLAS), chapter XI-2 on Special measures to enhance maritime security and the International Ship and Port Facility Security (ISPS) code in 2004. This code established enhanced security standards both for ships at sea and for port facilities. It mandated the implementation of a Ship Security Plan (SSP), the installation of ship alarms and Automatic Identification Systems (AIS), and the appointment of a Ship Security Officer (SSO), a Port Facility Security Plan (PFSP), a Port Facility Security Officer (PFSO) and a Company Security Officer (CSO).[7]

In 2005, the WCO adopted the SAFE Framework of Standards to Secure and Facilitate Global Trade, which established minimum standards and principles for all its members. These include the harmonization of advance electronic cargo information, the adoption of a risk management approach and the inspection of outbound cargo when requested by a receiving country.[8]

2.5 CONCLUSIONS

This chapter has provided a general overview of some of the most important factors that impact on maritime security. Technology can have both positive and detrimental effects on security given that it allows better management and control of transport by the use of information and communications technologies but it also provides more destructive weapons to terrorists and reduces the social and physical distance among terrorists and with respect to their targets. The reduction of physical distance is also an issue in the case of piracy. This phenomenon is sometimes connected to lack of stable governments in some countries or of coordination among states to tackle this issue. Moreover, a recent distressing trend is the ideological orientation of pirates that use ransoms obtained to finance large-scale terrorism. The latter has generated an important alert among politicians and practitioners in the last decades, especially with respect to ports, whose security depends on the efficient interaction of several agencies and stakeholders.

The topic of cooperation is also the most relevant one when considering the policies for ports and containers' security. All the initiatives enacted by the United States depend crucially on the collaboration of foreign governments. Probably, a more significant role of international agencies, such as the IMO or the WCO, is required for the deployment of inititatives that are based on the careful consideration of best practices. The rest of the chapters of Part I of the book will develop, among other issues, the topics described in this chapter while Part II will propose a comparative analysis of the policies and practices performed in various countries in several regions of the world.

NOTES

1. This chapter is based on Joseph Szyliowicz's keynote presentation at the opening ceremony of the Turkish Navy's Maritime Security Center, Marmaris, Turkey, October 2012.
2. http://www.tuttogreen.it/genova-festeggia-il-container-radioattivo-va-via/.
3. http://www.shippingandmarine.co.uk/article-page.php?contentid=17182&issueid=482 (accessed 7 May 2013).
4. http://www.polb.com/about/default.aspn.
5. http://www.supplychainsecurity.biz/ctpat/eligibility.htm (accessed 2011).
6. http://www.nti.org/gsn/article/napolitano-says-us-cannot-meet-cargo-screening-goal/ (accessed 2011).
7. http://www.worldtraderef.com/WTR_site/ISPS.asp (accessed 2011).
8. http://ec.europa.eu/taxation_customs/resources/documents/customs/policy_issues/ customs_security/normes_WCO_en.pdf (accessed 2011).

REFERENCES

Black, D. (2004), 'The geometry of terrorism', *Social Theory*, **3**, 14–25.
Eggers, W. (2005), *Prospering in the Secure Economy*, New York: Deloitte-Touche.
Papa, P. (2013), 'US and EU strategies for maritime transport security: a comparative perspective', *Transport Policy*, **28**, 75–85.
Papa, P. and L. Zamparini (2012), 'Security of Hazmat Ttansports in Italy', in R. Genserik and L. Zamparini (eds), *Security Aspects of Uni- and Multi-modal Hazmat Transportation Systems*, Berlin: Wiley, pp. 203–17.

RAND Database of Worldwide Terrorism Incidents (n.d.), http://www.rand.org/nsrd/projects/terrorism-incidents.html.

Reuters (2011), http://www.reuters.com/article/2011/01/06/us-security-usa-eu-napolitano-idUSTRE70550D20110106 (accessed 2011).

Robertson, N., P. Cruickshank and T. Lister (2012), 'Documents reveal al Qaeda's plans for seizing cruise ships, carnage in Europe', CNN, 1 May.

Rodrigue, J.P. (2010), 'Ports and maritime trade', available at http://people.hofstra.edu/jean-paul_rodrigue/downloads/Ports%20and%20Mariittime%20Trade.pdfy (accessed October 2013).

3. Overview of contemporary supply chain security initiatives

Khalid Bichou and Risto Talas

3.1 MANDATORY SUPPLY CHAIN SECURITY INITIATIVES

3.1.1 International Maritime Organization International Ship and Port Facility Security Code

The objective of the International Maritime Organization International Ship and Port Facility Security (ISPS) code is to establish an international framework involving cooperation between governments, government agencies, local administrations and the port and shipping industries to protect ships and ports engaged in international trade.

Name	International Ship and Port Facility Security (ISPS) Code
Originator	International Maritime Organization

Who can apply	• Ships engaged on international voyages:
	  ○ passenger ships including high-speed passenger craft
	  ○ cargo ships including high-speed craft of 500 gross tonnage and upwards
	  ○ mobile offshore drilling units
	• Port facilities serving such ships engaged on international voyages

Voluntary/ mandatory	Mandatory
Mission Requirements	The protection of ships and port facilities from unlawful acts For ships: • On scene security survey • Ship security assessment • Preparation of ship security plan • Implementation of ship security plan • Verification procedure • International ship security certificate

For ports:

- Port facility security assessment
- Preparation of port facility security plan
- Approval of port facility security plan
- Implementation of port facility security plan
- Statement of compliance of a port facility

Benefits	The full benefits of protected ships and port facilities will only come about once all contracting governments put in place and maintain the necessary arrangements for compliance with the ISPS code
Website	http://www.imo.org/

It is important that all terminals and port facilities that are not currently compliant with the ISPS code are encouraged to make the necessary changes as soon as possible. In addition to the benefits detailed above, compliance with the ISPS code is a requirement for many voluntary initiatives.

3.1.2   24-hour Rule

The 24-hour rule requires sea carriers and Non-Vessel Operating Common Carriers (NVOCCs) to provide US Customs with detailed descriptions of the contents of sea containers bound for the United States 24 hours before the container is loaded on board a vessel. The rule allows US Customs officers to analyse the container content information and identify potential terrorist threats before the US-bound container is loaded at the foreign seaport, not after it arrives in a US port. The use of such vague cargo descriptions as 'Freight-All-Kinds,' 'Said-To-Contain' or 'General Merchandise' is no longer tolerated. Sea carriers and NVOCCs that violate the 24-hour rule 2003 receive 'Do Not Load' messages. The 'Do Not Load' message instructs these parties not to load a specific container that has been found in violation of the 24-hour rule. Carriers and NVOCCs that disregard these 'Do Not Load' messages (and load the cited container) are denied permission to unload this container at any US port.

The tightened reporting requirements for containerized cargo entering the United States as prescribed by the 24-hour rule has forced companies' supply chains toward greater functionality. To meet the 24-hour rule requirements, shipowners and other NVOCCs have extended their electronic commerce technologies by developing e-commerce portals through which their customers can communicate more easily their shipping information and giving customers the capability to manage their shipments by increasing visibility in their supply chains.

3.2 VOLUNTARY SUPPLY CHAIN SECURITY INITIATIVES

3.2.1 Business Alliance for Secured Commerce (formerly Business Anti-Smuggling Coalition)

Business Alliance for Secured Commerce (BASC) was created in 1996 when a North American company, importing through the port of San Diego, California, submitted a proposal to the US Customs Service that would implement supply chain security procedures to reduce the risk of legitimate cargo being used by illegal organizations for narcotics trade, cargo theft and contaminated cargo. The proposal also sought to complement and strengthen the US Customs Service's Carrier Initiative Program (CIP) and Land Border Carrier Initiative Program (LBCIP), in order to modify the mentality of production companies toward implementing preventive measures in place of repressive measures.

BASC is a cooperation program between the private sector and national and international organizations, created to promote a secure global supply chain. The main goal is to encourage within its membership the development and implementation of voluntary steps to address the risks of narcotics and merchandise smuggling through legitimate trade, as well as the threat of a disruption in the global economy brought about by terrorism.

BASC procedures require a security program that consists of a number of operating measures adopted to protect an organization, its assets, properties, employees and customers.

Name	Business Alliance for Secured Commerce, World BASC Organization
Originator	A US importer with the US Customs in 1996; since then grown by business, supported by US Customs and Border Protection, International Chamber of Commerce, World Customs Organization
Who can apply	Member countries, customs administrations, international organizations, associations, businesses
Voluntary/ mandatory	Voluntary
Mission	Secure and facilitate international trade by the establishment and administration of global security standards and procedures applied to the supply chain in association with customs administrations and government authorities

Requirements   A security program that consists of a number of operating
measures adopted to protect an organization, its assets,
properties, employees and customers
The factors to consider in preparing a security program
include:

- Organizational security requirements
- Potential of the organization to meet those requirements
- Organization's vulnerability to current and future security
  risks
- Available options to the organization to cover its security
  needs

Other important aspects that should be included in a security
plan are:

- Clear definition of security requirements
- Written procedures for internal/external notification of
  security
- Mechanisms to establish accountability in case of theft or
  robbery
- Handling of document and files
- Procedures when checking lighting and perimeter fencing
- Procedures when closing facilities (doors, gates, windows
  etc.)
- Security systems to check entry and exit of people and/or
  vehicles
- Procedures for handling cargo
- Definition of policies for external monitoring
- Control and management of keys and conducting periodic
  inventory policies and procedures for personnel hiring
- Policies to be applied in criminal background checks
- Procedures for obtaining photographs and fingerprints of
  all employees
- Assignment of responsibilities for contract security
  personnel

To maintain the security program it is important to:

- Update the safety and security program at least once a year
- Update the security methods included in the plan
- Undertake an assessment of contract services
- Provide personnel training

Benefits
- Improve competitiveness and image of the companies
- Expand the opportunities of businesses in international
  markets
- Reduce the risks related to international trade

- Diminish economic losses due to inefficiency
- Promote an atmosphere of safe work
- Improve the control and traceability of the supply chain

Website   http://wbasco.org/index-eng.htm

3.2.2   Container Security Initiative

The Container Security Initiative (CSI) was launched in 2002 by the US Customs and Border Protection (CBP) agency with 20 of the world's largest container terminals. By June 2003, 23 ports representing at least 60 percent of container imports to the United States had signed CSI agreements and by September 2007, there were 55 CSI ports worldwide.

CSI addresses the threat to border security and global trade posed by the potential for terrorist use of a maritime container to deliver a weapon. CSI proposes a security regime to ensure all containers that pose a potential risk for terrorism are identified and inspected at foreign ports before they are placed on vessels destined for the United States. The US CBP has stationed multidisciplinary teams of US officers from both CBP and Immigration and Customs Enforcement (ICE) to work together with host foreign government counterparts.

Name	Container Security Initiative (CSI)
Originator	US Customs and Border Protection
Who can apply	All international container ports
Voluntary/ mandatory	Voluntary
Mission	Target and pre-screen containers and develop additional investigative leads related to the terrorist threat to cargo destined to the United States
Requirements	• The customs administration must be able to inspect cargo originating, transiting, exiting or being trans-shipped through a country. Non-intrusive inspection equipment (including equipment with gamma or X-ray imaging capabilities) and radiation detection equipment must be available and utilized for conducting such inspections. This equipment is necessary in order to meet the objective of quickly screening containers without disrupting the flow of legitimate trade
	• The seaport must have regular, direct and substantial container traffic to ports in the United States

- Commit to establishing a risk management system to identify potentially high-risk containers, and automating that system. This system should include a mechanism for validating threat assessments and targeting decisions and identifying best practices
- Commit to sharing critical data, intelligence and risk management information with the US Customs and Border Protection in order to do collaborative targeting, and develop an automated mechanism for these exchanges
- Conduct a thorough port assessment to ascertain vulnerable links in a port's infrastructure and commit to resolving those vulnerabilities
- Commit to maintaining integrity programs to prevent lapses in employee integrity and to identify and combat breaches in integrity

Benefits	• Significant measure of security for the participating port as well as the United States • CSI also provides better security for the global trading system as a whole
Website	http://www.cbp.gov/xp/cgov/border_security/international_activities/csi/

Through CSI, CBP officers work with host customs administrations to establish security criteria for identifying high-risk containers. Those administrations use non-intrusive inspection (NII) and radiation detection technology to screen high-risk containers before they are shipped to US ports. CSI, a reciprocal program, offers its participant countries the opportunity to send their customs officers to major US ports to target ocean-going, containerized cargo to be exported to their countries. Likewise, CBP shares information on a bilateral basis with its CSI partners. Japan and Canada currently station their customs personnel in some US ports as part of the CSI program.

CSI is now operational at ports in North America, Europe, Asia, Africa, the Middle East and Latin and Central America. CBP's 58 operational CSI ports (as at January 2008) make approximately 90 percent of all transatlantic and transpacific cargo imported into the United States subject to pre-screening prior to importation.

3.2.3 European Union Authorized Economic Operator

The European Union Authorized Economic Operator (EU AEO) designates the status that customs authorities from European member states should grant to reliable traders established in the European Community. AEOs will be able to benefit from facilitations for customs controls or simplifications for customs rules or both, depending on the type of AEO certificate. There are three certificate types:

- Customs simplifications. AEOs will be entitled to benefit from simplifications provided for under the customs rules.
- Security and safety. AEOs will be entitled to benefit from facilitations of customs controls relating to security and safety at the entry of the goods into the customs territory of the Community, or when the goods leave the customs territory of the Community.
- Customs simplifications/security and safety. AEOs will be entitled to benefit from both simplifications provided for under the customs rules and from facilitations of customs controls relating to security and safety (a combination of the above two points).

Name	European Union Authorized Economic Operator
Originator	European Commission
Who can apply	Manufacturers, importers, exporters, brokers, carriers, consolidators, intermediaries, ports, airports, terminal operators, integrated operators, warehouses, distributors
Voluntary / mandatory	Voluntary
Mission	Enhance security through granting recognition to reliable traders and encouraging best practice at all levels in the international supply chain
Requirements	• Customs compliance • Appropriate record keeping • Financial solvency • Security and safety standards
Benefits	• AEOs will be recognized worldwide as safe, secure and compliant business partners in international trade • AEOs will be given a lower risk score in risk analysis systems when profiling • If physical controls are to be conducted AEOs will be given priority treatment • Mutual recognition of AEO programs under Joint Customs Co-operation Agreements could result in faster movement of their goods through third country borders • Reduced data sets for entry and exit summary declarations – only for AEO safety and security • AEOs will be in a stronger position to benefit from simplified procedures

Website	http://ec.europa.eu/taxation_customs/resources/documents/ customs/policy_issues/customs_security/AEO_guidelines_ en.pdf

The main benefits of AEO status in the EU are:

- A lower risk score in customs' risk management systems.
- Consignments may be fast tracked through customs controls.
- Recognized status across the EU.
- Potential for future reciprocal arrangements and mutual recognition outside the EU.

3.2.4 World Customs Organization Framework of Standards to Secure and Facilitate Global Trade

The World Customs Organization (WCO) Framework of Security Standards is intended to provide a new and consolidated platform that will enhance world trade, ensure better security against terrorism and increase the contribution of customs and trade partners to the economic and social well-being of nations. It aims to improve the ability of customs to detect and deal with high-risk consignments and increase efficiency in the administration of goods, thereby expediting the clearance and release of goods. Specifically, the aims of the Framework are the following:

- Establish standards that provide supply chain security and facilitation at a global level to promote certainty and predictability.
- Enable integrated supply chain management for all modes of transport.
- Strengthen cooperation between customs administrations to improve their capability to detect high-risk consignments.
- Strengthen customs/business cooperation.
- Promote the seamless movement of goods through secure international trade supply chains.

Name	World Customs Organization Framework of Standards to Secure and Facilitate Global Trade
Originator	World Customs Organization
Who can apply	• Customs organizations • Businesses (as Authorised Economic Operators)
Voluntary/ mandatory	Voluntary

Mission	• Establish standards that provide supply chain security and facilitation at a global level to promote certainty and predictability
	• Enable integrated supply chain management for all modes of transport
	• Enhance the role, functions and capabilities of customs to meet the challenges and opportunities of the twenty-first century
	• Strengthen cooperation between customs administrations to improve their capability to detect high-risk consignments
	• Strengthen customs/business cooperation
	• Promote the seamless movement of goods through secure international trade supply chains
Requirements	• Appropriate record of compliance with customs requirements
	• Demonstrated commitment to supply chain security by being a participant in a customs/business partnership program
	• Satisfactory system for managing commercial records
Benefits	Obtaining enhanced competitiveness in national and international markets due to reduction in delays and costs that are achieved with predictable and efficient movement of goods across borders
Website	http://www.wcoomd.org/home.htm

3.3 VOLUNTARY LOCATION-SPECIFIC SUPPLY CHAIN SECURITY INITIATIVES

3.3.1 Customs-Trade Partnership Against Terrorism

Customs-Trade Partnership Against Terrorism (C-TPAT) is a joint government-business initiative to build cooperative relationships that strengthen overall supply chain and border security. Central to the security vision of C-TPAT is the core principle of increased facilitation for legitimate business entities that are compliant traders. Only importers and carriers based in the United States are eligible to participate in this program and one of its main motivations is to protect US borders from terrorist attacks occasioned by goods entering the country.

C-TPAT and non-US terminals
Non-US-based Marine Port Authority and Terminal Operators (MPTOs) may be eligible for membership of the C-TPAT scheme but only following an invitation from the US CBP to join. The terminal must handle cargo

vessels departing to the United States and have a designated company officer that will be the primary cargo security officer responsible for C-TPAT.

Name	Customs-Trade Partnership Against Terrorism (C-TPAT)
Originator	US Customs and Border Protection
Who can apply	<ul><li>US importers of record</li><li>US/Canada highway carriers</li><li>US/Mexico highway carriers</li><li>Rail carriers</li><li>Sea carriers</li><li>Air carriers</li><li>US Marine Port Authority and Terminal Operators</li><li>US air freight consolidators, ocean transportation intermediaries and Non-Vessel Operating Common Carriers (NVOCCs)</li><li>Mexican and Canadian manufacturers</li><li>Certain invited foreign manufacturers</li><li>Licensed US Customs brokers</li><li>Non-US Marine Port Authority and Terminal Operators (MPTOs)</li></ul>
Voluntary/ mandatory	Voluntary
Mission	To build cooperative relationships that strengthen and improve overall international supply chain and US border security
Requirements	<ul><li>US and foreign-based MPTOs must conduct a comprehensive assessment of their security practices based on the following C-TPAT minimum-security criteria. C-TPAT recognizes the complexity of marine port and terminal operations and endorses the application and implementation of security measures based upon risk. Therefore, the program allows for flexibility and the customization of security plans based on the C-TPAT member's business model, the port's geography, the commodities handled at the port and the terms and conditions of the lease agreement between the marine port authority and the terminal operator</li><li>ISPS code and MTSA compliance are a prerequisite for C-TPAT MPTO membership, and only terminals in compliance with the applicable ISPS code requirements may be utilized by C-TPAT members. The Physical Access Controls and Physical Security provisions of these criteria are satisfied for ISPS-regulated vessels and port facilities by those vessels' or facilities' compliance with the ISPS code and Coast Guard regulations</li></ul>

Benefits	• Incorporation of good sound security practices and procedures into existing logistical management methods and processes • Greater supply chain integrity • Reduced risk mitigation • Reduced cargo theft and pilferage • Stronger brand equity • Improved asset utilization • Greater efficiency between internal and external functions • Improved security for the workforce • Improved marketability • Understanding the end to end process, including knowing each entity along the supply chain
Website	http://cbp.gov/xp/cgov/import/commercial_enforcement/ctpat/what_ctpat/

C-TPAT also recognizes the unique role and relationship between the marine port authority and terminal operators' situation regarding terminal operators who operate as tenants within a marine port. For C-TPAT purposes, each terminal operator must implement the C-TPAT security criteria within the physical area and processes within the terminal operator's area of control and responsibility. Where a marine port authority does not control a specific process or element of the supply chain, such as a sea carrier, terminal operator or independent contractor, the MPTO should work with these business partners to seek to ensure that pertinent security measures are in place and adhered to within the overall port.

C-TPAT recognizes that MPTOs are already subject to defined security mandates created under the ISPS code and the Maritime Transportation Security Act (MTSA). It is not the intention of C-TPAT to duplicate these vessel and facility security requirements. Rather, C-TPAT seeks to build upon the ISPS and MTSA foundation and require additional security measures and practices that enhance the overall security throughout the international supply chain.

While much of the burden of these initiatives falls upon the carrier and the importer, the terminal's role as a C-TPAT MPTO requires full cooperation with these entities, as appropriate, in areas consisting of inspection, timely submission of trade data, cargo/container movement and high-risk targeting. An MPTO operating in an international port with a CSI contingent should make every effort to maintain regular liaison with the team leader of the CSI contingent, as a forum to discuss supply chain security issues and to gauge and evaluate current approaches to security and targeting.

3.3.2 Partners in Protection

Partners in Protection (PIP) is designed to enlist the cooperation of private industry in efforts to enhance border security, combat organized crime and terrorism, increase awareness of customs compliance issues and help detect and prevent contraband smuggling. This program does not have a 'certification' component. Companies may be refused if they do not fulfill the requirements, but once accepted in the program they work together with Canadian Customs to improve their supply chain security, even though they will not get a certification as such. A PIP participant can apply for a Customs Self-Assessment (CSA) program to expedite goods into Canada. By working with the Canadian Border Services Agency (CBSA), a company contributes to the protection of Canadian society and the facilitation of legitimate trade.

Name	Partners in Protection
Originator	Canadian Border Services Agency
Who can apply	Entire trade community, from importers, carriers, brokers, warehouse operators to associations engaged in trade with Canada
Voluntary/ mandatory	Voluntary
Mission	Enlist the cooperation of private industry in efforts to enhance border security, combat organized crime and terrorism, increase awareness of customs compliance issues and help detect and prevent contraband smuggling
Requirements	• Enhanced security • Exchange of information • Awareness sessions
Benefits	• Shipments and travelers will be processed more quickly • Improved security levels • Your staff will become more familiar with customs requirements • The CBSA will review your security procedures and suggest improvements, if necessary, to help reduce the possibility of your company being used unknowingly for contraband smuggling purposes • Enhanced reputation for your company by demonstrating a willingness to work with the CBSA in the fight against drugs and other contraband in Canada
Website	http://www.cbsa-asfc.gc.ca/security-securite/pip-pep/menu-eng.html

3.3.3   StairSec

StairSec is a new module introduced to the Swedish Customs program Stairway (originally created to facilitate customs processes for compliant traders). This module makes it possible to provide quality assurance for operators within the Stairway not only for quality in their customs routines but also for the security measures they have taken to prevent terrorists from using the operators' commercial flow of goods for transporting weapons of mass destruction.

Name	StairSec
Originator	Swedish Customs
Who can apply	Importers/exporters, brokers, forwarders (air/sea/land, i.e. multi-modal transport), terminals (seaports, hubs, warehouses etc.)
Voluntary/ mandatory	Voluntary
Mission	Flexible customs routines for foreign trade, within the framework of the legislation, a smooth border passage for travelers and efficient border protection
Requirements	● Customs compliant ● Low risk
Benefits	StairSec program leads to higher inspection rates of uncertified cargo, increasing likelihood of early warning and prevention
Website	http://www.tullverket.se/en/Business/the_stairsec/

3.3.4   Secure Export Partnership

The Secure Export Partnership is designed to protect cargo against tampering, sabotage, smuggling of terrorists or terrorist-related goods, and other transnational crime, from the point of packing to delivery. Exporters from New Zealand are eligible and encouraged to participate, especially those moving goods to the United States. The program emphasizes that security measures are customizable depending on the applicant's situation.

Name	Secure Export Partnership
Originator	New Zealand Customs Service
Who can apply	All exporters, by all modes of transport, to all destinations
Voluntary/ mandatory	Voluntary
Mission	Keeping trade flowing and secure

Requirements	• Accurate advance export information
	• Maintaining an agreed level of security
	• Working in partnership with customs
Benefits	• Secure supply chain from point of packing to time of loading for export
	• 'Green lane' status means cargo can be moved to port/airport facilities knowing the potential for customs intervention for security is low
	• Ability to demonstrate compliance with security standards when contracting to supply overseas importers that are committed to supply chain security
	• Joining the scheme will enhance your border clearance privileges in the United States provided your client is a member of C-TPAT initiated by the US CBP
	• In the event of trade disruption caused by security alerts, partners' exports are likely to experience minimal disruption as their security can be assured
	• The World Customs Organization's Framework of Standards to Secure and Facilitate Global Trade is being adopted and implemented by a large number of international customs administrations. By joining this scheme, partners will already have in place security measures that comply with these standards
	• Reduced fees for the lodgement of all export entries
	• Customs can provide advice and assistance if you strike unexpected issues with your export goods at overseas borders
Website	http://www.customs.govt.nz/exporters/Secure+Exports+Scheme.htm#howitworks

3.4   VOLUNTARY BUSINESS-SPECIFIC SUPPLY CHAIN SECURITY INITIATIVES

3.4.1   Technology Asset Protection Association

The Technology Asset Protection Association (TAPA) is an association of security professionals and related business partners from high-technology companies who have been working together to address emerging security threats that are common to the technology industry and high-tech businesses.

The goals of TAPA include:

- Security of goods from theft
  - o   in transit
  - o   in-transit storage
  - o   warehousing
- Specifies minimum standards for security throughout the supply chain
- Describes methods for maintaining standards
- Includes process for TAPA certification.

Name	Technology Asset Protection Association
Originator	Hi-tech companies
Who can apply	Hi-tech companies
Voluntary/ mandatory	Voluntary
Mission	To address the cargo theft problems facing the hi-tech industry on a collective level
Requirements	• Have a security policy, procedures and plan • Submit to periodic audits and certification
Benefits	• Reduced losses associated with transportation-related thefts • Economic benefits of more attractive freight carrier contract terms • Reduced customer inconvenience and disruptions • A reduction in the incidence of lost sales • The combined leverage of over 50 of the world's largest technology companies to negotiate more favorable terms with insurance companies and freight carriers
Website	http://www.tapaonline.org/new/engl/what_is_tapa.html

BIBLIOGRAPHY

Crutch, M. (2006), 'The benefits of investing in global supply chain security', Executive Summary, November 2006 CVCR Roundtable Meeting, Leigh University Center for Value Chain Research.

Jones, S. (2006), *Maritime Security: A Practical Guide*, London: Nautical Institute.

Lee, H. and S. Whang (2003), 'Higher supply chain security with lower cost: lessons from total quality management', Stanford GSB Research Paper No. 1824, 19 October.

Peleg-Gillai, B., G. Bhat and L. Sept (2006), *Innovators in Supply Chain Security: Better Security Drives Business Value*, Manufacturing Innovation Series, Stanford, CA: Stanford University.

Rice, J. and P. Spayd (2005), *Investing in Supply Chain Security: Collateral Benefits*, Special Report Series, IBM Center for The Business of Government.
Ya Deau, A. and P. Westley (1992), 'Terminal security', London: Through Transport Mutual Association Club.

4. Economic issues in maritime transport security

Luca Zamparini

4.1 INTRODUCTION

The maritime sector is definitely a pivotal one nowadays in economic systems. The large majority of international trade is carried by sea (80 per cent by volume according to the 2012 *Review of Maritime Transport* by the United Nations Conference on Trade and Development (UNCTAD)). Consequently, a high degree of security of the routes of vessels and ports, which are the critical links of globalized supply chains, is not only important for the maritime industry but also for many other sectors of the economy. A terrorist attack to a main port may not only cause damages to the port itself but would also paralyse, at least for a certain amount of time, world maritime trade. However, the deployment of security measures entails direct and indirect costs that must be borne by one or more of the stakeholders (that is, ports, shipping companies, insurance agencies) that are involved in the maritime industry. Maritime transport security and trade efficiency are two intertwined issues in the development of regional and global supply chains. There appears to be a lack of general consensus about the effects of increased security on efficiency and seamlessness of maritime trade. Some authors argue (see, among others, Thai, 2007) that the fulfillment of tighter security requirements can generate remarkable benefits in terms of enhanced service quality due to increased reliability of services, higher efficiency in operation and management, and also in terms of social responsibility awareness. All these may then lead to a better image in the market for the firm. Many of the improvements in security (that is, the Container Security Initiative (CSI)) require the integration of information technology and electronic data interchange systems in order to better manage shipment information (OECD, 2003). Moreover, security controls and advanced controls may also lead to a reduction in the variability of lead times and thus to an increased reliability of services (Wolfe, 2002) and to a decrease in loss and damage of shipments. Another benefit emerging from improved security is related to the possibility that improved protocols may lead to lower insurance premiums, especially with respect to pilferage and theft coverage. According to Wolfe (2002), security investments should take into account the integrity of the conveyance loading, documentation and sealing process, the reduction of the risk of tampering in transit and the provision of information about shipments in a timely manner.

The present chapter provides an overview of the economic issues that are connected to maritime transport security; emphasizing the possible trade-offs and synergies. The next two sections take into account two important topics in maritime security: the economic costs of an attack to a port by a dirty bomb and those of maritime piracy. In both sections, an indication of the wider costs to the global economic system will be accounted for and the available estimates provided. Section 4.4 discusses the economic costs and benefits that are connected to maritime security regulations. It first addresses the main international initiatives and then focuses on some US regulations before proposing a general framework of analysis, based on marginal social costs and benefits. The last section concludes.

4.2   THE ECONOMIC COSTS OF AN ATTACK TO A PORT

Nowadays, ports represent critical links in the globalized supply chains. Attacks to these facilities thus represent one of the most important security threats in maritime economics. A survey in 2003 (Frittelli et al., 2003) listed all possible sources of threat to a port infrastructure. They can be related to the use of commercial cargo containers to smuggle terrorists, nuclear, chemical or biological weapons; to the seizure of a large commercial cargo ship and its use as a collision weapon; to the sinking of a large commercial cargo ship in a major shipping channel in order to block all traffic to and from the port; to the attack of a large ship carrying a volatile fuel in order to detonate it in a port; to the attack of a large oil tanker in order to disrupt world oil trade and to cause large-scale environmental damage; to the seizure of a ferry or of a cruise ship in order to ask a ransom for passengers; or to the use of the land around the port in order to stage attacks on bridges, refineries or other port facilities. An example on which part of the maritime security literature has concentrated is related to the economic consequences of a dirty bomb on a large port facility that is represented by the twin ports of Los Angeles and Long Beach. They constitute one of world's most important maritime complexes in terms of traffic and trade and handle roughly half of US seaborne trade (Gordon et al., 2005). Three different studies (Gordon et al., 2005; Rosoff and von

Winterfeldt, 2007; Park, 2008) have tried to estimate, in recent years, the economic consequences of a dirty (radiological) bomb attack to the ports of Los Angeles and Long Beach.

The first study (Gordon et al., 2005) stated that the main consequence related to an attack on a port is its effect on business activities. The study estimated that the economic impact of this attack could exceed $34 billion and 212,000 jobs. The proposed model also distinguishes between direct losses arising from the loss of opportunities to produce goods and services and the capacity to ship goods. The indirect impact pertains to suppliers whose products are no longer purchased by the impacted firms and people. Moreover, the induced losses are due for the diminishing secondary consumption once workers are laid off. The impacts on the transportation network that is tightly linked to the port facility are two-fold. On the one hand, given port closure, many fewer freight trips to and from the port will be originated, thus reducing the traffic load on the region. On the other hand, the closure of facilities adjoining the port would increase traffic congestion on the network.

The second study (Rosoff and von Winterfeldt, 2007) is also based on the analysis of the effects of a dirty bomb planted in the Los Angeles and Long Beach harbour areas and proposes three different scenarios (low radioactivity, medium radioactivity and high radioactivity) with four possible modes of delivery of the bomb (truck, ship, train and plane/ helicopter). The paper distinguishes among the immediate fatalities and injuries related to the bomb blast, the medium and long-term health effects due to air dispersion of radioactive material and, together with the paper by Gordon et al. (2005), the economic consequences emerging from shutting down port operations. Interestingly, in the paper a huge difference in terms of costs emerges between the medium and high impact scenario. In the former case, the economic costs would be between $10 and $300 million and the fatalities between 0 and 30. In the latter case, the fatalities would be between 0 and 1000 and the economic costs would be in the order of hundreds of billions of dollars; mainly due to port shutdown and related business losses (between $30 and $100 billion) and decontamination costs (between $10 and $100 billion).

The third study (Park, 2008) complements the previous ones by taking into account the effects on all of the states of the USA by means of a model considering inter-state and inter-industry forward linkages. The model is related to short-term effects before goods substitutions and price adjustments take place. It emerges that in the case of a dirty bomb attack, all states would be affected because of the indirect impacts of the episode for a total cost of more than $4 billion that should be summed to almost $500 million in the rest of the world. Despite the variability in figures that may emerge by using different estimation models, it is clear that the effects of a terrorist episode in a major port go beyond the area of the port itself. This calls for a more thorough consideration of the implied costs at the local, national and international levels and justifies the international cooperation in issues related to maritime security.

4.3 ECONOMIC COSTS OF MARITIME PIRACY

As stated in the introduction to this chapter, maritime shipping routes are of vital importance for economic systems in terms both of merchandise trade and of energy security. In this context, the five most important maritime routes are the Suez Canal, the Strait of Hormuz, the Panama Canal, the Gulf of Aden and the Straits of Malacca (Mildner and Gross, 2011); the latter being the two choke points that have been more severely affected by maritime piracy in recent years. The Gulf of Aden is strategic for the connections between Asia, the Arabian peninsula and Europe while the Straits of Malacca links the Indian Ocean with the South China Sea and witnessed the passage of more than 50,000 ships in 2007. It appears evident that the closing of one of these choke points would not only imply problems at the local scale but may also be the cause of a global recession. It is then clear that combating piracy is not only important for local economic systems (that is, Somalia, Malaysia, Indonesia) but also for countries that depend on the trades through these important maritime routes. A complete taxonomy of the different categories of the cost of piracy has been proposed by two studies by Bowden and Basnet (2012) and Bellish (2013) that analysed Somali piracy and estimated the total cost to the global economy as between 6.6 and 6.9 billion dollars in 2011 and between 5.7 and 6.1 billion dollars in 2012. The categories are the following: (a) cost of ransoms and associated payments; (b) cost of military operations; (c) cost of security equipment and guards; (d) cost of re-routing; (e) cost of increased speed; (f) cost of labour; (g) cost of prosecution and imprisonment; (h) cost of piracy-related insurance; and (i) cost of counter-piracy organizations.

The first, and most direct, cost of piracy is the one related to the ransoms that have to be paid to pirates once they hijack one ship. It appears that in the latest years, despite the diminishing number of hostage ships, the negotiation period has been longer and, in 2012, it reached on average almost one year (316 days). In some cases, the cost of ransoms increases given the possibility that the pirates, once they release the ship, keep part of the crew hostage and ask for a second ransom. Moreover, the total cost of a ransom should also include its delivery, the damage caused to the vessel, the cost of negotiators and the counselling for crew members held hostage. These further costs increase with the increased length of time the vessel is kept hostage.

With respect to the cost of military operations, it is important to notice that they can take different forms. They may either be navy vessels deployed or maritime patrol airplanes or vessel protection detachment teams or military staff assigned to headquarters or onboard units. Furthermore, the cost of piracy is related to incremental operations with respect to the normal patrolling activity. In this context, it is necessary to compute specific training operations, specific equipment, personnel rotation, basing costs and fuel consumption.

The costs of security equipment and guards are borne by the shipping firms. The security equipment necessary for anti-piracy purposes is mainly razor wire, electrified barriers, water cannons, warning signs, acoustic devices and sandbags. Private guards must be allowed to operate by the flag states and are normally dependent on accreditation provided by a recognized body (the main one being the Security Association for the Maritime Industry).

The cost of re-routing was an important cost component in previous decades. However, the employment of private guards and extension of the risk zone has caused a reduction in the use of this strategy to counter piracy. Another, and apparently the most important, strategy against piracy is the increase in vessel speed. It appears that no successful piracy attack has been accomplished against vessels travelling at 18 knots or faster. The increased speed implies higher bunker costs, charter hire, insurance and opportunity costs. This cost component is among the largest with respect to overall piracy costs (Table 4.1).

The cost to labour component refers to the excess wages that are paid by companies to seafarers when the vessels they work in transit by routes that are at risk of piracy acts. In the agreement stipulated between the International Transport Workers' Federation and the shipping companies, the seafarers are entitled to a double wage and doubled compensation in the case of death or disability when they pass through a high risk area. Another labour cost to be considered is the replacement cost of the seaman that is being held hostage.

The cost of prosecution and imprisonment is based on the United Nations (UN) Convention on the Law of the Sea, on the UN Convention for the Suppression of Unlawful Acts Against the Safety of Maritime Navigation and on the jurisdictions of the various countries. Their combined regulation implies that any country affected by a piracy act can prosecute and arrest pirates. This has generated momentous problems in terms of diplomatic relationships among countries and a general

Table 4.1 Cost components of Somali piracy 2011–12

	Cost in 2011 ($)	Cost in 2012 ($)
Ransoms	160 million	63.5 million
Military operations	1.27 billion	1.09 billion
Security equipment and guards	1.064–1.16 billion	1.65–2.06 billion
Re-routing	486–681 million	290.5 million
Increased speed	2.71 billion	1.53 billion
Cost to labour	195 million	471.6 million
Prosecutions and imprisonment	16.4 million	14.89 million
Insurance	635 million	550.7 million
Counter-piracy organizations	21.3 million	24.08 million
Total cost	6.6–6.9 billion	5.7–6.1 billion

Sources: Bellish (2013) and Bowden and Basnet (2012).

unwillingness of Western countries to manage these trials and delegate them to the countries bordering the high risk areas.

There are basically two insurance forms related to the piracy phenomenon. The first is the 'war risk' insurance that covers vessels transiting through the war risk areas identified by the Lloyd's Market Association Joint War Committee. The insurance premium is normally reduced if the ship is equipped with security tools or armed guards. The other possible insurance is the 'kidnap and ransom' one, which normally covers the crew but not the vessel.

The last cost component related to piracy is connected with the creation and management of counter-piracy organizations. The most relevant ones, in the case of Somali piracy, are the Trust fund to support initiatives of states to counter piracy off the coast of Somalia, the UN Office of Drugs and Crime, the contact group on piracy off the coast of Somalia and the Djibouti Code of Conduct.[1]

Table 4.1 details the cost components related to Somali piracy in 2011 and 2012. It emerges that ransoms paid to pirates are among the lowest cost components, jointly with prosecution and imprisonment and the funding of counter-piracy organizations.

On the other hand, it appears that the two largest cost components are represented by the increased speed, the security equipment and guards, and the military operations. It is therefore apparent that piracy represents a cost for both private organizations and public administrations. However large, the costs to counter piracy in the Somali area are justified if one considers the necessity to secure the provision of fossil fuel energy to several regions of the world. It has been estimated[2] that 17 per cent of all oil traded in the world passes by the Somali coast and about 8 per cent of world seaborne trade transit the Suez Canal.

The momentous outcomes of terrorist acts and of piracy, both at the local level and on a global scale, have called for regulations that would tackle these issues in order to minimize their possibility and consequences. The following section will discuss some of these regulations, highlighting both costs and benefits. It will then consider a general benefit-cost model of transport security initiatives to try and ascertain its relevance in maritime security.

4.4   ECONOMIC COSTS AND BENEFITS OF MARITIME SECURITY REGULATIONS

An analysis of the costs and benefits of maritime security regulations must take into account the fact that such initiatives have both direct and indirect costs but, on the other hand, reduce the probability that a terrorist attack or any other (lack of) security-related event may take place. It is therefore necessary that the economic value of the latter be higher than the overall costs of an initiative.

A study by the Organisation for Economic Co-operation and Development (OECD, 2003) had proposed an estimation of the direct and indirect costs connected to various security measures. It first considered the Safety of Life at Sea Convention (SOLAS) chapter X1-2 and the International Ship and Port Facility Security (ISPS) code by dividing their measures into five main categories: (a) related to contracting governments; (b) targeting ships; (c) targeting maritime carrier companies: (d) targeting ports; and (e) certification/documentary requirements. In the case of contracting governments, their main responsibilities are related to setting the security level and (possible) alert levels and to communicate them to all actors involved in maritime transport. In this case, the direct cost of enacting such measures would be low but the indirect cost of an improper security level or missing alert would potentially be very high.

The second set of measures is targeted at ships and is composed of three main initiatives. The first is the automatic identification system, ship-borne automatic devices that allow the ship's position to be transmitted to other transponders. Although originally intended to enhance safety, these devices would allow governments and port authorities to have a clear picture of the ships travelling in a determined territory and to control those ships that pose a potential risk in terms of security. Another possible measure is represented by the ship identification number being clearly shown by vessels. Lastly, all ships weighing more than 500 gross tonnage (gt) should be equipped with a security alert system that would transmit a security alert to a designated authority, not send the alert to any other ship, not raise any alarm onboard the ship and keep transmitting the alert until it is deactivated because the security threat has ceased or the security issue has been resolved. This security alert should be started from the navigation bridge and should be of comparable standards to those required by the IMO.

The third set of measures is directed at shipping companies and consists of: (a) designating a company security officer; (b) deploying a ship security assessment for each vessel of the firm; (c) developing a ship security plan; (d) appointing a ship security officer; (e) supplying an appropriate level of training to all officers of the company; (f) equipping all vessels with the tools that are necessary to deploy security measures; and (g) producing a record of all security-related events.[3] The two largest cost components of the security measures related to companies are the appointment of a company security officer and the vessel security equipment. The designation of a ship security officer and record keeping of security-related events are two initiatives with the lowest costs.

The measures related to ports are similar to the ones related to shipping companies. Ports are required to develop a facility security assessment that would identify the assets and infrastructures that it is more important to protect. This would be followed by the definition of possible threats to these assets and infrastructures together with the likelihood of these events. Countermeasures would then have to be selected with the recognition of weaknesses in terms of procedures, policies and human factors. The port security assessment should then be followed by the port facility security plan that should take into account several different elements[4] in order to enhance the degree of security at the port, which would also imply a continuous review of each measure and the general plan. Moreover, ports should appoint a security officer that would be in charge of all the measures proposed in the security plan. The direct costs connected with the measures related to ports and their authorities are in general of a lower magnitude than those required for ships and shipping companies.

Three measures, enacted by the USA in order to increase the degree of security of maritime transport, are the 24-hour advance manifest rule, the CSI and the Customs-Trade Partnership Against Terrorism (C-TPAT).[5] They all involve the cooperation of US trading partners and shipping companies. It appears evident that compliance with the requirements of these initiatives is very burdensome for companies. In the case of the 24-hour advance manifest rule, this is a variable cost that has to be paid for each container that is shipped to the USA and so its relevance may be invariant with respect to the dimension of the firm. On the other hand, the CSI and, above all, the C-TPAT initiative may have a huge impact on the competitive power of firms whose potential market (or part of it) is in the USA (Thai, 2007; Papa, 2013). At the general level, a paper by Limao and Venables (2001) has estimated a high elasticity of international trade to cost. It appears that a 1 per cent increase in cost (that may be due to complying with security regulations) can determine a 2–3 per cent decrease in trade. Moreover, these initiatives may have the effect of making some of the ports non-competitive because of the increased monetary and time costs that these measures entail.

A paper by Farrow and Shapiro (2009) adopted a wider perspective and proposed a taxonomy of the categories of possible interventions to enhance (maritime) security (Table 4.2) by highlighting the possibility that

Table 4.2   Benefit-cost models of transport security initiatives

Issue/Model	Recommended action	Key variables for estimation
Allocating a fixed expenditure amount among independent sites	Equate the marginal expected social costs avoided (MESCA)	Social costs avoided and their change with expenditures, probabilities and costs of implementation
Displacement of probability of attack	Determine the net MESCA, net of probability increasing effects at other sites	As above, plus adjustments in probability for diverted attacks
Constraint on probability or cost reductions	Results in an optimal inequality among sites even where investment occurs	As above, but break-even will be different at sites with constraints
Both prevention and mitigation reducing activities	Equate the marginal social cost avoided of each type of expenditure	As above, but also separates effect of each activity
General rules: public goods	Invest until the sum of marginal damages avoided equals the individual site MESCA	As above, but identify the multiple sites that are positively linked
All hazards: multiple sources of probability and cost	The form of decision is the same (e.g. equate MESCA), but all costs and probabilities are taken into account	As above, but more complex probabilities
Dynamic uncertainty and irreversibility	There can be an optimal 'overinvestment' in security	More complex uncertainties

Source: Farrow and Shapiro (2009).

the strategy of intervention can take into consideration several objectives at the same time. The methodology that is adopted considers the marginal expected social costs avoided, which identifies the main benefit category of the suggested strategies.

Security activities are then justified if their costs are lower than the expected benefits. The consideration of a benefit-cost analysis also implies that a marginal increase in cost for each of the proposed activities is justified if it determines a higher marginal benefit. Moreover, this methodology can provide guidance on the optimal quantities of funding to different security activities (that is, prevention and mitigation).

The framework of analysis proposed by Farrow and Shapiro (2009) can usefully be adopted to analyse security plans at the country level. An example is the National Strategy for Maritime Security (Helmick, 2008) issued in the USA in 2005, or other national security plans, that normally take several different goals into consideration: prevent terrorist attacks and hostile acts; protect maritime-related population centres and critical infrastructure; safeguard the ocean and its resources; and minimize damage and expedite recovery. The methodology of marginal social cost avoided can help to optimally allocate the funds that are destined to maritime security in general in order to maximize the effectiveness of the proposed actions and the general welfare and security for a community.

4.5 CONCLUDING REMARKS

The models' estimations of possible terrorist attacks to a port and the actual estimations of the costs of piracy have shown that the magnitude of both phenomena are extremely relevant, both at the local and global scales. Such costs are not only related to private firms but are mainly incurred by society. The consideration of such momentous consequences paves the way for regulations that try and minimize the effects of such acts. However, it must be taken into account that any regulation should be subject to a benefit-cost analysis, given that they all imply costs to the various economic actors that are involved in maritime trade and to local and global communities. A possible strategy, suggested in this chapter, would imply investment in security until the point at which the marginal benefit of the investment equates its marginal cost. On the other hand, it would be important to consider the best practices that have been deployed in order to optimize the strategic regulation. Part II of the book will compare the policy applications in maritime security in various countries and regions of the world in order to provide such reference points for the administrations that want to pursue maritime security.

NOTES

1. For a complete description of these organizations, see Bowden and Basnet (2012).
2. See http://www.defenceweb.co.za/index.php?option=com_content&view=article&id=1 3540:somali-piracy-is-a-threat-to-global-oil-supplies (accessed 1 October 2013).
3. For a list and discussion of all tasks related to the listed measures, refer to OECD (2003).
4. A tentative list of the port security plan was proposed by the OECD (2003) report and includes: (a) measures to prevent the introduction of weapons and other dangerous substances in the port; (b) measures to prevent unauthorized access to port facilities and to the ships therein; (c) procedures to respond effectively and timely to security threats; (d) procedures to comply with the requirements of the contracting government once the security alert level is very high; (e) procedures for evacuation in case of security threats; (f) duties of personnel assigned to security tasks; (g) procedures to interact with ships' security activities; (h) periodic assessment and enhancement of the security plan; (i) report of security incidents; (j) identification of the security officer of the port; (k) insurance of the security of the information contained in the plan; (l) measures targeted at enhancing the security of cargo and its handling in the port; (m) auditing of the port facility security plan; (n) protocols to react in case a security alert system in a ship moored at the port has been activated; and (o) protocols to facilitate shore leave for the personnel of the ships.
5. For a description of these measures, see Chapter 2.

REFERENCES

Bellish, J. (2013), *The Economic Cost of Somali Piracy 2012*, Broomfield, CO: OneEarthFuture Foundation.

Bowden, A. and S. Basnet (2012), *The Economic Cost of Somali Piracy 2011*, Broomfield, CO: OneEarthFuture Foundation.

Farrow, S. and S. Shapiro (2009), 'The benefit-cost analysis of security focused regulations', *Journal of Homeland Security and Emergency Management*, **6** (1), article 25.

Frittelli, J., L. Martin, M. Jonathan, R. O'Rourke and R. Perl (2003), *Port and Maritime Security: Background and Issues*, New York: Novinka.

Gordon, P., J. Moore II, H. Richardson and P. Qisheng (2005), 'The economic impact of a terrorist attack on the twin ports of Los Angeles-Long Beach', in H. Richardson, P. Gordon and J. Moore (eds), *The Economic Impact of Terrorist Attacks*, Cheltenham, UK and Northampton, MA, USA: Edward Elgar, pp. 262–86.

Helmick, J.S. (2008), 'Port and maritime security: a research perspective', *Journal of Transportation Security*, **1** (1), 15–28.

Limao, N. and A. Venables (2001), 'Infrastructure, geographical disadvantage, transport costs and trade', *World Bank Economic Review*, **15** (3), 451–79.

Mildner, S.A. and F. Gross (2011), 'Piracy and world trade: the economic costs', in S. Mair (ed.), *Piracy and Maritime Security*, SWP Research Paper Series, Berlin: Stiftung Wissenschaft und Politik (German Institute for International and Security Affairs), pp. 20–7.

OECD (2003), *Security in Maritime Transport: Risk Factors and Economic Impact*, available at http://www.oecd.org/newsroom/4375896.pdf (accessed 25 October 2012).

Papa, P. (2013), 'US and EU strategies for maritime transport security: a comparative perspective', *Transport Policy*, **28**, 75–85.

Park, J.Y. (2008), 'The economic impacts of dirty bomb attacks on the Los Angeles and Long Beach ports: applying the supply driven NIEMO (National interstate economic model)', *Journal of Homeland Security and Emergency Management*, **5** (1), article 21.

Rosoff, H. and D. von Winterfeldt (2007), 'A risk and economic analysis of dirty bomb attacks on the ports of Los Angeles and Long Beach', *Risk Analysis*, **27** (3), 533–46.

Thai, V.V. (2007), 'Impacts of security improvements on service quality in maritime transport: an empirical study of Vietnam', *Maritime Economics and Logistics*, **9** (4), 335–56.

UNCTAD (2012), *Review of Maritime Transport 2012*, New York and Geneva: UNCTAD.

Wolfe, M. (2002), 'Freight transportation security and productivity: executive summary', Fifth EU/US Forum on Intermodal Freight Transport, Jacksonville, Florida, 11–13 April 2001.

5.   Risks and costs of maritime security: review and critical analysis

Khalid Bichou

5.1   THE NEW FRAMEWORK FOR MARITIME SECURITY

Since the 9/11 terrorist attacks in the USA, the international community has acknowledged the new security threats to maritime transportation systems and the need for an improved regulatory regime. As a result, a new international framework for enhancing maritime security has been introduced by the International Maritime Organization (IMO). Essentially, this has been done through (a) dividing the 1974 Safety of Life at Sea (SOLAS) Convention chapter XI into two parts: chapter XI-1 for 'Special measures to enhance maritime safety' and a new chapter XI-2 for 'Special measures to enhance maritime security', and (b) establishing a new International Ship and Port Facility Security (ISPS) code to support the security regulations incorporated in the SLOAS XI-2 regulations. In addition, SOLAS XI-1 introduces the new regulation XI-1/5 requiring ships to be issued with a Continuous Synopsis Record (CSR), and modifies regulation XI-1/3 for ships' identification numbers to be permanently marked in a visible place on ships. There has been a further modification to SOLAS chapter V/19, with a timetable for the fitting of Automated Identification Systems (AIS).

The ISPS code itself is divided into two parts: part A is a mandatory section, while part B is a non-compulsory guidance detailing procedures to be undertaken when implementing the provisions of part A and of SOLAS XI-2. The code sets three maritime security (MARSEC) levels ranging from low/normal (1) to high (3) in proportion to the nature/scope of the incident or the perceived security threat. MARSEC level 1 is compulsory and is enclosed under ISPS A. MARSEC level 2 indicates a heightened threat of security incident, while MARSEC level 3 refers to a probable or imminent threat of a security incident. Both the ISPS code and the SOLAS amendments were adopted in December 2002 and came into force in July 2004.

Other statutory instruments have been developed and implemented at various national and regional levels. For instance, the European Community (EC) regulation 725/2004 incorporates the IMO mandatory requirements as well other non-compulsory measures. Parallel initiatives include national regulations such as Canada's own 24-hour rule; regional initiatives such as the Association of South East Asian Nations (ASEAN)/Japan Maritime Transport Security and the Secure Trade in the Asia Pacific Economic Cooperation (APEC) Region (STAR); and additional international programmes such as the IMO/International Labour Organization (ILO) code of practice on security in ports. Finally, it is worth underlying other initiatives currently under development; and in particular the World Customs Organization (WCO) framework on trade security.

The US-led maritime security initiatives are, however, the most significant in both scope/scale and implications. Such programmes range from the incorporation of both mandatory and voluntary ISPS provisions into the US Maritime Transportation Security Act (MTSA) of 2002, to the introduction of a set of further security measures that go beyond what was agreed at the IMO. Among these are the Container Security Initiative (CSI), the Customs-Trade Partnership against Terrorism (C-TPAT) and the 24-hour advance vessel manifest rule, commonly known as the '24-hour rule'. The Public Health Security and Bioterrorism Preparedness and Response Act (Bioterrorism Act) of 2002 is another important piece of legislation requiring detailed information on food shipments before their arrivals to US ports. Programmes targeting domestic participants include the Importer Self-assessment Program (ISA) whereby participating C-TPAT US importers assume responsibility for self-assessment; and the Operation Safe Commerce (OSC), a pilot project targeting cargo entering the USA and starting with three major container load centres (namely, the ports of Los Angeles/Long Beach, Seattle/Tacoma and New York/New Jersey) with a view to analysing security procedures and developing improved methods for securing the global supply chain. Note that in addition to maritime security regulations, similar security programmes for air and inland transportation systems have been introduced by the US administration. Examples include foreign airport pre-inspection; the advanced passenger manifest; and the advanced cargo manifest for rail, truck and air (respectively, 2 hours, 1 hour and 4 hours prior to arrival in/departure for the USA).

Among the few industry-led initiatives, the Smart and Secure Tradelanes (SST) programme, launched by the Strategic Council on Security Technology (SCST), is worth mentioning. The programme is driven by major global port operating companies and seeks to develop a technology platform to track global container movements through the incorporation of a range of automatic identification technologies such as anti-intrusion sensor devices, Radio Frequency Identification (RFID) technologies and satellite (GPS, IMMARSAT) tracking systems. Other relevant schemes include the Star-Best programme and a series of ISO initiatives (ISO 28000, 28001, 28004 and 20858 series).

Table 5.1 provides a summary of major maritime security regulations and initiatives. Although some of these programmes are yet to be fully operational, it is believed they build up a more formal and effective framework and ensure a higher level of security assurance within and beyond the maritime industry.

5.2 RISK ASSESSMENT AND MANAGEMENT OF MARITIME SECURITY

With such complexities in the current maritime security framework, much of the literature on the subject has focused on prescriptive details of the measures being put in place as well as their compliance costs and economic impacts. However, there has been little work on security risk assessment and management models, be it at the physical or transaction levels.

5.2.1 Safety Risk-based Models to Maritime Security

The primary aim of maritime security assessment models is to assess the level of security within and across the maritime network. When introducing the risk factor, the concept and measure of uncertainty must be considered. The conventional approach to risk defines it as being the chance, in quantifiable terms, of an adverse occurrence. It therefore combines a probabilistic measure of the occurrence of an event with a measure of the consequence, or impact, of that event. The process of risk assessment and management is generally based on three sets of sequenced and interrelated activities:

1. The assessment of risk in terms of what can go wrong, the probability of it going wrong and the possible consequences.
2. The management of risk in terms of what can be done, the options and trade-offs available between the costs, the benefits and the risks.
3. The impacts of the risk management decisions and policies on future options and undertakings.

Performing each set of activities requires multi-perspective analysis and modelling of all conceivable sources and impacts of risks as well as viable

Table 5.1 Outline of IMO and US regulatory frameworks for maritime security

	Aim	Legal arrangements	Targets/ participants	Main requirements and responsibilities	Inspection and certification	Observation
IMO Package	Security of maritime network Prevention of terrorism threats	International amendments to SOLAS 1974 mainly: ISPS code and the new SOLAS XI-2 chapter	1. Ship: 500+ gt vessels engaged in international voyage 2. Ship-owning/ operating company	1. Install SSAS and AIS. Keep security records. Display SIS. Provide security equipment 2. Develop SSP. Appoint SSO and CSO. Undertake SSA. Keep records. Carry out training and drills. → Obtain ISSS	ISSC issued by flag state government or RSO (e.g. classification society) for ships and shipping companies Maintenance of certification up to 5 years for ISSC. Interim ISSC valid for 6 months	Part A mandatory Part B guidelines are non-compulsory, but some countries have incorporated them on a mandatory basis in their national security regulations

Table 5.1 (continued)

		Aim	Legal arrangements	Targets/ participants	Main requirements and responsibilities	Inspection and certification	Observation
Selected non-ISPS US Initiatives	CSI	Secure container trading systems/ lanes between major foreign ports and the USA	Bilateral agreement/ partnership between the USA and foreign trade country port partners	Foreign ports (US ports under reciprocity) with substantial and direct waterborne container traffic to the USA	Establish security procedures to identify high-risk container cargo. Work with deployed CBP officers to target containers at risk. Provide NII equipment for container screening and inspection	Validation process and risk assessment mechanism (updated regularly)	CBP offers CSI reciprocity (from April 2005, Canada and Japan customs personnel already deployed in US ports)
	C-TPAT	Develop, maintain and implement effective security processes across the US-bound global	Voluntary agreement between CBP and the private sector New issued criteria for importers in March 2005	US importers and their supply chain partners (carriers, US seaports/ terminals, foreign manu- facturers,	Three-tier certification programme: (1) the certified C-TPAT companies; (2) the validated C-TPAT companies; and (3) 'the green	C-TPAT certification and continuous validation process New criteria for listed importers scaled in	C-TPAT participants are offered reduced frequency screening as well as reduced risk scores in the ACS/ATS

	supply chain	may be interpreted as mandatory	suppliers and sub-contractors, FF, brokers, warehouse providers etc.)	lane' corresponding to the certified and validated C-TPAT companies	three phases from 25 March 2005: phase 1 (2 months) hardening the physical SC, phase 2 (4 months) internal SC security, phase 3 (6 months) business partner requirements	Under the new criteria, there is likely impact on foreign manufacturers exporting to US C-TPAT members
24-hour Rule	Identify/ target high-risk US-bound cargo (including cargo being trans-shipped or remaining onboard the ships) 24-hours	Compulsory regulation, not applicable to bulk cargo	Ocean carriers or their agents. Licensed or registered NVOCCs	Electronic reporting to CBP, via AMS and 24-hours prior to loading at foreign ports, of complete manifest information (14 data elements) for all cargo on board ships	CBP identification/ clearance of transmitted information Non-issuance or delay of permits to unload suspected cargo, or cargo with	Exception may be made for break-bulk cargo shipments Importers may request confidentiality of their identity and the identity

Table 5.1 (continued)

	Aim	Legal arrangements	Targets/ participants	Main requirements and responsibilities	Inspection and certification	Observation
Selected non-ISPS US. Initiatives	24-hour Rule	in advance of loading onboard vessels destined for or transiting via US ports		calling in US ports, even if the cargo is being transhipped or continues on the ship to a third country after it departs the USA	incomplete/ late advance manifest Penalties may also apply	of their shippers Generic descriptions (FAK, STC, general cargo) are not accepted

Notes: ACS: Automated Commercial System; AIS: Automated Identification System; AMS: Automated Manifest System; ATS: Automated Targeting System; CBP: US Customs and Border Protection; CSO: Company Security Officer; CSR: Continuous Synopsis Record; DHS: Department of Homeland Security; FAK: Freight-all-Kind; FF: Freight Forwarders; gt: Gross Tonnage; ISSC: International Ship Security Certificate; MODUs: Mobile Offshore Drilling Units; NNI: Non-Intrusive Inspectional (equipment); NVOCCs: Non-Vessel Operating Common Carriers; RSO: Recognized Security Organization; SC: Supply Chain; SIS: Ship Identification Number; SSA: Ship Security Assessment; SSAS: Ship Security Alert System; SSO: Ship Security Officer; SSP: Ship Security Plan; STC: Said to Contain.

Table 5.2 Major hazard analysis tools

	Consequence analysis	Cause analysis
Sequence dependent	Event Tree Analysis	Markov Process
Sequence independent	Failure Mode and Effects	Fault Tree Analysis

options for decision making and management. The empiricist approach is to regard accidents as random events whose frequency is influenced by certain factors. Under this approach, the immediate cause of an accident is known in the system safety literature as a hazardous event. A hazardous event has both causes and consequences. The sum of the consequences constitutes the size of the accident. Hazardous events range in frequency and severity from high-frequency, low-consequence events, which tend to be routine and well reported, to low-frequency, high-consequence events, which tend to be rare but more complex. Several analytical tools have been developed for hazard analysis. The choice of tool depends on (1) whether the causes or the consequences of a hazardous event are to be analysed and (2) whether the techniques used take into consideration or not the sequence of the causes or consequences (Table 5.2).

The causes of a hazardous event are usually represented by a fault tree, which is a logical process that examines all potential incidents leading up to a critical incident. A popular methodology that relates the occurrence and sequence of different types of incidents is the Fault Tree Analysis (FTA). Under the FTA, a mathematical model is fitted to past accident data in order to identify the most influential factors (top events) and estimate their effects on the accident rate. The model is then used to predict the likelihood of future accidents. The extent to which the tree is developed (from top to basic events) is usually governed by the availability of data with which to calculate the frequencies of the causes at the extremities of the tree, so that these may be assigned likelihoods. From these, the likelihood of the top event is deduced. A simplified application of FTA in the context of maritime security would be to categorize and grade scenario risks according to their overall threat potentials using a scale system from (1) for minor to (3) for severe to fit into the ISPS provisions of MARSEC levels.

FTA has a number of limitations. For instance, the approach assumes that the causes are random and statistically independent but certain common causes can lead to correlations in event probabilities that violate the independence assumptions and could exaggerate the likelihood of an event fault. In a similar vein, missed or unrecorded causes may equally bias the calculated likelihood of a hazardous event. Another shortcoming of the FTA is the assumption that the sequence of causes is not relevant. Where the sequence does matter, Markov chain techniques may be applied.

The consequences of a hazardous event may be analysed using an event tree. Event Tree Analysis (ETA) is a logical process that works the opposite way of FTA by focusing on events that could occur after a critical accident. Under ETA, a statistical analysis of past accidents is performed to estimate the consequences of each type of accident in order to predict risk and consequences of future accidents. The event tree approach implies that the events following the initial accident, if they occur, follow a particular sequence. Where a particular sequence is not implied, Failure Modes and Effects Analysis may be used. This technique seeks to identify the different failure modes that could occur in a system and the effects that these failures would have on the system as a whole. Both are logical processes with the difference being that the first examines all potential incidents leading up to a critical event while the second works the opposite way by focusing on events that could occur after a critical incident. In both models, risks are identified, estimated, assessed and prioritized through a combination of probability and impact.

Most of the general tools described above have been successfully applied across many areas of transport safety, and there seems to be a general consensus among researchers on standardized processes of assessment and management. Methodological questions, such as in terms of selecting or adjusting the appropriate tool, may not constitute a problem as much as data availability and accuracy. Nonetheless, these tools may not be relevant to assessing and managing transport security, including for the port and maritime network. The essence of safety risk models is a probabilistic approach based on the assumption of unintentional human and system behaviour to cause harm. This is not the case for security incidents stemming from terrorism and we are not aware of the existence of any risk models being applied to malicious acts. Another major problem with assessing security threats is that much of the assessment process is intelligence-based, which does not always follow the scrutiny of statistical reasoning. Even with a sound intelligence risk approach, there are many uncertainties involved such as in terms of higher levels of noise in background data. An additional instance of the inadequacy of conventional risk models to maritime security is the lack of historical data given the rarity of occurrence of large-scale terrorist incidents. Another important issue stems from the supply chain dimension of the international shipping network, and as such data on the scope and levels of externalities are extremely difficult to extract and analyse. In either case, the security of the maritime network must be considered in both its physical and supply chain dimensions, the latter evolving around disruptions and risk-driven uncertainties in the supply chain.

5.2.2 Security Incidents and Precursor Analysis

Accident precursors, which are also referred to as accident sequence precursors, can be defined in different ways depending on the approach used such as in terms of causation or correlation. A broad definition of precursors may involve any internal or external condition, event, sequence or any combination of these that precedes and ultimately leads to adverse events. More focused definitions reduce the range of precursors to specific conditions or limit their scope to a specified level of an accident's outcome. For instance, the US Nuclear Regulatory Commission (NRC) defines a precursor as any event that exceeds a specified level of severity (US NRC, 1978), while other organizations incorporate a wider range of severities. In either case, a quantitative threshold may be established for the conditional probability of an incident given a certain precursor, with events of lesser severity being considered either as non-precursors with no further analysis or as non-precursors that need categorization and further investigation.

Several formalized programmes are available for observing, analysing and managing accident precursors including comparison charts and reporting systems. The latter have taken the lead in recent years as many organizations have designed and implemented them to take advantage of precursor information, with the most recognizable reporting system being the colour alert system used by the US Department of Homeland Security (DHS). Relevant examples in the maritime industry include voluntary reporting initiatives for maritime safety (BTS, 2002) and the International Maritime Bureau (IMB, n.d.) reports of piracy attacks.

A major drawback resulting from the combination of warning thresholds and event reporting is that the system may depict several flaws and errors. If precursors are defined too precisely or the threshold is set too high, several risk-significant events may not be reported. On the other hand, setting the threshold for reporting too low may overwhelm the system by depicting many false alarms, and ultimately a loss of trust in the system. Table 5.3 shows the types of errors that may occur given these conflicting approaches. Type I error refers to a false negative and occurs in situations of missed signals when an incident (for example, terrorist attack) occurs with no warning being issued. Type II error refers to a false positive whereby a false alert is issued, leading, for instance, to mass evacuation or a general disturbance of the system.

Another issue arises when reporting precursor events under regulatory constraints. The fact that much reported data remains in the hands of the

Table 5.3   Errors resulting from the interplay between threshold settings and event reporting

	Significant	Not significant
Event reported	True positive (Significant event)	False positive (Type II error)
Event not reported	False negative (Type I error)	True negative (Non-significant event)

Source: Phimister et al. (2004).

regulator raises questions about (a) the reliability and validity of information since fears of regulatory actions may discourage organizations from reporting precursor events, and (b) the dissemination of reported information given that the regulator may restrict access to data that is considered too sensitive to be shared. The argument here is that the purpose of reporting must emphasize organizational learning along with a guarantee of privacy and immunity from penalties for those reporting the information.

A particularly useful concept developed from precursor analysis is the so-called 'near miss', also referred to as the near hit or the close call. A near miss is a particular kind of precursor with elements that can be observed in isolation without the occurrence of an accident. The advantage of the concept is that organizations with little or no history of major incidents can establish systems for reporting and analysing near misses. This is because it has been found that near misses occur with greater frequency than the actual event (Bird and Germain, 1996). This argument is strengthened with much of the literature on reported transport accidents confirming that near misses have usually preceded the actual incidents (Cullen, 2000; BEA, 2002).

In ports and shipping, implementing programmes of security assessment based on precursor analysis would have a number of benefits including for such aspects as identifying unknown failure modes and analysing the effectiveness of actions taken to reduce risk. Another opportunity from precursor analysis is the development of trends in reported data, which may be used for the purpose of risk management and mitigation. (Even though, we are not aware of any formal precursor programme being implemented in the context of port and maritime security, except for ongoing research into potential security hazards for liquid-bulk and specialized ships such as liquefied natural gas (LNG) and liquefied petroleum gas (LPG) vessels.) On the one hand, inherently secure designs against the threats of terrorism and other similar acts are yet to be developed, although improvements have been made in ship design for safer and sustainable transportation. On the other hand, existing reporting schemes of security incidents in shipping and ports depict noticeable gaps in both content and methodology. This is the case, for instance, for piracy and armed robbery incidents whereby available reports show general information with no sufficiently detailed data to display and analyse incident precursors.

Analysis of accident precursors can also be useful in conjunction with Probabilistic Risk Analysis (PRA). PRA is a quantitative risk assessment method for estimating risk failure based on a system's process mapping and decomposition into components (Bier, 1993; Bedford and Cooke, 2001). PRA has been used in a variety of applications including risk analysis in transportation systems. PRA can be combined with precursor analysis to quantify the probability of accidents given a certain precursor, thus helping to prioritize precursors for further analysis or corrective actions. The method can also be improved based on precursor data analysis, for instance, by checking on the validity of PRA model assumptions.

Hence, against conventional approaches of risk assessment based on probabilistic measurements of observed accident frequencies, precursor analysis ideally combined with other techniques such as near misses and PRA methods provides an effective framework for risk assessment and management in the context of maritime security. Security assessment and management in shipping and ports may also be analysed by examining the reliability and robustness of the maritime network.

5.2.3   Applications in Maritime Security

Most of the general tools described above have been successfully applied across most areas of environmental management in shipping and ports, with the Formal Safety Assessment (FSA) being the most standardized framework of risk analysis in regulated maritime systems. The FSA was first developed by the UK Maritime and Coast Guard Agency (MCA) and later incorporated into the IMO's interim guidelines for safety assessment (IMO, 1997). The FSA methodology consists of a five-step process: hazards identification; risk assessment; risk management; cost-benefit analysis; and decision making.

Despite the variety of analytical tools available, the FSA and other conventional risk assessment models involve a substantial element of subjective judgement for both the causes and the consequences. The assumption of randomness of the causes of hazardous events is particularly problematic for low-frequency, high-consequence events such as environmental disasters. As a result of the new and frequent security threats, the traditionally low-frequency, high-consequence security events are predicted to

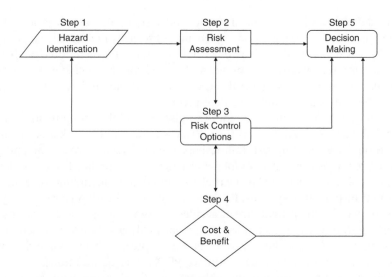

Source: Adapted by the author from IMO (1997).

Figure 5.1   FSA methodology

become more frequent and even more severe. Moreover, there is a growing debate on (1) the premise and extent of randomness of security attacks and (2) the assumption that the sequence and interdependency of the causes of such attacks is not relevant. On the other hand, any analytical tool for risk assessment and management requires that the boundaries, components and functioning of the system under study are well established. However, this is not always evident in shipping and ports given the combination of several elements related to vehicle (ship), facility (port), cargo, equipment, communication, labour and other exogenous factors. Since several of the causes and the consequences of maritime incidents are global in nature, it would be difficult to place spatial or geographical boundaries on them.

The calculation of the consequences of a security accident can also be subjective. Once identified, the level of seriousness of a hazard or an event should be traced down as far as relevant, and should account for various types of impacts; human, economic, social, cultural and so on. An important element in any valuation method of decision making is the cost of preventing a fatality (CPF) and other principal losses in transport and infrastructure, a key component of which stems from human casualties, that is, fatalities and injuries. In most countries, specific regulatory frameworks set out the value of preventing a fatality (VPF) and other values for the prevention of injuries on transport infrastructure. For example, the UK currently operates with a VPF of a just over £1.38 million while the USA uses a VPF figure of around $6 million. This variation may stem from differences in methodologies of calculations, social priorities and values or other reasons. A major issue with regard to maritime security impacts is how to collectively define and quantify the value of preserving global trading and preventing maritime accidents. Even if a standard VPF from changes in global maritime systems is achieved, such value is based on life saving rather than observable market transactions of risk reduction. Most economists believe that VPF valuations should be based on the preferences of those who benefit from preventative security measures and who also pay for them, either directly or through taxation. In the context of casualty prevention, these preferences are often measured using the willingness to pay (WTP) approach, that is, the amount that the average member of the general public is willing to pay to reduce the level of risk to the average victim. The WTP approach has been extensively used in the context of international transport and maritime safety, but no global consensus exists on the use of the methodology in the context of maritime security.

A further difficulty stems from the dissimilarity between stakeholders' perceptions as to the allocation and distribution of the costs and benefits associated with a precautionary policy decision or a risk management programme. Page (1978) has described some of these problems in the context of environmental risk management:

- Poor knowledge of the processes that determine the probability and impact of risk.
- Potential for catastrophic loss in that the occurrence of an environmental disaster would engender great individual, corporate and societal losses.
- Combination of low subjective probability, high uncertainty and lack of consensus.
- Rarity of the occurrence of similar events with only few estimates based on historical figures.
- Unclear pattern regarding the value, allocation, transfer and distribution of costs and benefits among both participating and non-participating parties.

The primary aim of security risk assessment models in shipping and ports is to assess the level of maritime security within and across the international maritime network. From the above discussion, we have pointed out the limitations of conventional risk models in providing an integrated and effective approach to global maritime security threats, risks and impacts. In particular, when assessing a system's risk and reliability to security risk, conventional approaches seem to overlook the network structure and interdependencies of port and shipping operations as well as the global dimension of security risks and impacts.

5.3   THE SUPPLY CHAIN RISK DIMENSION OF MARITIME SECURITY

Since the introduction of the new security regime in shipping and ports, researchers and practitioners alike have questioned the wisdom of such a plethora of regulations. Others have justified the overlap of these pro-grammes by the need to establish a multi-layered regulatory system in an effort to fill potential security gaps (Flynn, 2004; Willis and Ortiz, 2004). The concept of layered security is not entirely new to transport systems and dates back to the 1970s. Prior to the introduction of new maritime security measures, the concept was also cited in 1997 in the context of avia-tion security (Gore Commission, 1997).

To illustrate the application of the layered approach to shipping and port security, we develop a conceptual construct of the structure and functioning of the international maritime and port network. The system is portrayed in terms of three channels (logistics, trade and supply) and three flows (payment, information and physical). A channel is a pathway tracing the movement of a cargo shipment across a 'typology' of multi-institutional and cross-functional cluster alignments, while flows are the derived interactions (business transactions) between various 'functional institutions' within each channel. Figure 5.2 depicts the hierarchy of regu-latory programmes by level of security and maritime network coverage. The levels relative to each programme are hypothetical but typical.

In our model, the supply chain (or supply channel) encompasses both the logistics and trade channels, but rarely oversees the different arrange-ments within each of them. The logistics channel consists primarily of specialists (carriers, freight forwarders, third party logistics providers (3PLs) and so on) that facilitate the efficient progress of cargo through, for example, warehousing and transportation. Both the trade channel and supply channel are associated with the ownership of goods moving through the system, with the difference that the trade channel is normally perceived to be at the level of the sector, the industry or the nation (for example, the oil trade, the containerized trade, the US-Canada trade) and the supply channel at the level of the firm (Toyota or Wall-Mart respec-tive supply chains). For each channel, one or a combination of physical, information and/or payment flows is taking place. Figure 5.3 depicts the

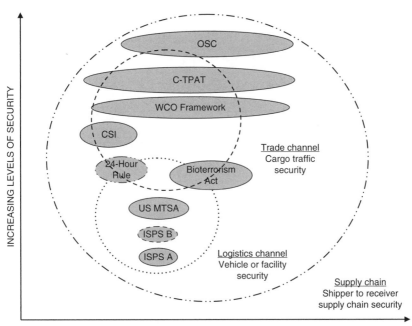

INCREASING LEVELS OF MARITIME NETWORK COVERAGE

Note: OSC = Operation Safe Commerce.

Figure 5.2 Hierarchy of security regulations by level of security and maritime coverage

interactions between channels and flows in a maritime network system. For simplification, channel and flow configurations are depicted in linear path combinations, although a better illustration would be in terms of web-type networked relationships.

To illustrate the need for a layered framework to maritime security, consider a typical global movement of a containerized cargo, which is estimated to involve as many as 25 parties and a compound number of flow configurations within and across the maritime network (Russell and Saldana, 2003). The role and scope of control exercised by members of the supply channel (mainly manufacturers, shippers and receivers) would only oversee the management of direct interactions between them rather than the details of logistical arrangements. Arrangements such as cargo consolidation and break-bulk, multi-modal combinations, trans-shipment and reverse logistics are typically performed by third parties including carriers, ports and other intermediaries. In a similar vein, the trade channel stakeholders (customs,

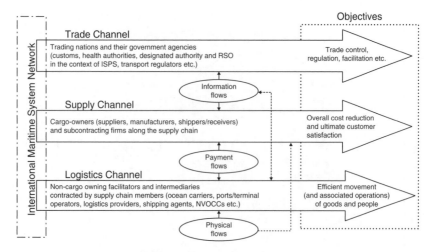

Note: RSC = Recognized Security Organization.

Figure 5.3   Channel typologies and components of the maritime network system

health authorities, regulators and so on) may be able to scrutinize and monitor the logistical segment within their own national territory, but would have little or no control over arrangements taking place in a foreign country including at transit and trans-shipment locations. Thus, the combination of intersecting functional and institutional arrangements across the supply chain makes it almost impossible for a single actor within a single channel to effectively trace and monitor operations across different channels.

One can argue, however, that the layered approach, as being currently implemented, has not yet materialized into an integrated and comprehensive system capable of overcoming existing and potential security gaps. For instance, the emphasis on goods and passenger movements has diverted attention away from non-physical movements such as financial and information flows. Similar observations can be made for outbound cargo and associated flows and processes. Other gaps include the exclusion from the current regulatory regime of fishing vessels, pleasure crafts and yachts, and other commercial ships of less than 500 gt. There is also lack of harmonization between the new security regime and other maritime environmental and safety programmes such as the Standards for Training, Certification and Watch keeping (STCW) code and the International Ship Management (ISM) and International Maritime Dangerous Goods (IMDG) codes. No wonder why the emphasis has been shifting to more comprehensive tools such as C-TPAT and ISO programmes.

Another aspect of interest when examining maritime network security is the interplay between supply chain security and supply chain risk, the latter being closely related to uncertainties stemming from specific supply chain configurations. Juttiner et al. (2003) review the literature on supply chain risk management and categorize sources of supply chain risk into three major groups:

- Environmental risk sources corresponding to uncertainties associated with external sources such as terrorism or environmental risks.
- Organizational risk sources relating to internal uncertainties within the supply chain, for instance, strikes or production failures.
- Network-related risk sources referring to uncertainties arising from the interactions between organizations in the supply chain.

The current maritime security framework strongly emphasizes environmental and organizational risk sources, but there is less focus on network-related vulnerabilities. However, excluding or minimizing network-related risk sources may overlook the capacity of the system to either absorb or amplify the impact of events arising from environmental or organizational sources. Examples of network-related risk drivers in maritime security include uncertainties caused by contracting with non-compliant (non-certified) supply chain partners. A recent study involving 20 top US firms has shown that there is a tendency among American shippers towards trading off lowest bidders with known suppliers (MIT/CTS Interim Report, 2003). In the context of C-TPAT, this could imply trading off foreign manufacturers with national suppliers; and for a US firm with a global sale outreach, this could even imply trading off producing in the USA against transferring operations abroad. There have been similar examples across the shipping and port industry, for instance, shipping lines changing their ports of call because of the existence or absence of a regulatory programme.

5.4 ECONOMIC EVALUATION AND APPRAISAL OF MARITIME SECURITY MEASURES

Several attempts have been made to assess the cost impacts of new security regulations, mainly the ISPS code. Table 5.4 summarizes aggregate estimates for ISPS cost compliance. Note that all such estimates were based on national risk assessment models such as the US national risk assessment tool and the UK risk assessment exercise (US N-RAT, 2003; UK RAE, 2004), and thus they were calculated for the purpose of cost

Table 5.4 Summary of ISPS cost estimates as calculated by various regulatory risk assessment tools

Source of estimate	Cost items	Scope	Costs in $ million		
			Initial costs	Annual costs	Overall cost over 10 years (2003–13) @ 7% discount rate
USCG	Total ISPS US ports	226 port authorities, of which 5000 facilities are computed (from Fairplay) (ISPS Parts A and B, MARSEC Level 1)	1125	656	5399
	Total ISPS US-SOLAS and non-SOLAS vessels subject to the regulation	3500 US flag vessels, as well as domestic and foreign non-SOLAS vessels (i.e. operating in US waters) (ISPS Parts A and B, MARSEC Level 1)	218	176	1368
	Automated Identification System (AIS)		30	1	50
	Maritime Area (contracting government)	47 COTP US zones	120 (+ 106 for 2004)	46	477
	OSC facility (offshore installations)	40 US OSC facilities under US jurisdiction	3	5	37
	US cost for ISPS implementation	(ISPS Parts A and B)	115	884	7331
	Aggregate cost of elevating MARSEC level from 1 to 2	Based on a twice MARSEC level 2 per annum, each for 21 days		16 per day	

UK	Total ISPS UK port facilities	430 facilities (ISPS Part A, MARSEC Level 1)	26	2.5
	Total ISPS UK flagged ships and company-related costs	620 UK flag vessels (ISPS Part A, MARSEC Level 1) (calculations based on an exchange rate of US$ = UK £1.6)	7.4	5.2
OECD	AIS	Based on 43,291 international commercial fleet of more than 1000 gt (passenger and cruise vessels not included), MARSEC Level 1, ISPS Part A only	649.3	Undetermined
	Other vessel measures		115.11	14.6
	Ship operating companies		1163.89	715.4
	Total ships and shipping companies		1279	730
	PFSA, PFSO		390.8	336.6
	Total ISPS ports	2180 port authorities worldwide, of which 6500 facilities are computed (from Fairplay) (ISPS Part A only, MARSEC Level 1) (MARESC level 1, ISPS Part A only)	Undetermined	Undetermined
	Global cost for ISPS implementation		Undetermined	Undetermined
Australian Government	Total costs for Australia	70 ports, of which 300 port facilities. 70 Australian flag ships	240	74

Notes: COTP = Captain of the Port; OSC = Operation Safe Commerce; PFSA = Port Facility Security Assessment; USCG = US Coast Guard.

Sources: US Federal Register (2003), N-RAT Assessment Exercise, 204 (68), 60464–6046 and OECD (2003).

assessment of what was at the time 'the ISPS proposal', and in any case before its adoption and implementation.

In evaluating the costs and benefits for optimal regulatory decisions, cost-benefit analysis (CBA) is regarded as a fairly objective method of making assessments. Cost-efficiency analysis (CEA) is an alternative method to CBA usually applied when the output is fixed and the economic benefits cannot be expressed in monetary terms. CBA and CEA are widely used to assess the efficiency of various measures and alternatives such as in terms of a new regulatory regime or a new investment (for example, in infrastructure or technology). In the context of maritime regulation, CBA was first introduced by the FSA guidelines as approved by the IMO in 2001; and later adopted in most subsequent regulatory programmes including for regulatory assessment of the ISPS code and other related measures.

However, in a typical CBA or CEA model, the results of implementing a regulation can be entirely different from one stakeholder (firm, nation-state and so on) to another. The concept of externality is very difficult to apprehend in the context of malicious incidents. According to the definition of externality, costs arising from accidents are external when one person or entity causes harm to another person involved in the accident, or a third party, without providing appropriate compensation. Risk decisions regarding the introduction of regulatory measures involve multiple stakeholders who influence decisions through a complex set of legal and deliberative processes. Whether this is beneficial to the whole community or not is very debatable given the differences between stakeholders' values and perspectives. In a typically fragmented maritime industry, this focus raises the important question: costs or benefits to whom? In other words, who will bear the cost of or gain the benefits from the compliance with statutory measures?

To correct CBA or CEA deficiencies particularly with regard to cost sharing and distribution, Stakeholder Analysis (SHA) was introduced in the early 1980s. SHA is designed to identify the key players (stakeholders) of a project or a regulation, and assess their interests and power differentials for the purpose of project formulation and impact analysis. Several procedures have been proposed for SHA implementation, with the World Bank four-step formula (stakeholders' identification, stakeholders' interests, power and influence interrelationships, and strategy formulation) being the most recognized and widely used. It must be noted, however, that there is no clear-cut predominance of one method over another, and quite often not all the conditions for the implementation of a complete regulatory assessment exercise are met.

An important element in any valuation method of new regulatory decisions is the cost of preventing principal losses in security incidents, a key component of which stems from human casualties, that is, fatalities and injuries. However, since the value of these losses is not observable in market transactions, most economists believe that these valuations should be based on the preferences of those who benefit from security measures and who also pay for them, either directly or through taxation. In the context of casualty prevention, these preferences are often measured using the WTP approach, that is, the amount people or society are willing to pay to reduce the risk of death or injury before the events. There are two major empirical approaches to estimating WTP values for risk reductions, namely, the revealed preference method (RPM) and the stated preference method (SPM). RPM involves identifying situations where people (or society) do actually trade off money against risk, such as when they may buy safety (or security) measures or when they may take more or less risky jobs for more or less wages. SPM, on the other hand, involves asking people more or less directly about their hypothetical WTP for safety or security measures that give them specified reductions in risk in specified contexts. The WTP approach has been extensively used in the context of road safety, but little literature exists on the use of the methodology in the context of shipping safety, let alone in the context of maritime and port security. The problem with the WTP approach in the latter context is that it is difficult to assume that people or society are capable of estimating the risks they face from terrorism (RPM) or that they are willing to answer questions about trading off their security, or safety, against a given amount of money (SPM).

In addition to compliance cost, other costs arise from implementing the new regulatory requirement. These mainly refer to commercial and operational costs stemming from potential inefficiencies brought about by the new measures. For instance, one study has estimated that the security measures introduced in the wake of the 9/11 terrorist attacks, including transport-related initiatives, would cost the US economy as much as $151 billion annually, of which $65 billion is just for logistical changes to supply chains (Damas, 2001). Against this, a simulation game exercise of a terrorist attack on a major US port has found that it could cost as much as $50 billion with a backlog of up to 60 days (Grenscer et al., 2003).

Another way to analyse the cost-benefit of a regulatory change is to contrast transfer costs against efficiency costs. The first refers to the costs incurred and recovered by market players through transferring them to final customers (for example, from ports to carriers to shippers), while the second represents net losses in consumer/producer surpluses. Note that such analysis is not without bias, including the common practice of cost spin-off and exponential computations of security expenses. Table 5.5

Table 5.5   Summary of press reports on ports' container security charges

Example of average terminal security fees		$/TEU
Australian ports (those operated by P&O Ports)		3.8
Europe	Belgian ports	10.98
	Danish ports	61
	Dutch ports	10.37
	French ports	10.98
	Italian ports	9.76
	Latvian ports	7.32
	Norwegian ports	2.44
	Spanish ports	6.1
	Irish ports	8.54
	Swedish ports (Gothenburg)	2.6
	UK ports Felixstowe (HPH)	19 for import and 10 for export
	Harwich	19 for import and 10 for export
	Thames	19 for import and 10 for export
	Tilbury	12.7
Canada	Vancouver	2.7% increase in harbour dues
	TSI Terminal handling charges	1.5
USA	Charleston, Houston, Miami	5
	Gulf seaports marine terminal conference	2
Others	Shenzhen	6.25
	Hong Kong	6.41
	Mexico	10

Note: TEU is Twenty-foot Equivalent Unit.

Sources: Various news articles from Lloyd's List, Fairplay and Containerisation International.

provides a sample list of terminal security fees as charged by major ports and terminal operators.

5.5   CONCLUSION

This chapter is intended to serve as a conceptual piece that draws from the interplay between engineering and supply chain approaches to risk in the context of recent maritime security regulations. It is hoped that cross-disciplinary analysis of the perception and impact of the security risk will stimulate thinking on appropriate tools and analytical frameworks for enhancing port and maritime security. In so doing, it may be possible to develop new approaches to security assessment and management, including such aspects as supply chain security.

The framework and methods reviewed in this chapter could serve as a roadmap for academics, practitioners and other maritime interests to formulate risk assessment and management standards and procedures in line with the new security threats. Equally, further research can build on this to investigate the mechanisms and implications of security measures on port and shipping operations, including such aspects as the cost and economic impacts on operational and supply chain efficiency.

REFERENCES

BEA (Bureau d'Enquêtes et d'Analyse pour la Sécurité de l'Aviation Civile) (2002), *Rapport sur l'Accident de Air France Concorde F-BTSC ayant lieu le 25 Juillet 2000 à la Platte d'Oie*, Paris: Ministère de l'Equipement, du Transport et du Logement.

Bedford, T. and R. Cooke (2001), *Probabilistic Risk Analysis: Foundations and Methods*, Cambridge: Cambridge University Press.

Bier, V.M. (1993), 'Statistical methods for the use of accident precursor data in estimating the frequency of rare events', *Reliability Engineering and System Safety*, **42**, 267–80.

Bird, F.E. and G.L. Germain (1996), *Practical Loss Control Leadership*, Alberta: Det Norske Veritas.

BTS (Bureau of Transportation Statistics) (2002), 'Project 6 overview: develop better data on accident precursors or leading indicators', in *Safety Numbers Conference Compendium*, Washington, DC: BTS, available at http://www.bts.gov/publications/safety_in_numbers_conference_2002/project07/project7_overview.html (accessed October 2013).

Cullen, W.D. (2000), *The Ladbroke Grove Rail Inquiry*, Norwich: Her Majesty's Stationery Office.

Damas, P. (2001), 'Supply chains at war', *American Shipper*, November, 17–18.

Flynn, S. (2004), *America the Vulnerable: How our Government is Failing to Protect Us from Terrorism*, New York: Harper-Collins Publishing.

Gore Commission (1997), *Report to the White House on Aviation Safety and Security*, available at http://www.fas.org/irp/threat/212fin~1.html (accessed 2008).

Grencser, M., J. Weinberg and D. Vincent (2003), *Port Security War Game: Implications for U.S. Supply Chains*, Washington, DC: Booz Aallen Hamilton.

IMB (International Maritime Bureau) (n.d.), http://www.icc-ccs.org (accessed 2009).

IMO (1997), 'Interim guidelines for the application of formal safety assessment (FSA) to the IMO rule making process', MSC/Circular 829 and MPEC/Circular 355, International Maritime Organization, London.

Juttner, U., U.H. Peck and M. Christopher (2003), 'Supply chain risk management: outlining an agenda for future research', *International Journal of Logistics: Research and Applications*, **6** (4), 197–210.

MIT/CTS Interim Report (2003), *Supply Chain Response to Terrorism: Creating Resilient and Secure Supply Chains*, available at http://web.mit.edu/scresponse/repository/SC_Resp_Report_Interim_Final_8803.pdf (accessed 2010).

OECD (2003), *Security in Maritime Transport: Risk Factors and Economic Impact*, Maritime Transport Committee Report, Paris: OECD.

Page, T. (1978), 'A generic view of toxic chemicals and similar risks', *Ecology Law Quarterly*, **7**, 204–44.

Phimister, J.A., V.M. Bier and H.C. Kunreuther (eds) (2004), *Accident Precursor Analysis and Management: Reducing Technological Risk through Diligence*, National Academy of Engineering, Washington, DC: The National Academies Press.

Russell, D.M. and J.P. Saldana (2003), 'Five tenets of security-aware logistics and supply chain operation', *Transportation Journal*, **42** (4), 44–54.

US Federal Register (2003), *N-RAT Assessment Exercise*, **204** (68), 60464–6.

US NRC (US Nuclear Regulatory Commission) (1978), Risk *Assessment Review Group Report*, NUREG/CR- 400, NRC: Washington, DC.

Willis, H.H. and D. Ortiz (2004), *Evaluating the Security of the Global Containerised Supply Chain*, RAND Technical Report Series, Pittsburg, PA: RAND Corporation.

6. Maritime terrorist attacks against seaports 1968–2007

Risto Talas and David Menachof

6.1 INTRODUCTION

The motivation for researching maritime terrorism came from Dr Talas's PhD thesis, which was mainly concerned with maritime port security efficiency modelling. One of the key elements of the research was collecting data from specialist terrorism underwriters at Lloyd's of London on the likelihood of the occurrence of certain prescribed types of terrorist attack on a maritime port facility. As part of the literature review for the PhD thesis, data on terrorist attacks against ports and against shipping in ports were collected from RAND Corporation and analysed. It was in the analysis of the data that the pattern of terrorist attacks began to emerge and thus Gleason's (1980) and Jenkins et al.'s (1983) method of modelling (general) terrorism risk using the Poisson distribution and the application of the Kolmogorov-Smirnov test on the data from the RAND database of worldwide maritime terrorist attacks[1] from 1968 to 2007 was repeated. The importance of the research is in the validation of the actual terrorism insurance prices quoted by terrorism underwriters when compared with the theoretical predictor of the likelihood of a terrorist attack against ports and against shipping in ports using empirical data and the Poisson distribution.

In the chapter we propose new definitions of port security risk. The port security risk model is described, which is based on Talas and Menachof (2009) and Willis et al. (2005). We show how empirical data of the terrorist incidents in ports and on vessels in ports can be used to predict the probability of future terrorist attacks of this nature and provide the model for port security risk with a coefficient of port security terrorism risk, albeit with two important assumptions.

6.2   PORT SECURITY RISK

As risk is present in all walks of daily life it is logical that an extensive literature exists on the subject. Whether considering individuals' attitudes to risk and decision making under uncertainty (Kahneman and Tversky, 1979) or risk as a factor in decision making (March and Shapira, 1987), the interpretation of risk varies from person to person. Definitions of risk also vary according to the discipline in which the discussion is framed, be it supply chain (Juttner et al., 2003; Chopra and Sodhi, 2004; Zsidisin et al., 2004; Christopher, 2005; Rao and Goldsby, 2009), supply chain security (Williams et al., 2008), port security (Bichou, 2004, 2009; Talas and Menachof, 2009), terrorism (Sheffi, 2001; Woo, 2003; Price, 2004; Willis et al., 2005; Greenberg et al., 2006; Raymond, 2006), sociology and psychology (Heimer, 1988) or more established disciplines such as economics, finance or management (Juttner et al., 2003). Rao and Goldsby (2009) present selected definitions of risk from the literature including from Lowrance (1980) as 'risk is a measure of the probability and severity of adverse effects' and from Yates and Stone (1992), 'risk is an inherently subjective construct that deals with the possibility of loss'.

Definitions of risk relevant to this research can be found in Robinson (2008), March and Shapira (1987), Bedford and Cooke (2001), Markowitz (1952), Broder (2006), Greenberg et al. (2006), Bakshi and Gans (2010), Price (2004) and Willis et al. (2005). Robinson (2008, p. 182) describes risk from a security perspective as 'the probability that harm may result from a given threat'. March and Shapira (1987, p. 1404) review managerial perspectives on risk and risk taking and define risk as 'reflecting variation in the distribution of possible outcomes, their likelihoods and their subjective values'. Bedford and Cooke's (2001) analysis of probabilistic risk analysis describes risk as having two particular elements: hazard and uncertainty. Markowitz (1952, p. 89) describes risk as 'variance of return'. Broder (2006, p. 3) describes risk as 'the uncertainty of financial loss, the variations between actual and expected results or the probability that a loss has occurred or will occur'. Greenberg et al. (2006, p. 143) state that terrorism risk 'does not exist without existence of threat, the presence of vulnerability and the potential for consequences'. Bakshi and Gans (2010) define their risk score, x, to be the conditional probability that given a terrorist targets a (shipping) container for infiltration, the attempt would escape detection by security precautions in place up through the primary inspection at the port of debarkation: $P\{no\ alarm\ |\ threat\}$. Price (2004, p. 335) claims that ports (in the context of terrorism) are actually faced with uncertainty, not risk because uncertainty implies that while the range of events is known, the associated probabilities of each type of event are not. To an insurance underwriter, risk can represent not only the vessel, aircraft or property under consideration for insurance (Broder, 2006, p. 3) but also the product of the probability of the occurrence of an insured event and the financial consequences of such an event. Willis et al. (2005) describe terrorism risk as consisting of the product of threat, vulnerability and consequence: where threat is the probability that an attack occurs; vulnerability is the probability that an attack results in damage, given that an attack has occurred; and consequence is the expected damage, given that an attack has occurred which resulted in damage. Drawing on this definition and the definitions by Robinson (2008), Broder (2006) and Bedford and Cooke (2001), the proposed definition for port security risk is: the product of the probability of a threat to port facility assets, cargoes and the ship–port interface that may give rise to a loss and the size of the financial consequences that might result.

These definitions can be summarized and expressed as:

Risk = *P* (attack occurs) * *P* (attack results in damage | attack occurs) * *E*
     (damage | attack occurs and results in damage)
   = Threat * Vulnerability * Consequence

In order to estimate the terrorist risk, it is necessary to be able to estimate the probability of the threat manifesting itself in an attack, the probability that the attack results in damage and an estimate of the expected damage that might follow.

6.3   GLEASON'S (1980) MODELLING OF TERRORISM RISK IN THE UNITED STATES

Gleason (1980) modelled terrorism risk using the Poisson distribution and focused exclusively on acts of international terrorism in the United States that occurred between 1968 and 1974. Gleason (1980) describes the Poisson distribution as a good model for occurrences such as terrorist events for three reasons: first, 'the probability than an event of terrorism occurs during a time interval increases with the length of the time interval'; second, 'the probability is almost negligible that two events of terrorism will occur in a very small time interval'; and third, 'events of terrorism which occur during one time interval are independent of those which occur in any other time interval'.

The Poisson distribution is described by Equation 6.1:

$$p(N = n) = \frac{\lambda^n e^{-\lambda}}{n!} \qquad (6.1)$$

where n = number of occurrences of an event and λ = expected number of occurrences during a given time interval.

6.4   ANALYSIS OF THE RAND DATABASE OF TERRORIST ATTACKS

The data in the RAND terrorism databases found in Jenkins et al. (1983), Gardela and Hoffman (1990, 1991, 1992) and the online RAND database of terrorism incidents were analysed and only terrorist attacks on seaports as well as attacks on vessels while alongside or at anchor in any seaport were recorded. See Appendix 6.A1 for the list of terrorist attacks. There are some identifiable patterns that emerge from the data in terms of the geographic locations and modus operandi of the terrorist attacks. In the late 1960s and early 1970s, many of the attacks were by anti-Castro groups seeking to attack Soviet or communist country origin shipping calling in Cuba. Throughout the 1970s, the anti-Castro groups were joined by anti-Israeli groups, Black September (Greece) and Irish terrorist groups. The majority of attacks used limpet mines attached to the hulls of vessels.

In the 1980s, the growing trend of terrorism was the rise of the Middle Eastern terrorist groups such as the Palestinian Liberation Organization and the Popular Front for the Liberation of Palestine. In Europe, the Basque terrorist group ETA began to operate in the maritime domain and in North Africa, the Polisario began to attack shipping in Moroccan ports. The modus operandi also evolved from the use of limpet mines in the 1970s to include bombing, shelling and highjacking.

In the 1990s, maritime terrorism was dominated by the Tamil Tiger Sea Arm in Sri Lanka and the emergence of terrorist groups that would later become affiliated to Al-Qaeda and the modus operandi further evolved to include suicide bombings, especially in Sri Lankan waters.

In the first decade of the twenty-first century, maritime terrorist attacks have occurred in Yemen, Russia, Iraq, Pakistan, the Philippines, Corsica and Indonesia. The geographic spread seems to have widened to include many more countries. During the last 30 years of the twentieth century, terrorist attacks followed almost a migratory path beginning in Cuba and stretching gradually to the Middle East. Today it appears that terrorist attacks can occur in places where previously they would have been thought extremely unlikely. The globalization of supply chains and the

Table 6.1   *Number of worldwide maritime terrorist attacks in ports: years 1968–2007*

Year	No. of attacks	Year	No. of attacks	Year	No. of attacks	Year	No. of attacks	Year	No. of Attacks
1968	2	1970	1	1980	3	1990	0	2000	1
1969	0	1971	1	1981	2	1991	0	2001	1
		1972	2	1982	4	1992	0	2002	1
		1973	2	1983	2	1993	1	2003	2
		1974	6	1984	5	1994	1	2004	3
		1975	5	1985	2	1995	1	2005	1
		1976	3	1986	2	1996	2	2006	1
		1977	1	1987	3	1997	4	2007	2
		1978	2	1988	3	1998	0		
		1979	2	1989	0	1999	0		

proliferation of social media channels means that an attack in an obscure part of the world will still eventually reach a wide audience.

A summary of the number of terrorist attacks in each year of the study is found in Table 6.1. The mean, $\lambda = 1.85$, represents 74 attacks over 40 years from 1968 to 2007. Performing the calculation in Equation 6.1, the probabilities of the number of attacks in any given year are shown in Table 6.2.

Figure 6.1 shows the probabilities of actual versus expected attacks in seaports. The overall fit of the actual situation appears to replicate a Poisson distribution.

Gleason (1980) hypothesized that the Poisson distribution was a good model for incidents of international terrorism in the United States and performed two goodness of fit tests, namely, Chi-square and the Kolmogorov-Smirnov (K-S) tests to test the hypothesis. Owing to the nature of his data, Gleason (1980, p. 261) combined the 'Number of Incidents' classes in order to ensure a valid Chi-square test, that is, the expected frequency in each class was at least five. Owing to this combination of classes, he decided to follow up with the K-S test as this 'test treats individual observations separately; consequently, information is not lost through the combining of categories'. The K-S test, specifically the one-sample K-S test, is a nonparametric test used to compare a sample distribution with a reference probability distribution; in this case, the Poisson distribution. Gleason (1980) showed that the results of both the Chi-square and the K-S tests suggested that the Poisson distribution was a good model.

Following Gleason's (1980) example, it was decided to test the hypothesis that the Poisson distribution is a good model for the maritime terrorism attack data contained in column (4) of Table 6.2. However, in order to

Table 6.2   Probabilities of a given number of attacks in a year in the maritime domain calculated using the Poisson distribution, the actual number of attacks and the expected number of attacks

(1) No. of attacks	(2) Expected probability	(3) Expected number of years in which there were the number of attacks	(4) Actual number of years in which there were the number of attacks	(5) Actual probability
0	0.157,237,166	6.289,487	7	0.170
1	0.290,888,758	11.635,550	11	0.275
2	0.269,072,101	10.762,884	12	0.300
3	0.165,927,796	6.637,112	5	0.125
4	0.076,741,605	3.069,664	2	0.050
5	0.028,394,394	1.135,776	2	0.050
6	0.008,754,938	0.350,198	1	0.025
7	0.002,313,805	0.092,552	0	0.000
8	0.000,535,067	0.021,403	0	0.000
9	0.000,109,986	0.004,399	0	0.000
10	2.034,74E-05	0.000,814	0	0.000

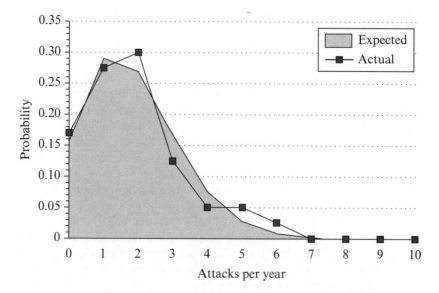

Figure 6.1   Probabilities of actual versus expected attacks in the maritime domain

Table 6.3   *Results of the one-sample Kolmogorov-Smirnov test from*
              SPSS

		VAR00001
N		40
Poisson Parameter[a,b]	Mean	1.8500
Most Extreme	Absolute	0.035
Differences	Positive	0.033
	Negative	−0.035
Kolmogorov-Smirnov Z		0.221
Asymp.Sig. (2-tailed)		1.000

Notes:
a. Test distribution is Poisson.
b. Calculated from data.

apply the Chi-square test, the data would have to be aggregated into three combinations and as this was the same problem that Gleason (1980) had encountered with the data on terrorism attacks on the United States, it was decided to apply the K-S goodness of fit test in isolation. The K-S test rejects the null hypothesis that the sample distribution is drawn from the (in this case) Poisson distribution if the Z-value is greater than the critical values in the one-sample K-S test table in Appendix 6.A2. The results of the K-S test performed using SPSS are shown in Table 6.3.

The K-S Z-value of 0.221 means that the data in column (4) of Table 6.2 describe a Poisson distribution as the K-S Z-value is critical at the alpha = 0.01 level. This means that the probability of future terrorist incidents in ports or on vessels in ports can be modelled using the Poisson distribution and the data in Table 6.2.

The model for port security risk is based on Talas and Menachof (2009), Willis et al. (2005), Gleason (1980) and the RAND terrorism database data in Table 6.2.

If l_j is the loss (consequence) from an attack type j and the probability of the occurrence of l_j is $p(l_j)$ and the vulnerability of the port facility from l_j is defined as $1-p(s_{ij})$ where s_{ij} is the ability of security system i to prevent l_j then it follows that the

$$\text{aggregate port security risk is } \sum_{i=1}^{n} \sum_{j=1}^{m} p(l_j) \times (1 - p(s_{ij})) \times l_j \quad (6.2)$$

for n security systems against m different types of security incident. Furthermore, we can use Poisson to calculate $p(l_j)$ for any given terminal. However, this requires two important assumptions: first, that each terrorist attack is independent and second, that each port facility is equally likely to be attacked.

The probability for n attacks in a given year ($0 \leq n \leq 10$) is shown in column (2) of Table 6.2 and what is required for our model is the probability of 1 or more attacks in any year. This is calculated by summing the probabilities of n attacks where $1 \leq n \leq 10$. The probabilities of $n > 10$ were disregarded as they are very small and unlikely to affect the overall result.

Given that there are 4339 ports in the world,[2] if we were to model the probability of one or more attacks in any year on one of those port facilities with $\lambda = 1.85$, the probability would be 0.000426355 (see Equation 6.3).

$$p(l) = \sum_{n=1}^{10} \frac{p(n) \times n}{4339} = 0.000426355 \qquad (6.3)$$

The resulting model for port security terrorism risk is shown in Equation 6.4.

$$PortSecurityRisk = 0.000426355 \times \sum_{i=1}^{n} \sum_{j=1}^{m} (1 - p(s_{ij})) \times l_j \qquad (6.4)$$

While this model holds for the assumption that each port is equally likely to be attacked, it is interesting to compare the coefficient derived from the Poisson process with that of the expert opinion of a specialist terrorism underwriter regarding the terrorism risks in ports in different countries around the world. A specialist terrorism underwriter from Lloyd's of London was approached for a sample of his premium pricing of terrorism risks and the sample premiums are shown in Table 6.4.

The average of the sample terrorism premiums is 0.0313 per cent, whereby the Poisson forecast of 0.0426 per cent per annum may be considered to be 'in the ballpark'.

Table 6.4   Sample of terrorism insurance premiums provided by a Lloyd's Underwriter

Location	Terrorism Insurance Premium (% per annum)
North America	0.0152
Europe	0.018
South Asia	0.07
North Asia	0.03
Australasia	0.023

Source: Interview 23 April 2009.

6.5 CONCLUSIONS AND FUTURE RESEARCH

The research develops a model of port security risk, based on Talas and Menachof (2009), also incorporating Willis et al.'s (2005) definition of terrorism risk and continues the work of Gleason (1980) adapted for terrorist attacks against ports or against shipping in ports from 1968 to 2007. The results show that the attack patterns resemble a Poisson distribution, as confirmed by the K-S test. This means that we are able to calculate a worldwide port security terrorism attack probability, while noting the two key assumptions of attack independence and that every port is equally likely to be attacked. While the second assumption may not always hold in practice, the research has shown that the predicted coefficient is in the 'ballpark' of the premium charging levels for terrorism insurance charged in the Lloyd's Insurance Market. Nevertheless, with the trend of terrorism becoming more globalized in the first decade of the twenty-first century, this assumption should not be ruled as unrealistic.

Managerial implications from this research are that those involved in the maritime and shipping industry are able to quantify the risk, and subsequently the insurance premiums that they should be paying or charging. The researchers recognize that there have been massive improvements in port security over the period the data cover, but have also seen 'improvements' in the terrorists' ability to strike. There is an implicit recognition that stopping any and all terrorist attack attempts may be impossible on a global scale, but this is not the goal of this chapter, and that the results of the research allow the risk from terrorist attacks in seaports and on ships in seaports to be properly quantified.

NOTES

1. RAND Terrorism Incidents Database, http://www.rand.org/nsrd/projects/terrorism-incidents (accessed 23 April 2010).
2. http://www.ports.com (accessed 23 April 2010).

REFERENCES

Bakshi, N. and N. Gans (2010), 'Securing the containerized supply chain: analysis of government incentives for private investment', *Management Science*, **56** (2), 219–33.

Bedford T. and R. Cooke (2001), *Probabilistic Risk Analysis: Foundations and Methods*, Cambridge: Cambridge University Press.

Bichou, K. (2004), 'The ISPS code and the cost of port facility compliance: an initial logistics and supply chain framework for port security assessment and management', *Journal of Maritime Economics and Logistics*, **6**, 322–48.

Bichou, K. (2009), 'Security and risk-based models in shipping and ports: review and critical analysis', in *OECD/ITF Roundtable 144, Terrorism and International Transport: Towards Risk-based Security Policy*, OECD/ITF Transport Research Centre, pp. 111–37.

Broder, J. (2006), *Risk Analysis and the Security Survey*, 3rd edn, Boston, MA: Elsevier Butterworth Heinemann.

Chopra, S. and M.S. Sodhi (2004), 'Managing risk to avoid supply chain breakdown', *MIT Sloan Management Review*, **46** (1), 53–61.

Christopher, M. (2005), *Logistics and Supply Chain Management*, 3rd edn, Harlow, Essex: FT Prentice Hall.

Gardela, K. and B. Hoffman (1990), *The RAND Chronology of International Terrorism for 1986*, Santa Monica, CA: RAND Corporation.

Gardela, K. and B. Hoffman (1991), *The RAND Chronology of International Terrorism for 1987*, Santa Monica, CA: RAND Corporation.

Gardela, K. and B. Hoffman (1992), *The RAND Chronology of International Terrorism for 1988*, Santa Monica, CA: RAND Corporation.

Gleason, J.M. (1980), 'A Poisson model of incidents of international terrorism in the United States', *Studies in Conflict and Terrorism*, **4** (1), 259–65.

Greenberg, M., P. Chalk, H. Willis, I. Khilko and D. Ortiz (2006), *Maritime Terrorism: Risk and Liability*, Santa Monica, CA: RAND Corporation Centre for Terrorism and Risk Management Policy.

Heimer, C. (1988), 'Social structure, psychology and the estimation of risk', *Annual Review of Sociology*, **14**, 491–519.

Jenkins, B., B. Cordes, K. Gardela and G. Petty (1983), *A Chronology of Terrorist Attacks and Other Criminal Actions Against Maritime Targets*, Santa Monica, CA: RAND Corporation.

Juttner, U., H. Peck and M. Christopher (2003), 'Supply chain risk management: outlining an agenda for future research', *International Journal of Logistics: Research and Applications*, **6** (4), 199–213.

Kahneman, D. and A. Tversky (1979), 'Prospect theory: an analysis of decision under risk', *Econometrica*, **47** (2), 263–92.

Lowrance, W.W. (1980), 'The nature of risk', in R.C. Schwing and W.A. Albers (eds), *How Safe is Safe Enough?*, New York: Plenum Press, pp. 5–14.

March, J.G. and Z. Shapira (1987), 'Managerial perspectives on risk and risk taking', *Management Science*, **33** (11), 1404–18.

Markowitz, H. (1952), 'Portfolio selection', *Journal of Finance*, **7** (1), 77–91.

Price, W. (2004), 'Reducing the risk of terror events at ports', *Review of Policy Research*, **21** (3), 329–49.

RAND Terrorism Incidents Database, http://www.rand.org/nsrd/projects/terrorism-incidents (accessed 23 April 2010).

Rao, S. and T.J. Goldsby (2009), 'Supply chain risks: a review and typology', *International Journal of Logistics Management*, **20** (1), 97–123.

Raymond, C.Z. (2006), 'Maritime terrorism in Southeast Asia: a risk assessment', *Terrorism and Political Violence*, **18** (2), 239–57.

Robinson, P. (2008), *Dictionary of International Security*, Cambridge: Polity Press.

Sheffi, Y. (2001), 'Supply chain management under the threat of international terrorism', *International Journal of Logistics Management*, **12** (2), 1–11.

Talas, R. and D. Menachof (2009), 'The efficient trade off between security and cost for sea ports: a conceptual model', *International Journal of Risk Assessment and Management*, **13** (1), 46–59.

Williams, Z., J.E. Lueg and S.A. LeMay (2008), 'Supply chain security: an overview and research agenda', *International Journal of Logistics Management*, **19** (2), 254–81.

Willis, H., A. Morral, T. Kelly and J. Medby (2005), *Estimating Terrorism Risks*, Santa Monica, CA: RAND Corporation.

Woo, G. (2003), 'Insuring against al-Qaeda', National Bureau of Economic Research Meeting, Cambridge, Massachusetts, 1 February.

Yates, J.F and E.R. Stone (1992), 'The risk construct', in J.F. Yates (ed.), *Risk Taking Behaviour*, New York: Wiley, pp.1–25.

Zsidisin, G.A., L.M. Ellram, J.R. Carter and J.L. Cavinato (2004), 'An analysis of supply risk assessment techniques', *International Journal of Physical Distribution and Logistics Management*, **34** (5), 397–413.

APPENDIX 6.A1: ATTACKS ON PORT FACILITIES 1968–2007

1 June 1968
UNITED STATES, GALVESTON, TEXAS
The Japanese vessel *Mikagasan Maru* was extensively damaged by a bomb allegedly placed by El Poder Cubano, a Cuban exile group.

16 September 1968
UNITED STATES, MIAMI HARBOUR
El Poder Cubano terrorists fired at the Polish general cargo vessel *Polancia*.

24 January 1970
ISRAEL
Al Fatah and the Popular Front for the Liberation of Palestine jointly claim credit for an explosion in an ammunition truck unloading in the docks.

19 February 1971
TURKEY, ISTANBUL
A US army passenger vessel was damaged by a bomb.

29 March 1972
UNITED STATES, BISCAYNE, FLORIDA
A Soviet research vessel was bombed by the JCN, an anti-Castro Cuban group.

1 December 1972
CYPRUS
An attempt by the Black September organization to hijack an Italian passenger vessel was thwarted by Coast Guard police.

4 March 1973
LEBANON
The Greek charter vessel *Sanya* sank in Beirut harbour following an explosion onboard. The official investigation revealed that the explosion was caused by a limpet mine. Black September claimed credit for the attack.

30 December 1973
UNITED STATES, MIAMI, FLORIDA
Two bombs damaged the 573-ton *Mereghan II* while moored alongside waiting to lift cargo in Miami River docks.

2 February 1974
PAKISTAN, KARACHI
Three gunmen, members of the Muslim International Guerrillas, seized a Greek general cargo vessel and threatened to blow up the ship unless the Greek government freed two Arab prisoners.

2 March 1974
FRANCE
The Pierre Overnay brigade attacked the barge *Ouest France* while moored alongside the quay and firebombed 180 Renault cars.

May 1974
UNITED STATES, LOS ANGELES, CALIFORNIA
The *Caribe Star* was sunk in the harbour by a bomb placed onboard. The 120 ft former ferry had been fitted out for Arab interests. The Jewish Defence League claimed responsibility.

9 April 1974
PORTUGAL
The Revolutionary Brigades attacked the Portuguese troop ship *Niassa*. The vessel's hull was holed in two places on the waterline.

20 July 1974
IRELAND, BELFAST
A bomb exploded on board the ferry *Ulster Queen*. Provisional Irish Republican Army (IRA) suspected after coded telephone warning to a newspaper.

16 December 1974
UNITED STATES, MIAMI, FLORIDA
A bomb exploded in the port offices of the Eastern Steamship Lines. Frente de Liberacion Nacional Cubana suspected.

9 March 1975
IRELAND, GREENCASTLE HARBOUR
Over 30 incendiary devices were planted on trawlers in the harbour. Only two exploded, destroying the vessels. Ulster Defence Association suspected.

23 July 1975
JAPAN, OKINAWA
A Chilean training vessel and a Kobe University vessel docked at the International Ocean Expo were attacked by terrorists using Molotov cocktails. Radical leftists suspected.

1 August 1975
ARGENTINA, SANTA FE
The Montoneros and the People's Revolutionary Army made lightning bomb strikes on the river port.

2 November 1975
PUERTO RICO, SAN JUAN
Russian vessel *Maxim Gorkiy* damaged by two bomb blasts below the waterline while at anchor in the port.

28 November 1975
PUERTO RICO
Russian vessel *Maxim Gorkiy* hit by a second attack when a bomb was thrown onboard injuring one crew member and causing minor damage.

August 1976
LEBANON
The Greek vessel *Tina* was sunk by three limpet mines believed to be planted by members of a right-wing Lebanese Christian group while the vessel was part loaded with a cargo of arms for Fatah.

16 September 1976
UNITED STATES, PORT ELIZABETH, JERSEY
A Soviet cargo vessel was damaged by a limpet mine planted by an anti-Castro refugee.

23 October 1976
LEBANON
Three Greek vessels *Eko*, *Riri* and *Spiro* were attacked in port with limpet mines. All vessels sank at their moorings.

22 July 1977
PERU
A Cuban trawler docked at a port near Lima was bombed and the vessel sank. The International Commandos of Zone 6 of CORU claimed responsibility.

30 April 1978
PHILIPPINES
The *Don Carlos* was boarded by armed members of a Muslim Separatist rebel group of the South Philippines. Cargo offloaded and passengers taken hostage.

3 October 1978
ISRAEL
Israeli Navy sank a bomb-laden vessel belonging to Fatah heading for Eilat with the intention of destroying the Eilat-Ashkelon pipeline and oil tank farms in the port.

March–June 1979
UNITED STATES, MASSACHUSETTS
Multiple bomb threats against vessels and petroleum storage site disrupt port operations.

1979 (month unknown)
PORTUGAL
Whaler *Sierra* rammed by *Sea Shepherd*. Perpetrators arrested but escaped. Members of Greenpeace or Fund for Animals suspected.

9 January 1980
UNITED STATES, SACRAMENTO, CALIFORNIA
Port closed for three days following threats to bomb the Soviet vessel *Nicolay Karamzin* and that the harbour had been mined.

16 June 1980
BELGIUM
Demonstrators smashed navigational and radio equipment onboard *Andrea Smits* while loading nuclear waste for disposal in the Atlantic.

29 October 1980
ITALY, GENOA
A Libyan vessel under repair almost sank following a limpet mine explosion on the waterline. Maltese National Front suspected.

2 October 1981
SPAIN, SANTANDER
A powerful bomb caused a 6 foot hole in the hull of a destroyer moored in
the port. ETA military wing suspected.

2 November 1981
FRANCE, NANTES
British hydrographic survey vessel *Hecate* suffered minor explosion on the
hull while docked. Divers subsequently found another bomb with 2.2 lbs
of plastic explosive that had failed to explode. Irish National Liberation
Army terrorists suspected.

2 January 1982
LEBANON, TRIPOLI
The Lebanese-registered tanker *Babanaft* was shelled while lifting Iraqi
crude in the port. Fire on deck extinguished and vessel sailed immediately.

9 March 1982
LEBANON, TYRE
Lebanese general cargo vessel bombed in the port despite strict security.

16 March 1982
BRAZIL, RIO DE JANEIRO
Liberian-flagged tanker *Hercules* ordered to leave after a bomb was found
onboard. Outcome unknown.

16 December 1982
PHILIPPINES
The ferry *Santa Lucia* was damaged while in Pagadian by an explosive
device planted by the Moro National Liberation Front.

23 February 1983
IRELAND, LOUGH FOYLE
A British cargo vessel was seized in an inlet by the IRA and the ship was
blown up.

5 August 1983
FALKLAND ISLANDS, PORT STANLEY
An ultra-nationalist Argentine group claimed responsibility for an explo-
sion on board the Danish vessel *Kraka* moored in the harbour. The vessel
was unloading granite blocks to be used to build a memorial to fallen
British soldiers during the Falklands War.

20 March 1984
NICARAGUA, PUERTO SANDINO
Explosive device planted at port entrance that damaged a Soviet tanker.

January–March 1984
NICARAGUA, CORINTO, BLUEFIELDS and EL BLUFF
Mine laying operations in three ports caused a total of 11 ships to sink, including Soviet, Panamanian Dutch, Liberian and Nicaraguan registered.

28 June 1984
ARGENTINA, BUENOS AIRES
Two tankers, the *Perito Morena* and *Belgrano*, were set ablaze by the Sargento Cisneros Commandos.

25 September 1985
CYPRUS
Three members of the PLO's elite Force-17 seized an Israeli yacht on Yom Kippur and killed the three inhabitants.

7 October 1985
EGYPT
The Italian cruise vessel *Achille Lauro* was seized with 511 passengers onboard by four members of the Popular Front for the Liberation of Palestine. An American passenger, Leon Klinghoffer, was shot in the head and thrown overboard in his wheelchair.

30 January 1986
ITALY, MESSINA
Two 135 ton Cypriot-flagged hydrofoils were bombed and sunk while docked for repairs.

14 September 1986
MOROCCO
A Spanish vessel was attacked by Polisario guerrillas.

23 January 1987
MAURITANIA
Panamanian bulker *Maritime King* attacked with rocket fire by Polisario guerrillas.

1 February 1987
LEBANON
Egyptian vessel *Fast Carrier* damaged by two limpet mines placed on the port side.

25 March 1987
GERMANY, HAMBURG
Molotov cocktails thrown at British truck and trailer parked in the port.

14 February 1988
CYPRUS, LIMASSOL
A ferry boat damaged by an explosion in the port.

11 July 1988
GREECE
Two men preparing an explosive device to attack the vessel *City of Poros* died when the bomb went off prematurely in the port. Middle Eastern gunmen then attacked the *City of Poros* firing automatic weapons at the crowd of passengers and throwing grenades.

1 August 1988
NICARAGUA
A ferryboat with a ten-person US delegation was ambushed by guerrillas in the southeast of the country.

25 December 1993
ISRAEL, EILAT
An Israeli vessel *Jrush Shalom* was bombed while docked in the port.

8 July 1994
ALGERIA, JIJEL
GIA attackers boarded a cargo vessel moored in the port and murdered seven Italian sailors.

16 January 1995
TURKEY, TRABZON
A ferry *Avraysa* was hijacked in the port by Turkish-Abkhaz terrorists.

April 1996
SRI LANKA, COLOMBO
Van Ommeren vessel docked in the port came under mortar attack by two LTTE gunboats. Damage to accommodation block and two sailors injured.

9 August 1996
SRI LANKA, TRINCOMALEE
A Philippine-registered vessel was bombed under the waterline by LTTE while loading sand.

1 July 1997
SRI LANKA, JAFFNA
The LTTE abducted the Indonesia crew of a ferry and blew up the ship.

7 July 1997
SRI LANKA, JAFFNA
LTTE hijacked *Morang Bong* and abducted 37 North Korean sailors.

1 September 1997
SRI LANKA, TRINCOMALEE
A Chinese-owned vessel attacked by the LTTE. Crew members killed, wounded or missing.

9 September 1997
SRI LANKA, TRINCOMALEE
LTTE attacked vessel *Athena* with a limpet mine while at anchor in the roads. Main engine room fire and vessel was in danger of sinking.

12 October 2000
YEMEN, ADEN
USS Cole attacked by suicide boat causing 20 ft by 40 ft hole in the port side. Seventeen sailors killed.

11 September 2001
UNITED STATES, NEW YORK
Ports of New York and New Jersey severely disrupted following the terrorist attacks on the World Trade Center.

October 2002
YEMEN, ADEN
The French tanker *Limburg* was attacked by a suicide boat while waiting to take on a pilot for docking in Aden causing explosion and fire. One sailor drowned.

15 March 2003
RUSSIA
Explosion in Khasan district killed a naval lieutenant and a former military officer.

30 November 2003
IRAQ
A Turkish tanker was attacked.

25 May 2004
PAKISTAN, KARACHI
A bomb exploded in the port, killing two and injuring two others.

23 June 2004
PAKISTAN, GWADAR
Chinese engineers developing deep-sea port came under rocket attack.

31 July 2004
PAKISTAN, GWADAR
A series of explosions in the port city with the first occurring by the port.

28 August 2005
PHILIPPINES, LAMITAN
A bomb exploded among the liquefied petroleum gas (LPG) tanks on the ferry *Dona Ramona* injuring at least 30, including nine children.

13 May 2006
CORSICA, BASTIA
A bomb exploded in the Bastia Maritime Authority complex.

3 March 2007
INDONESIA, AMBON
A bomb exploded at the port gates in the Yos Sudarso port in Ambon.

8 September 2007
ALGERIA, DELLYS
Coast Guard troops targeted by suicide truck bomber during a flag-raising ceremony.

APPENDIX 6.A2:   KOLMOGOROV-SMIRNOV ONE-SIDED TEST

Table 6.A2.1   Kolmogorov-Smirnov One-sided Test critical values

n	0.1	0.05	0.025	0.01	0.006
1	0.9000	0.9500	0.9750	0.9900	0.9950
2	0.6838	0.7764	0.8419	0.9000	0.9293
3	0.5648	0.6360	0.7076	0.7846	0.8290
4	0.4927	0.5652	0.6239	0.6889	0.7342
5	0.4470	0.5094	0.5633	0.6272	0.6685
6	0.4104	0.4680	0.5193	0.5774	0.6166
7	0.3815	0.4361	0.4834	0.5384	0.5758
8	0.3583	0.4096	0.4543	0.5065	0.5418
9	0.3391	0.3875	0.4300	0.4796	0.5133
10	0.3226	0.3687	0.4092	0.4566	0.4889
11	0.3083	0.3524	0.3912	0.4367	0.4677
12	0.2958	0.3382	0.3754	0.4192	0.4490
13	0.2847	0.3255	0.3614	0.4036	0.4325
14	0.2748	0.3142	0.3489	0.3897	0.4176
15	0.2659	0.3040	0.3376	0.3771	0.4042
16	0.2578	0.2947	0.3273	0.3657	0.3920
17	0.2504	0.2863	0.3180	0.3553	0.3809
18	0.2436	0.2785	0.3094	0.3457	0.3706
19	0.2373	0.2714	0.3014	0.3369	0.3612
20	0.2316	0.2647	0.2941	0.3287	0.3524
21	0.2262	0.2586	0.2872	0.3210	0.3443
22	0.2212	0.2528	0.2809	0.3139	0.3367
23	0.2165	0.2475	0.2749	0.3073	0.3296
24	0.2120	0.2424	0.2693	0.3010	0.3229
25	0.2079	0.2377	0.2640	0.2952	0.3166
26	0.2040	0.2332	0.2591	0.2896	0.3106
27	0.2003	0.2290	0.2544	0.2844	0.3050
28	0.1968	0.2250	0.2499	0.2794	0.2997
29	0.1935	0.2212	0.2457	0.2747	0.2947
30	0.1903	0.2176	0.2417	0.2702	0.2899
31	0.1873	0.2141	0.2379	0.2660	0.2853
32	0.1844	0.2108	0.2342	0.2619	0.2809
33	0.1817	0.2077	0.2308	0.2580	0.2768
34	0.1791	0.2047	0.2274	0.2543	0.2728
35	0.1766	0.2018	0.2242	0.2507	0.2690
36	0.1742	0.1991	0.2212	0.2473	0.2653
37	0.1719	0.1965	0.2183	0.2440	0.2618
38	0.1697	0.1939	0.2154	0.2409	0.2584
39	0.1675	0.1915	0.2127	0.2379	0.2552
40	0.1655	0.1891	0.2101	0.2349	0.2521
>40	$1.07/\sqrt{n}$	$1.22/\sqrt{n}$	$1.36/\sqrt{n}$	$1.52/\sqrt{n}$	$1.63/\sqrt{n}$

Source: http://www.york.ac.uk/depts/maths/tables/kolmogorovsmirnov.pdf (accessed 1 June 2010).

7. Maritime piracy analysis

Alec D. Coutroubis and George Kiourktsoglou

7.1 INTRODUCTION

Ancient Romans considered pirates to be enemies of the human race (*hostes humani generis*). Pirates (Thracian) first turned up in the early sixth century BCE in the Mediterranean Sea (Andersen et al., 2009) and since then they have repeatedly made their presence felt in different geographical hotspots and time periods throughout history.

In the early twenty-first century, almost 90 per cent of global trade (and 60 per cent of crude oil trade) is seaborne (UNCTAD, 2011), a fact that renders maritime piracy a clear and present danger to global growth and prosperity.

In the early and mid 1990s, piracy used to revolve in and around the Malacca Straits in South East Asia, a 900 km (550 miles) narrow sea lane skirting Indonesia, Singapore, Malaysia and Thailand. Close cooperation among the above littoral nations supported through donors' funds (mainly Japanese) led the phenomenon to subside long before the turn of the century.

Since 2005, the international community has observed a remarkable surge of piracy in the West Indian Ocean, off the Somali Shelf, the Horn of Africa, around the Gulf of Aden and (lately) in the Arabian Sea. This fairly recent development in the millennia-long timeline of the scourge is of a different nature though. It has repeatedly involved kidnap hijackings. The aim in similar cases is not merely to commandeer ship (and cargo), but intriguingly, to hold vessel and crew to ransom. Successful attacks are followed by months (in some cases years) of long negotiations between gangs of pirates and ship owners. These 'rituals' wreak havoc on the lives of seafarers while at the same time they ravage shipping business ventures.

Last but not least, during the period of two to three years after 2008, there has been a remarkable surge of criminal activity in the Gulf of Guinea, attributed mainly to Nigerian criminals (IMB, 2012b). In this case, there are hints of a political agenda (the Movement for the Emancipation of the Niger Delta (MEND) Army) that occasionally mutates into something more criminal and less political like piracy.

Piracy in the twenty-first century carries on challenging the international community to an unprecedented degree and, as such, it demands a coordinated and well-orchestrated response.

7.2 STRUCTURE OF THE CHAPTER

The present chapter begins with some basic definitions and issues related to the corresponding terminology. As a first step, the authors analyse contemporary criminal business model(s) on the high seas, as well as potential targets and vulnerability. Next, the analysis shifts to counter-piracy policies. In this case, the issues of interest are political willingness (underpinning such policies), information and intelligence (along with methods for the collection of the latter), technical cooperation and assistance, reporting, operational responses on land, 'catch and release' policies, youth involvement in piracy and armed protection of merchant ships. The final chapter offers some basic conclusions.

7.3 DEFINITIONS

Maritime piracy does not have a single definition. The prevailing one though is set out in the United Nations Convention on the Law of the Seas 1982 (UNCLOS) and more specifically in Article 101 (with further clarifications in Articles 102 and 103).

7.3.1 Article 101: Definition of Piracy

Piracy consists of any of the following acts:

(a) any illegal acts of violence or detention, or any act of depredation, committed for private ends by the crew or the passengers of a private ship or a private aircraft, and directed:
(i) on the high seas, against another ship or aircraft, or against persons or property on board such ship or aircraft;
(ii) against a ship, aircraft, persons or property in a place outside the jurisdiction of any State;
(b) any act of voluntary participation in the operation of a ship or of an aircraft with knowledge of facts making it a pirate ship or aircraft;
(c) any act inciting or of intentionally facilitating an act described in subparagraph (a) or (b).

For the last 30 years the above definition has been the ultimate legal 'yardstick', promptly used in cases of maritime piracy. Lately though, the same definition has stirred a lively debate (if not controversy) mainly triggered by its wording. It has conspicuously failed to recognize as such, blatant cases of piracy (usually off Somalia) just because of a technicality: the fact that they had taken place within the jurisdiction(s) (the Exclusive Economic Zone, in other words, 12 nautical miles off the coast) of sovereign states. It is therefore a narrow definition and unsuitable for private law purposes at least in the early twenty-first century (Todd, 2010).

On the contrary, until 2009 the International Maritime Bureau (IMB) had a broader definition of piracy (it switched thereafter to the one of UNCLOS) (IMB, 2009): Piracy is 'an act of boarding or attempting to board any ship with the apparent intent to commit theft or any other crime and with the apparent intent or capability to use force in the furtherance of that act'. This definition was tailor-made to match IMB's purposes of statistical analysis and, interestingly, it was more of a functional and less of a legal nature. It is worth noting though that by changing it the IMB managed (at least in its 2010 and 2011 reports) to 'artificially' alter the statistical landscape of piracy, especially in the Somali basin and the West Indian Ocean.

For all their utilitarian nature, the majority of piracy's definitions converge on the most striking trait of the phenomenon and at the same time its quintessential hallmark: the use of violence and more specifically the forcible seizure of property (the merchant ship) (Todd, 2010).

7.3.2   The Current Status Quo

Patricia O'Brien, the UN Under Secretary-General for Legal Affairs, said at the Expo 2012 UN Pavilion (de Grave, 2012):

> Piracy has existed for thousands of years. It had substantially diminished in the end of the nineteenth century and seemed to have become one of the legends of the past, gradually disappearing from criminal law legislation . . . A few decades ago, the 'pirate phoenix' appeared to be rising again to become a regional, if not a global scourge . . .

7.4   UNDERSTANDING THE CRIMINAL BUSINESS MODEL

The analysis of current practices of high seas piracy throughout the world leads to the conclusion that, at present, there are four distinctive business models. More specifically:

1.   In West Africa/Gulf of Guinea, Nigerian (mostly) pirates target diesel and oil tankers, taking aim mainly at the precious commodity, hoping

to reap benefits by reselling it in the black market (Saul, 2012; Strategy Page, 2012b).

2. In East Africa/Indian Ocean, Somali pirates target (mostly) crews for hostage taking, with the ultimate goal to extract ransom payments from ship owners and/or seafarers' families (One Earth Future, 2012).

3. In the Caribbean/Latin America, robbers go after the valuables of the crew and the ship. This is a highly opportunistic criminal venture and usually takes place when the vessel is at berth (IMB, 2011).

4. In South East Asia (Malacca Straits), where, just like in the case of Latin America, comparatively more violence-prone pirates go after the valuables of crews and ships. In this case though the difference is that the ship is attacked when (mostly) at sea (Raymond, 2012).

Understanding the above business models is therefore crucial if operational responses are to be targeted directly at the heart of pirates' ability to operate and launch assaults.

Throughout the centuries, unparalleled resilience and remarkable versatility have been the hallmarks of high seas piracy. In the twenty-first century, a typical manifestation of the above features comes through the use of the so-called 'mother-ships' by Somali pirates (IMB, 2011). As a first step, the technique comprises the hijacking of a large fishing trawler. Next, the pirated vessel (along with her crew) blends in with the international fishing fleet on the high seas. At the same time, though, it is commissioned as an attack springboard for raids waged hundreds of nautical miles away from the Horn of Africa (and the Gulf of Aden) to the western coastline of India. Skiffs launched from the hijacked trawlers intercept and attack innocent merchant vessels, rendering the whole criminal venture both more efficient and highly effective.

Pirates are adaptive and applying pressure to their business models, or their own desire to increase their revenue, causes their models to be adjusted. Agencies and organizations involved in countering piracy must therefore be at least as adaptive if they are to be able to react to changes in a timely manner or, ideally, to pre-empt those changes.

7.4.1 Some More Elaborate Elements of Piracy's Business Model(s)

Piracy is largely a crime of opportunity, and pirates go where naval patrols are absent. Off the coast of Somalia, with the decrease in success rates in maritime attacks, kidnappings on land are increasing, either perpetrated by or involving Somalis from clans associated with maritime piracy. There were several cases in 2012 of aid workers and tourists being kidnapped by or sold to pirate gangs for hostages. Furthermore, hostages are increasingly held for longer periods of time and subsequently ransomed for smaller amounts of money. The rising trend indicates that the pirates are modifying their own goals and aspirations, probably due to the pressure exerted by their dwindling success at sea (Aries Risk Group, 2012).

On a different vein, armed security is effective; not a single ship protected by armed guards has been hijacked to date. However, it is not without its challenges. Pirates have taken notice of the presence of armed security teams on ships, typically breaking off approaches when confronted and seeking softer targets to attack. Roaming over an extremely large maritime territory in their mother-ships, even using mid-size dhows, Somali pirates seek victim-ships travelling less-obvious routes, less likely to be protected by naval forces. They are also looking for 'targets' unlikely to be armed, poorly exercising security 'best management practices' or, to summarize, unable to effectively defend themselves.

Piracy is also only one of a range of threats to security, and the problem needs to be treated holistically, with an understanding of the impact of one criminal activity on another. An excerpt from the article 'A buccaneering spirit is not piracy's only gift to business' (Phillips and Clay, 2012) presents some alternative and highly intriguing views on piracy:

> Steve Jobs's now famous maxim, originally said to the Macintosh team in 1982, started it all: 'It's better to be a pirate than to join the navy'. This rebel spirit has since trickled into the rest of Silicon Valley. Mark Zuckerberg has continued the spirit with his own rebellious maxim: 'Move fast and break things'. Silicon Valley and its disruptors run on rebellion, a low regard for risk, and phenomenal innovation. The pirates of Somalia happen to use the same exact recipe.

Why has the term 'pirate' come to characterize all that is admirable in an entrepreneur? Probably because behind modern-day piracy's unrepentant criminality analysts can identify seriously bright innovators. Piracy is far more sophisticated and complex than its media image, for pirates must also develop structures, streamline logistics and stay adaptable.

Harardheere, a village on the northern coast of Somalia, established the world's first pirate 'stock exchange' in 2009, where locals can buy shares in pirate gangs planning hijacking ventures. Although credible statistics are difficult to come by, sources point to an exchange that lists 72 'companies' (Minney, 2010).

Like any business startup, a piracy mission begins with a search for venture capital. 'Pirate capitalists' court investors who will, according to J. Peter Pham of the Atlantic Council, offer $250,000 or more in seed money (Masterplan, 2012). The capital is then spent on recruitment (gangsters, tech-savvy savants, caterers), intelligence (negotiators) and materials (speedboats).

Key to the radical success of pirates is their stealth-and-surprise approach. David James of Henley Business School notes that pirates' decision to avoid 'symmetrical' conflict helps them a lot (Economist, 2010). Rather than challenging their targets head on, pirates surprise and attack their enemies at their weakest points, giving them no time to react.

Somalia has not always been a hotbed of piracy. Following its government's collapse in 1991, its territorial waters could not be enforced, so foreign fleets trawled Somalia's waters, stealing its fishing stock and destroying livelihoods. At the same time, the Chinese began prolifically exporting to Europe via the Suez Canal, exposing Puntland's ex-fishermen to billions of dollars in cargo floating past them. So they pivoted from fishermen to pirates. 'Boya', the most infamous pirate, tells of a small band of ten raiders who started attacking fleets, then grew into a large, well-run criminal organization (C-Span Video Library, 2011).

Innovation has long come from misfits. Historically, pirates far from being economic anarchists, opened up international trading markets. Historian Thomas Gallant argues that illegal networks of armed predators actually facilitated the spread of capitalism (Gallant, 2001). In Gallant's words: 'Bandits helped make states and states helped make bandits. . . . Pirates are ruthless criminals, yet their innovative and adaptable business model is not without its lessons. We do ourselves a disservice should we neglect to learn from those who innovate on the high seas' (Gallant, 2001, p. 25).

7.4.2 Targeting and Vulnerability

It is no surprise that the low and slow are the most vulnerable, but there are studies that suggest that older vessels are also more vulnerable, even if newer vessels are more valuable (Coutroubis and Kiourktsoglou, 2011a, 2011b). Interestingly, one out of every three vessels attacked off Somalia is less than five years old (Coutroubis and Kiourktsoglou, 2011a), a statistic that further corroborates the fact that pirates base their criminal activities on a rock-solid business plan (and strategy). The authors claim the following in their study 'Age profiles of attacked and pirated vessels off Somalia':

> In this case, it is clear that Somali pirates have a strong preference for young, if not very young vessels. Almost one out of every three (32%) attacks has been mounted against a vessel aged up to five years old. Tellingly, as the vessel population grows older the frequency of attacks dies away (57% of the international fleet's vessels are older than twenty years but only 31% of the vessels attacked belong to the same age group). (Coutroubis and Kiourktsoglou, 2011a)

7.5 CURRENT COUNTER-PIRACY POLICIES

7.5.1 Political Willingness

The key issues in countering both the sea- and shore-based elements of piracy's business model(s) are political willingness and backing that will result with the necessary actions. It is argued that the former without the latter results in ineffective responses such as the catch and release practice. The House of Commons in its latest report on Somali piracy (and the European Union's (EU) Operation Atalanta) graphically describes the fruits of political will and cooperation among different stakeholders:

> We note with satisfaction the extent of practical international cooperation in countering piracy, including by China, and the cooperation with regional organizations such as the African Union. We believe, however, that the Gulf States should make a greater effort to assist in solving the problems of piracy and Somalia. We concluded in our previous report that piracy would not be ended until the root causes of the problems in Somalia were successfully tackled. Since that report, the EU has developed its activity by formulating a Strategy for the Horn of Africa and appointing a Special Representative for the area, as well as launching EUTM [EU Training Mission] Somalia and EUCAP Nestor [EU capacity building mission]. We believe that the missions should be taken forward pro-actively and that the EU's development aid should focus on providing alternative livelihoods for the Somali people. These missions must continue until the incentives for piracy are removed and the coastal states of the region are able to police their own coastlines. (House of Commons, 2012, Summary)

7.5.2 Information and Intelligence

Given the will to act, understanding the situation in order to identify the most effective counters to piracy requires effective surveillance and the subsequent analysis and dissemination of information and intelligence. Information sharing is vital, and needs to be extended to all those engaged in a particular aspect.

Within this context, one can easily identify three different 'tools' of counter-piracy information, intelligence gathering and dissemination (outlined below).

7.5.3 (1) The Djibouti Code of Contact

The Djibouti Meeting adopted the Code of Conduct concerning the Repression of Piracy and Armed Robbery against Ships in the Western Indian Ocean and the Gulf of Aden, which was signed on 29 January

2009 by the representatives of Djibouti, Ethiopia, Kenya, Madagascar, Maldives, Seychelles, Somalia, the United Republic of Tanzania and Yemen. It remains open for signature at the International Maritime Organization (IMO) Headquarters by other countries in the region. Comoros, Egypt, Eritrea, Jordan, Mauritius, Mozambique, Oman, Saudi Arabia, South Africa, Sudan and the United Arab Emirates have since signed making the current total 20 countries from the 21 eligible to sign the Djibouti Code of Conduct.

The Code, which became effective from the date it was signed (29 January 2009), takes into account and promotes the implementation of those aspects of UN Security Council Resolutions 1816 (2008), 1838 (2008), 1846 (2008) and 1851 (2008) and of UN General Assembly Resolution 63/111 that fall within the competence of IMO. The Code provides for sharing of related information through a number of centres and national focal points using existing infrastructures and arrangements for ship to shore to ship communications (that is, the Regional Maritime Rescue Coordination Centre in Mombasa, Kenya, and the Rescue Coordination Sub-Centre in Dar el Salaam, United Republic of Tanzania) and the regional maritime information centre, which is being established in Sana'a, Yemen.

Technical cooperation and assistance (Resolutions 2 and 3)
In another resolution, the Djibouti Meeting requested states, the IMO, the United Nations Development Programme (UNDP), the United Nations Office on Drugs and Crime (UNODC), the European Commission (EC), the Regional Co-operation Agreement on Combating Piracy and Robbery Against Ships in Asia – Information Sharing Centre (ReCAAP-ISC) and the maritime industry to provide assistance, either directly or through the IMO, to those states that require support in the effective implementation of the Djibouti Code of Conduct. It further recommended the establishment of a regional training centre for the purpose of promoting the implementation of the Code and accepted, with appreciation, the offer of the Government of Djibouti to host a regional training centre within the scope of the Code (IMO, 2009).

7.5.4 (2) The Satellite Automated Identification System Data Resource

Regulation 19 of SOLAS chapter V, 'Carriage requirements for shipborne navigational systems and equipment', sets out navigational equipment to be carried onboard ships, according to ship type. In 2000, the IMO adopted a new requirement (as part of a revised new chapter V) for all ships to carry Automatic Identification Systems (AIS) capable of providing information about the ship to other ships and to coastal authorities automatically. The regulation requires AIS to be fitted aboard all ships of 300 gross tonnage (gt) and upwards engaged on international voyages, cargo ships of 500 gt and upwards not engaged on international voyages and all passenger ships irrespective of size. The requirement became effective for all ships on 31 December 2004. Ships fitted with AIS maintain AIS in operation at all times except where international agreements, rules or standards provide for the protection of navigational information.

Maritime security: AIS ship data
At its 79th session in December 2004, the Maritime Safety Committee (MSC) of the IMO agreed that in relation to the issue of freely available AIS-generated ship data on the World Wide Web, the publication on the World Wide Web or elsewhere of AIS data transmitted by ships could be detrimental to the safety and security of ships and port facilities and was undermining the efforts of the IMO and its member states to enhance the safety of navigation and security in the international maritime transport sector (IMO, 2003). In view of the above, the North Atlantic Treaty Organization (NATO) recently signed a contract with a commercial satellite operator to take advantage of the latest technical developments in the field:

> The NATO Maritime Operation Centres (MOC Northwood and MOC Naples) and NATO Shipping Centre (NSC) will be acquiring exactAIS® data to be used within Operation Ocean Shield, a counter-piracy operation in the Arabian Sea, Gulf of Aden and Somali Basin, consisting of naval vessels from NATO nations as well as elements ashore. Exact AIS data will also be used in support of Operation Active Endeavour, NATO's maritime counter-terrorism operation in the Mediterranean. (ExactEarth, 2012)

7.5.5   (3) Unmanned Underwater Vehicles

The British Ministry of Defence (MoD) is seeking to develop a new generation of unmanned maritime 'drones' that would be used for anti-submarine warfare and possible missile attacks on enemy ships: 'It is entirely possible that we will see drones off the coast of Somalia,' said a defense official. 'They could be used for tracking ships and providing intelligence to the other maritime forces. This is one of the potential uses of UUV [Unmanned Underwater Vehicle] technology.' With fewer frigates available because of defence cuts, the UK is currently unable to dedicate one of these ships solely to counter-piracy operations, and UUVs are regarded as one way of shoring up and extending diminishing capabilities. An MoD spokesperson said: 'Exploring innovation in maritime defence is part of the work we do to exploit the latest technology and ensure the Royal Navy is best equipped to meet future requirements' (Hopkins, 2012).

7.5.6 Reporting

It is a fact that a large number of piracy attacks go unreported:

> Industry analysts say some owners and masters of commercial boats prefer not to report relatively small losses from piracy, or attempted boarding, because they worry about clean records, costly delays in the event of an investigation in the nearest port, jittery clients who might take business elsewhere, and the likelihood of higher insurance rates if they log an attack with authorities.

'Shipping culture often dictates that a company or captain will stay silent about minor piracy, partly because they don't think much can be done about it and because a boarding can reflect poorly on their vessel's security', said Nick Davis of Britain-based Gulf of Aden Group Transits, which provides security to ships. 'You don't want to stick your head above the parapets,' Davis said. 'As long as the crew doesn't get hurt, you tend to leave it be' (Torchia, 2009).

The pattern includes a raft of attacks on fishing trawlers (which can be a precursor to a wider outbreak of piracy in a region). Without the information concerning the full extent of piracy attacks, authorities are unaware of both an existing problem and the potential for a larger one.

At this point, it needs to be mentioned that unreported (by the shipping industry) piracy attacks, successful or not, take place not only off the coast of Somalia but, interestingly, all over the world. Nigeria is another prime example:

> Pirates/Robbers are often violent and have attacked, hijacked and robbed vessels/kidnapped crews along the coast, rivers, anchorages, ports and surrounding waters. A number of crew members were injured in past attacks. Generally all waters in Nigeria remain risky. Vessels are advised to be vigilant as many attacks may have gone unreported. (IMB, 2012b)

7.5.7 Operational Responses on Land

Up to now, operational responses on land have mainly included (but not been strictly limited to) traditional counters to crime by local law enforcement, quasi-national bodies (Shiine, 2012). Interestingly, though, the EU was the latest body to reach a decision to assist ongoing law enforcement efforts in Somalia by less traditional means like direct military operations on land:

On Friday 23 March 2012 the Council of the European Union confirmed its intention to extend the EU Naval Force (EU NAVFOR) counter-piracy mission, Operation ATLANATA off the Somali coast until December 2014. At the same time the Council also extended the area of operations to include Somali coastal territory and internal waters. (EU NAVFOR, 2012)

For all the attractiveness of international forces conducting operations against piracy on land, there are negative (as well as positive aspects) to such actions. It is also identified that circumstances ashore might prevent effective action being taken against pirates, in which case, the only option will be to address the symptoms at sea.

Despite these restrictions, military experts think this new approach will hurt the pirates. But risks to civilians remain, they warn. 'It could have a coercive effect: The navy is taking the fight into the pirates' own backyard,' said Lee Willett, senior research fellow in maritime studies at the Royal United Services Institute in London. He added that using force ashore increases the risk of affecting innocent civilians. The pirates, depending on where they are based, are embedded among the local population. Analysts suggest that they have contributed a share of the ransom money to poor communities, but they have also brought prostitution, alcoholism and other problems. Under threat from helicopters, the pirates could be tempted to use villagers as human shields for their boats. Or they could simply take their boats off the shore and transport them farther inland. And then what? How far would the European Union be prepared to give chase? What if the pirates paid civilians to guard the boats on the beaches? How far does the beach stretch, in military terms, anyway? (Dempsey, 2012)

7.5.8 Catch and Release

The catch and release policy used by a number of navies off East Africa results from three distinctive reasons:

1. A reluctance of the corresponding country to assume the burden associated with prosecuting pirates.
2. The potential for captives to claim asylum in the holding country.
3. Concerns about the ability to prove the piracy charge because of the difficulties involved in gathering evidence that will stand up in court.

The anti-piracy patrol off Somalia has captured and prosecuted about 800 pirates so far. But more than five times that number have been captured and released. More prisons are being built in Somaliland and Puntland but these must be paid for and supervised by Western nations if they are to be effective. The key problem is that most nations contributing ships to the anti-piracy patrol are not willing to prosecute and imprison Somali pirates. This led to the 'catch and release' method used by most European navies, mainly because the legal systems back home makes it difficult for the pirates to be prosecuted and easy for the pirates to claim asylum if brought back. (Strategy Page, 2012a)

In addition to the above, legal officers in countries willing to initiate legal proceedings came to realize many times in the past the unwillingness of vessel operators and seafarers to actively contribute to the prosecution of alleged pirates.

> Regrettably, without sufficient evidence to prove piracy and the reluctance of the two crew members to testify against their captors, the 19 men were returned to Somalia. The dhow, with a crew of German sailors onboard, has sailed towards the port of Al Mukalla on the Yemen coast where it will be handed over to the Yemen Coastguard for return to its owners and for the two crew members to be reunited with their families. (EU NAVFOR, 2011)

The lack of cooperation could be potentially attributed to high travel expenses, the involved seafarers' effort to overcome the psychological trauma and, among other things, a potential increase in the insurance costs of the vessel operator as a byproduct of further scrutiny.

In a country with a shortage of pirate volunteers, limited access to weapons and other supplies and poor shore support, this 'catch and release' policy could conceivably work. In Somalia's case, none of those conditions apply. Catch and release is therefore a flawed policy that is no more than a very short-term threat reduction and needs to be replaced with the apprehension and trial of the suspects.

7.5.9 Youth Involvement in Piracy

The fact that the UN endorsed classification of a child as anyone under the age of 18 poses a legal problem for those who capture young pirates, whether at sea or on land, particularly if a catch and release policy is being followed (Isenberg, 2012): 'Off the Horn of Africa, about one-third of pirates are children, some as young as 10 or 11.' 'Nobody knows what to do with them . . . Under international law, we have to treat children, and children who are being used as criminals, differently than we treat adult criminals. And the problem is that we haven't got the mechanisms in place to deal with them . . . That leads to military forces encountering child pirates, but then letting them go, in a sort of "catch and release" . . . the problem is "you're returning children to adult criminals".'

The issue of child piracy has attracted the interest of Senator Roméo Dallaire's Child Soldiers Initiative, which works towards the prevention of use of children as child soldiers. Dallaire and his compatriots 'don't see major difference between a child soldier and a child pirate . . . They are children being used by adults for criminal or political purposes, and they are extremely vulnerable, and there are a lot of them' (CBC News, 2012).

7.5.10 Armed Protection of Merchant Ships

The IMB in its latest report claims that 'Successful hijackings (off Somalia) have been reduced due to efforts and actions of the naval forces and preventive measures used by the merchant vessels including the use of citadels and employment of Privately Contracted Armed Security Personnel (PCASP)' (IMB, 2012a, p. 21).

The issue of armed security personnel (either military or private) on board merchant vessels has proved to be fairly controversial (in some cases not without good reason) (IBN Live, 2012). Pundits agree that

> even if the industry is not a major proponent of armed guards, all elements of the maritime industry want a code of conduct for the use of force and a clear legal structure for the provision of security. Currently the industry is 'self-regulating', which at its best interpretation means that management teams set standards or competitive forces create a Darwinian rise to the top. Historically, if the industry of private security companies in Iraq is a fair comparison, there is a 'race to the bottom' as vendors respond to competitive pricing in an unregulated environment to meet the letter but not the spirit of the contract. That means more lower cost 'Third Country Nationals' than 'Tier One' contractors and more potential for problems. Although the industry boasts US Navy SEALS and retired British Special Boat Service (SBS) veterans, you are more likely to meet ex-Royal Marines and U.S. Navy security professionals bolstered by armed Ghurkas to Yemenis. That is not a slight to the skills but it is a financial reality that shipowners are tight fisted. (Isenberg, 2012)

On the Vessel Protection Detachment (jargon for national military forces onboard merchant ships) issue, countries like the Netherlands remain adamant that ships under the Dutch flag cannot legally make use of Private Companies of Armed Security Personnel (PCASP) (Dutch Ministry of Defence, 2012). On the other side of the spectrum, Cyprus (and Singapore) has recently passed a law that explicitly allows the use of armed private security personnel as a means of protection against piracy (Neocleous & Co. LLC, 2012).

All in all, the thing that has been made clear through the latest developments in the sector of armed protection services is that the industry craves for a uniform 'level playing field' of quality standards (and regulation) mainly on an international level.

7.6 CONCLUSIONS

Based on the above analysis, piracy features on a global level three major groups of 'interests/stakeholders':

1. national (state) interests (that is, governments)
2. supra-national/international interests (that is, IMO, IMB inter alia)
3. business interests (that is, ships owners, charterers, shippers, private maritime security companies inter alia).

All three are ineluctably interwoven with each other, always within the broader context of piracy and maritime security. It is therefore for this reason that on a national level, political will is absolutely necessary if security problems on the high seas are to be effectively addressed. By the same token, the adoption of a holistic solution renders military (naval) measures, both on land and at sea, absolutely indispensable to the security of global supply chains and the corresponding trade flows. Piracy is a form of organized crime and, as such, inter-state and inter-agency cooperation (on a regional level they can break grounds against both seaborne and land-based criminality) are essential to its discouragement and/or suppression. The latter though cannot be effectively implemented unless the shipping industry assumes its fair share of responsibility within a framework of 'bona fide' regulation.

Interestingly, within the last three to four years, such regulation has been made increasingly pertinent to the industry of armed security services too. The ultimate goal remains to ensure the creation of a 'level playing field' for fair competition among all providers of armed security services on the high seas.

Understanding the business model used by pirates in a particular geographical region is also key to the development of effective operational and strategic responses. Too many attacks go unreported. Because of under-reporting, the full extent of the problem is unknown, a fact that has a serious impact on the way the international community responds to the rising challenge(s). One cannot stress enough the paramount importance of both raw data (information) and intelligence (analysis) to counter-piracy operations and strategy given that pirates continuously adapt (and hone) their tactics.

Lastly, the UNCLOS definition of piracy should be revisited and made potentially more 'inclusive' (like the one up until 2009), encompassing attacks against vessels inside Exclusive Economic Zones and removing the distinction between personal and politically motivated financial gain.

REFERENCES

Andersen, E., Brockman-Hawe, B. and Goff, P. (2009), *Suppressing Maritime Piracy: Exploring the Options in International Law Workshop Report*, One Earth Future, available at http://goo.gl/h32Vw (accessed 28 July 2012).

Aries Risk Group (2012), *The Evolution of Piracy in Somalia*, available at http://goo.gl/xREBm (accessed 14 August 2012).

C-Span Video Library (2011), *After Words with Jay Bahadur*, available at http://goo.gl/8xLMe (accessed 08 September 2012).

CBC News (2012), 'International piracy experts meet in Halifax', available at http://goo.gl/cMxRG (accessed 8 September 2012).

Coutroubis, A. and G. Kiourktsoglou (2011a), 'Age profiles of attacked and pirated vessels off Somalia', *Maritime Interdiction Operations Journal*, NATO Maritime Interdiction Operations Center, May, available at http://goo.gl/DkmQg (accessed 24 August 2012).

Coutroubis, A. and G. Kiourktsoglou (2011b), 'Written evidence, piracy off the Coast of Somalia', House of Commons, Foreign Affairs Committee, August, available at http://goo.gl/kDD0I (accessed 24 August 2012).

De Grave, I. (2012), 'Q&A: U.N. spotlights pirates in the Malacca Strait at Expo 2012', Inter Press Service News Agency, available at http://goo.gl/1S196 (accessed 4 August 2012).

Dempsey, J. (2012), 'The risks of chasing pirates on land', *New York Times*, available at http://goo.gl/9ATTm (accessed 1 September 2012).

Dutch Ministry of Defence (2012), *Defense Organization Makes Security for Merchant Shipping Cheaper*, available at http://goo.gl/R9wRp (accessed 11 September 2012).

Economist, The (2010), 'Pirate copy', available at http://goo.gl/dBK4L (accessed 29 September 2012).

EU NAVFOR (2011), *Failed Pirates Returned to Somalia*, available at http://goo.gl/kxSXO (accessed 6 September 2012).

EU NAVFOR (2012), *EU Extends Counter Piracy Mission Off Coast of Somalia*, available at http://goo.gl/7rIX0 (accessed 1 September 2012).

ExactEarth (2012), *ExactEarth Announces New Contract with NATO*, available at http://goo.gl/c4uJD (accessed 29 August 2012).

Gallant, T. (2001), *Brigandage, Piracy, Capitalism, and State-formation: Transnational Crime from a Historical World-systems Perspective*, London: Berg Publishers.

Hopkins, N. (2012), 'Ministry of Defence plans new wave of unmanned marine drones', *Guardian*, available at http://goo.gl/V5FWN (accessed 29 August 2012).

House of Commons (2012), *Turning the Tide on Piracy*, available at http://goo.gl/TNoey (accessed 20 August 2012).

IBN Live (2012), *Fishermen Killed: India Summons Italian Envoy*, available at http://goo.gl/IVkFL (accessed 11 September 2012).

IMB (International Maritime Bureau) (2009), *Piracy & Armed Robbery Against Ships, Annual Report*, 1 January–30 June, available at http://goo.gl/2BQZe (accessed 29 August 2012).

IMB (International Maritime Bureau) (2011), *Piracy & Armed Robbery Against Ships, Annual Report*, 1 January–30 June, available at http://goo.gl/2BQZe (accessed 29 August 2012).

IMB (International Maritime Bureau) (2012a), *Piracy & Armed Robbery Against Ships, Annual Report*, 1 January–30 June, available at http://goo.gl/2BQZe (accessed 29 August 2012).

IMB (International Maritime Bureau) (2012b), *Piracy & Armed Robbery Prone Areas and Warnings*, available at http://goo.gl/i2DEc (accessed 31 July 2012).

IMO (International Maritime Organization) (2003), *AIS Transponders*, available at http://goo.gl/a4OtZ (accessed 25 August 2012).

IMO (International Maritime Organization (2009), *The Djibouti Code of Contact*, available at http://goo.gl/Q2epT (accessed 25 August 2012).

Isenberg, D. (2012), *The Rise of Private Maritime Security Companies, Somalia Report*, available at http://goo.gl/pwg81 (accessed 11 September 2012).

Masterplan (2012), *Pirates Need a Business Plan Too*, available at http://goo.gl/EjVzX (accessed 29 September 2012).

Minney, T. (2010), 'Somali pirates stock exchange finances sea ventures', available at http://goo.gl/nremH (accessed 29 September 2012).

Neocleous Andreas & Co. LLC (2012), 'Anti-piracy law enters into force', available at http://goo.gl/oxvmU (accessed 11 September 2012).

One Earth Future (2012), *The Human Cost of Somali Piracy 2011*, available at http://goo.gl/jKaW7 (accessed 14 August 2012).

Phillips, M.Kyra and A. Clay (2012), 'A buccaneering spirit is not piracy's only gift to business', *Wired Magazine*, available at http://goo.gl/rZZd0 (accessed 22 August 2012).

Raymond, Z.C. (2012), 'Piracy and armed robbery in the Malacca Strait', available at http://goo.gl/XNEPw (accessed 14 August 2012).

Saul, J. and J. Mark (2012), 'Pirates eye share of Gulf of Guinea riches', Reuters, available at http://goo.gl/h0Oov (accessed 14 August 2012).

Shiine, O. (2012), *Puntland, Somaliland Prepare to Fight Pirates, Somalia Report*, available at http://goo.gl/1CP5b (accessed 1 September 2012).

Strategy Page (2012a), *Catch and Release*, available at http://goo.gl/XlQn6 (accessed 7 September 2012).

Strategy Page (2012b), *Raiders of the Lost Oil*, available at http://goo.gl/TL7P5 (accessed 1 September 2012).

Todd, P. (ed.) (2010), *Maritime Fraud and Piracy*, London: Lloyds List.

Torchia, C. (2009), 'Pirate attacks go unreported', News24, available at http://goo.gl/ekWEJ (accessed 29 August 2012).

UNCLOS (United Nations Convention on the Law of the Seas) (1982), Article 101, available at http://goo.gl/ogTVX (accessed 31 July 2012).

UNCTAD (United Nations Conference on Trade and Development) (2011), *Review of Maritime Transport*, available at http://goo.gl/S1W7X (accessed 28 July 2012).

PART II

Policy applications

8. US maritime security policy: achievements and challenges

Joseph S. Szyliowicz*

8.1 INTRODUCTION

Although merchants and traders have engaged in international trade for centuries, the level of such trade has increased dramatically over time and, in recent years, has come to play a dominant role in the economic wellbeing of nations. These changes in the international economy can be attributed to developments such as the end of the Cold War, the liberalization of economies and the impact of technology. Advances in transportation and communications technology have made for greater and easier movement of both goods and people. Of particular significance has been the widespread adoption of the use of containers for transporting goods rather than loading and unloading individual items of cargo, which caused costs to decrease exponentially. Today an estimated 200 million containers travel around the world annually. The scope and scale of the global maritime system can best be illustrated by a few statistics: 80 percent of world trade by value and 90 percent of volume is sea trade; 4000 ports ship cargo around the world; 46,000 ships are engaged in international trade including about 3000 container vessels, the largest of which carries more than 10,000 20 foot equivalents.

The impact of these developments can be seen in US trade figures. According to the International Trade Administration, US imports have grown from $22 billion in 1960 to $1263.9 billion in 2004, exports from $25.1 billion to $1146.1. Imports now account for over 15 percent of the US economy compared to 3 percent in 1960, exports for 17 percent compared to 5 percent in 1970 (ITA, 2005). The increase in the overall transportation of goods has been paralleled by other international trends such as the rise in outsourcing and 'Just in Time' manufacturing techniques, both of which require a well-developed transportation and communication infrastructure and create additional security challenges. The effective, efficient and secure functioning of these ever more closely linked and integrated global supply chains is thus a matter of widespread international concern.

This is certainly the case for the USA, which is a major actor in global trade. About 8000 ships crewed by more than 200,000 foreign mariners arrive annually in US ports, delivering more than $700 billion in merchandise. Containers are an important component of this activity. The USA accounts for over 10 percent of the total world container traffic (over 100 million annually) and its role continues to increase, although the global recession has led to a temporary decline in year over year activity. Still, in 1995, US ports handled 37,000 20 foot containers daily, and in 2008, 77,000. Overall, maritime activities are estimated to account for about 20 percent of the total US economy ($2 trillion) and to provide two million jobs (Harrald, 2005; US Bureau of Transportation Statistics, 2009).

The high importance of maritime transport to the US economy exposes it to more than just traditional smuggling and theft threats. Terrorism represents a new diverse and dynamic threat that has rippled through the entire globalized supply chain. Therefore, twenty-first-century maritime security requires an international orientation rather than a policy that is designed primarily to meet domestic needs.

8.2   THE NATURE OF THE THREAT

Terrorists have historically paid little attention to ships and shipping because carrying out such an attack requires a significant investment in money and training. Between 1969 and 2007, attacks on the maritime sector accounted for only 2 percent of all attacks. However, these include successful operations by Al-Qaeda against both cargo ships (the *MV Limburg* in 2004) and military vessels (the *USS Cole* in 2000). The recent revelations that Osama Bin Laden considered attacks on oil tankers as well as the successful attacks by Somali pirates reinforces the importance of effective policies to ensure maritime security (Lorenz, 2007). The greatest concern is with the possibility of a successful attack on a port, especially one using a container that contained some kind of weapons of mass destruction (WMD) such as a dirty bomb. The economic cost of such an attack is difficult to quantify but anywhere between 50,000 and 1,000,000 lives would be lost and the financial costs could run as high as $1 trillion, assuming a prolonged economic slump would result from the cessation of trade (US DHS, 2005; Container Security Initiative 2006–11 Strategic Plan, 2006). Such costs could effectively be reduced through the creation of detailed plans to facilitate the restart of ports and container shipping systems in the wake of a terrorist attack or natural disaster (Greenberg et al., 2006). The extent to which such recovery planning has been carried out, however, is not clear and deserves further investigation.

Efforts to minimize the threat are hampered by several fundamental issues. The first is that supply chains are international in scope but the available international structures are not able to impose effective policies. The International Maritime Organization (IMO) has undertaken various initiatives to strengthen transportation security in its member states but the fragmented nature of the international system with its numerous private and public, national and international actors greatly complicates the achievement of transportation security in the USA and in other countries as well. The fundamental issue is the concept of state sovereignty, which remains the dominant paradigm. Thus, although the USA has actively pursued a strategy of placing customs agents at foreign ports, its implementation has involved difficult and contentious negotiations. We shall return to this fundamental issue below.

A second difficulty is that global freight now moves along an integrated intermodal system that links the individual modes, highway, rail and shipping. This development is due to the nature of modern economic systems, which are characterized by constant pressures to reduce costs by increasing productivity and reducing inefficiencies, and by increasing customer expectations on both freight and passenger systems. This development has important implications for security since the focus has been upon enhancing the security of modes individually. Such a specialized orientation, while necessary, is no longer adequate. Not only must attention be paid to the protection of each mode but the intermodal dimension also requires attention. The interdependent nature of today's system, including characteristics such as the increased number of stakeholders, the diversity of terminals that serve as critical elements in the infrastructure and the increasing reliance on information technology, further complicate the task of dealing with terrorism. This is especially important when one considers the devastating consequences a cyber attack could unleash. Furthermore, the intermodal movement often involves 'inbound' freight, sending a container from a port to its final destination in the USA or even to another port for export via road or rail. The shipment is obviously vulnerable during this period as it is not subject to the same level of scrutiny once inside US borders, and many experts believe that the US Customs and Border Protection (CBP) has not adequately addressed various vulnerabilities (Giermanski, 2011).

8.3   US POLICY

The need to enhance the security of the sea mode was recognized immediately after 9/11. Accordingly, in 2002, Congress passed the Maritime

Transportation Security Act (MTSA), which called for various initiatives to safeguard US ships and ports to be administered by the Department of Homeland Security (DHS). Subsequently, many other policies and programs have been introduced. Altogether, 19 US programs or initiatives dealing with maritime security have been enacted (US DHS, 2005; Harrald, 2005; Caldwell, 2007; North, 2009; US GAO, 2010). All of these are designed to implement the basic principle underlying the US approach to safeguarding maritime transportation – that of a layered security posture that integrates the intelligence collection and analysis, prevention, enforcement, response and recovery capabilities of both the domestic and international communities.

> Specifically, a layered approach to maritime security means applying some measure of security to each of the following points of vulnerability: transportation, staff, passengers, conveyances, access control, cargo and baggage, ports, and security en route.[1]

The broad scope and detailed attention of these various layers has most certainly improved security for maritime trade, but major weaknesses remain. In the sections that follow, we shall focus on the major initiatives for maritime security, and show how approaches have been implemented in two key areas – port security and container security. As shall become clear, the programs thus far remain US-centric in their goals, structures and procedures, creating or exposing dangerous gaps in security worldwide. Moreover, the inflexible nature of many initiatives has hindered or prohibited effective implementation in both domestic and foreign settings. By discussing the specific problems encountered, and revealing their related risks, the need for a balanced and cooperative plan on a global scale is apparent. We conclude by suggesting what such a system could entail.

8.4   THE PORT CHALLENGE

Ports are generally considered one of the major security weaknesses in the maritime system because of the many ways in which they are vulnerable to terrorism. An attack can be mounted against a docked ship or a storage facility from the seaside, from the land or even from the air. For economic and historical reasons, they tend to be located in areas that are easily accessible by land and sea since the goal was to create a structure that would permit the easy flow of goods into and out of the facility. They often contain petrochemical and other hazardous storage facilities that, like other infrastructure components, were built with limited attention to security, as this was traditionally focused on the threats of smuggling and stowaways. Moreover, thousands of workers, visitors and seamen move in and out of ports daily, as do a large number of trucks, many of which haul containers. These players are in fact intermodal nodes that link sea transport to rail and road, and thus may potentially enable terrorists and their weapons to gain access to locations throughout the country. There are 361 ports (including eight of the world's 50 highest-volume ports) in the USA, each of which possesses unique characteristics in terms of its geographic layout, operator, primary activities, linkages and security arrangements.

The Port of Long Beach (PLB), the second busiest port in the USA and the 17th busiest port in the world, provides a good illustration of the challenges. Located within a city of nearly 500,000 people, it includes 3200 acres of land, ten piers and 80 berths, operates every day of the year and employs 30,000 daily workers who handle on average 5,067,597 containers (an average of 13,900 containers per day) aboard 4746 vessels annually with cargo valued at more than \$120 billion. It generates more than \$5 billion in US Customs revenues; approximately \$4.9 billion in local, state and general federal taxes; more than \$47 billion in direct and indirect business sales; and nearly \$14.5 billion in annual trade-related wages.

Numerous entities are responsible for security. The US CBP Service is responsible for inspecting incoming cargo, including containers and also checks the credentials of crews and passengers; the US Coast Guard is responsible for protecting vessels and harbors and ensuring the safety and viability of US shipping lanes and inland waterways; the Long Beach Police Department is responsible for providing primary law enforcement and has jurisdiction for all criminal acts that are not covered by federal statute; the Long Beach Fire Department is responsible for providing fire and emergency medical services; the Harbor Police is responsible for enforcing city and county ordinances that specifically cover the waterfront and facilities owned by the PLB; and finally, the Long Beach Board of Harbor Commissioners are responsible for establishing policies that will facilitate a layered approach to safety and security without adversely impacting the flow of commerce through the PLB.

8.5 IMPLEMENTATION AND EFFECTIVENESS

How effectively each of these actors can carry out its functions is an important issue as is the extent to which their efforts add up to an integrated security posture. For example, the Coast Guard, the lead agency under the MTSA, is responsible for developing new regulations and conducting port and harbor security assessments. Though it has implemented a number of important measures in this and other areas, it is not obvious that it possess the manpower or the expertise to carry out such non-traditional functions. Three areas are of particular concern. To increase security, the Coast Guard is developing an Automatic Identification System (AIS) to track vessels but apparently lack adequate resources. Second, the port security assessments are not based on a 'defined management strategy, specific cost estimates, and a clear implementation schedule' so that this vital activity is not as effective as is necessary. Third, the Coast Guard's efforts to ensure that security measures are implemented appropriately are not adequate in such areas as staffing and training. The lack of clear guidance and unclear roles for port owners and operators has further delayed adequate implementation of appropriate solutions (Wrightson, 2005).

In addition, the existing structure creates difficult issues of coordination and implementation, given the varieties of functional activities that are carried out at Long Beach and other ports by federal, state and local agencies. Many have argued for some kind of structural reorganization but only minor progress has been achieved in this regard because of several factors including the difficulty of establishing common standards. These would have to apply to many different kinds of activities and personnel including workers and operators. Furthermore, there are numerous stakeholders (private and public) and the well-established tendency of public agencies to focus narrowly and to defend their activities constitutes a formidable barrier. Accordingly, one expert has suggested that as far as the federal agencies are concerned, the focus should be on producing a 'paradigm shift' that would incorporate two key ideas. First, the MTSA must be regarded from a systems perspective and the responsibilities of each federal actor evaluated and, if necessary, expanded to ensure that its functions and responsibilities are commensurate with the functional area (for example, intermodal transportation, cargo processing) for which it is responsible. Furthermore, the difference between security and law enforcement should be recognized in evaluating the success of policies and projects since the usual metrics are based on the latter (Henrikson, 2005).

The need for effective inter-agency cooperation is accentuated by the 'layered approach.' This is evidenced, for example, by the ways in which the problem of the arrival of large numbers of foreign sailors is dealt with. The 'layered' approach assigns responsibility for preventing illegal immigrants and security risks from entering the country to the State Department, which issues the visas, to the CBP, and to the Coast Guard, both part of the DHS. Since the CBP's onboard inspections are carried out without electronic verification of a seafarer's identity, questions have been raised about its ability to identify potential risks and it is not surprising that significant differences characterize the CBP and the Coast Guard's data regarding the number of 'absconders' (seamen who leave a vessel without permission) and 'deserters' (a seafarer who fails to return). Furthermore, the Coast Guard supports US ratification of the International Labour Organization (ILO) Seafarer's Convention (185) designed to prevent fraud and exploitation (which has been ratified by 18 countries that provide 30 percent of seafarers) while the CBP is opposed (US GAO, 2011c).

Similar problems characterize the effort to ensure that the thousands of workers in a port are not security risks. The Transportation Security Administration (TSA) and the US Coast Guard (both parts of the DHS) manage the Transportation Worker Identification Credential (TWIC) program. Here, too, the US Government Accountability Office (GAO) found serious deficiencies as its investigators were able to easily access ports using TWICs that were illegally acquired or forged through fake business practices. It concluded:

> Internal control weaknesses governing the enrollment, background checking, and use of TWIC potentially limit the program's ability to provide reasonable assurance that access to secure areas of Maritime Transportation Security Act (MTSA)-regulated facilities is restricted to qualified individuals. (US GAO, 2011a)

The situation had not changed by 2013 for the GAO found that all the shortcomings identified earlier in this program had not been corrected by the DHS, thus raising the issue of 'the program's premise and effectiveness in enhancing security' (GAO-13-198, 2013).

At the heart of many of the problems confronting efforts to enhance domestic port security is the funding issue. Any reorganization at the PLBeach, for example, would be expensive and it is not at all obvious who would be responsible for what amounts. This problem has wide ramifications, for experts agree that limited funding streams and questions about how to pay for maritime security measures are major barriers to improving maritime security. A debate continues to rage over who should provide the funds – the federal government, the state and local governments who profit from maritime activities or industry, and in what amounts and percentages. Many argue that US taxpayers should not provide funds to large and profitable corporations to secure infrastructure since enhancing security is in their own financial interest to do so. As a result, the federal funds provided to US port authorities to improve maritime security thus far are woefully inadequate, particularly when compared to the amounts devoted to aviation security. On average since 9/11, Congress has provided

$175 million annually to support improved maritime security measures. Since passage of the MTSA (which provided no funding mechanism) in 2002, Congress has allocated a total of $491 million, but the Coast Guard has estimated that $7.3 billion will be required to implement the security provisions mandated by the Act. At present funding levels, that goal will not be achieved until the middle of the century. Further complicating the issue is the requirement that federal funds be matched locally (25 percent) and inefficient grant management practices (Congressional Research Service, 2005).

Lack of funding, inadequate cooperation and coordination, and the lack of clear guidance and unclear roles for port owners and operators have delayed adequate implementation of appropriate solutions at the nation's seaports. Analysing the level of port security that has been achieved, the GAO concluded that although important steps had been taken: 'Assessing the progress made in securing seaports is difficult, as these efforts lack clear goals defining what they are to achieve and measures that track progress toward these goals.' Nevertheless, it identified the following major challenges: 'failure to develop necessary planning components to carry out the programs; difficulty in coordinating the activities of federal agencies and port stakeholders to implement programs; and difficulty in maintaining the financial support to continue implementation of security enhancement' (Wrightson, 2005).

8.6   THE CONTAINER CHALLENGE

The funding issue is also relevant in any effort to ensure that none of the millions of containers imported annually pose a security risk. The seriousness of this problem and the difficulties inherent in checking containers was recognized immediately after 9/11, and within two weeks, a multi-agency Container Working Group involving 16 government agencies and a large number of private sector organizations was established. Its goal was to enhance cargo security by addressing areas such as information sharing, security and container tracking technologies, cargo data, physical security, detection of WMD and international affairs. And also to establish criteria to identify high-risk containers and trucks, implement a pre-screening process at foreign points of origin, develop and deploy technologies to pre-screen high-risk cargoes and secure containers and trucks en route to US ports, and improve the security of containers as they are transported to their domestic destinations (Bemis, 2002). Its recommendations, published in 2002, led to the establishment of two significant programs, the Container Security Initiative (CSI), which was launched promptly by the CBP in January 2002, and the Customs Trade Partnership Against Terrorism (C-TPAT), among additional initiatives.

8.7   CONTAINER SECURITY PROGRAMS

CSI is one of the most significant and forward leaning of the post-9/11 layered response strategies. It is based on the principle that the most effective strategy to mitigate the container threat is the one that addresses and eliminates the threat before the container reaches the homeland. Under this program, participating countries sign a bilateral agreement with the USA, which allows the stationing of teams of CBP agents in foreign ports in order to identify potentially dangerous cargo using automated risk assessment cargo information and available intelligence. If necessary, CBP officials then ask the host authorities to subject the container to further inspection. To obtain the data necessary for risk assessment in a timely fashion, the '24 hour rule' requires that manifest and bill of lading information is available to CBP agents 24 hours prior to the loading of US-bound cargo at a foreign port. Failure to fully comply with this regulation can result in civil penalties and ultimately the denial of permission to ship to the USA. Once the CPB receives the manifest information, it is entered into the Automated Targeting System, which applies hundreds of classified and unclassified targeting metrics and assigns a level of risk for terrorism to each container. When a container is identified as high risk, CPB Inspectors conduct non-intrusive X-ray or gamma ray scans to generate an image of the contents of the container, which is reviewed for anomalies, or they physically inspect the container or both (Harrald, 2005; US Customs and Border Protection, 2006; Caldwell, 2007; Wilson, 2008; US GAO, 2010). Although the concept is relatively simple, consider the following information:

> Unlike other cargo ships whose loading process occurs at the port and whose cargo is often owned by a single company, container ships carry cargo from hundreds of companies and the containers are loaded away from the port at individual company warehouses. A typical single container shipment may involve a multitude of parties and generate 30 to 40 documents. A single container could also carry cargo for several customers, thus multiplying the number of parties and documents involved. The parties involved in a shipment usually include the exporter, the importer, a freight forwarder, a customs broker, a customs inspector, inland transportation providers, the port operators, possibly a feeder ship, and the ocean carrier. Each transfer of the container from one party to the next is a point of vulnerability in the supply chain. It is also important to keep in mind that not all U.S. bound containers arrive at U.S. ports. Half of the containers discharged at the Port of Montreal, for instance,

move by truck or rail to cities in the Northeastern or Midwestern United States. (Fritelli, 2003, pp. 53–4)

In addition, the sheer volume of imported containers ensures that no one single shipment can be scrutinized too carefully. On average since 2005, CBP Inspectors annually process over 11 million ship-born containers entering the USA. At the PLB, the second busiest container port in the country, one container is landed every 20 seconds. The Seaport Commission reported (prior to 9/11) that less than 2 percent of import cargo was physically inspected. To physically inspect a container, it takes five CBP Inspectors an average of three hours. Growing terminal congestion and 'just-in-time' delivery requirements put pressure on inspectors to expedite container releases.

To improve the screening process, the CPB relies heavily on technology and is constantly bringing on-line new and better tools. Emerging technologies such as electronic surveillance via Global Positioning System (GPS) will allow CPB Inspectors to monitor the movement of containers from the point of loading to the seaport. The CPB is also piloting the use of electronic seals or smart tags that can track and report on the integrity of a shipment. Traditional container seals provide evidence of unauthorized access or tampering only upon physical inspection, which may not occur until the container reaches its final destination. Smart tags (RF tags) combine robust mechanical features with sophisticated sensors that transmit container information as it passes a reader device and issues alerts if the container has been tampered with or damaged. The tags can also measure seal integrity, store data and provide communications while in transit, thereby automating the essential functions of seal checking and reporting in order to remove human intervention.

However, technology is not a 'magic bullet.' The DHS experience with technological innovation and deployment has not always yielded positive results. On many occasions, the DHS has tended to rush to procure and deploy new technologies before they have been adequately tested. The GAO recently criticized the DHS for such practices (US GAO, 2011b) and subsequently identified three weaknesses in the ways in which the DHS acquired and deployed technology: (1) a lack of program requirements; (2) not adequately testing and evaluating technologies; and (3) not considering the costs and benefits associated with a technology (US GAO, 2011b).

In 2008, Congress passed legislation adding the requirement of 100 percent scanning of US-bound cargo containers using non-intrusive imaging systems by 2012. On 27 June 2012 Congress announced a deferral until July 2014. However, this proposal raised numerous logistical and practical concerns in terms of its cost, disruption of supply chains, adequate staffing and unnecessary and uneven economic burdens on ports. The CBP has established minimum technical standards for the inspection equipment and processes used at domestic ports, but since it is not a standard-setting organization, there are no specific guidelines in CSI for when foreign ports look to install a scanning device. Nor is there any framework for assigning the costs of upgrading a foreign port to accommodate CSI compliance. All these issues aroused considerable opposition from the private sector as well as many governments and in late 2010, the Director of Homeland Security advised that this might not be possible or affordable. Soon thereafter, the deadline was extended by at least two years to 2014 (Brew, 2003; North, 2009; US GAO, 2010).

A second important program in the CBP's layered approach to maritime security with which CSI must synchronize is the C-TPAT, initiated in November 2001. Since supply chain and border security requires the cooperation of the private sector, this initiative is designed to safeguard supply chains by having private sector participants agree to meet certain standards and to ensure that all their suppliers, importers and shippers meet the same standards. While participation is voluntary, firms that cooperate and meet the standards along their entire supply chain benefit because their products are subjected to fewer inspections and their cargo thus encounters fewer delays. To join C-TPAT, a company submits a security profile, which the CBP compares to its minimum security requirements for the company's trade sector. The CBP then reviews the company's compliance with local and US customs laws and regulations and any violation history that might preclude the approval of benefits, which include reduced scrutiny or expedited processing of the company's shipments. This is a powerful incentive for it gives firms a competitive advantage and, as a result, has enjoyed great success. As of May 2008, there were over 8400 C-TPAT members representing roughly 30 percent of US-bound cargo (Harrald, 2005; Wilson, 2008; US GAO, 2010).

A third major program, the Megaports Initiative, is operated by the US Department of Energy's National Nuclear Safety Administration (DOE NNSA). It focuses explicitly on preventing terrorists from placing WMD in containers from foreign ports. The DOE installs radiation detection equipment at foreign ports for use by foreign authorities and port operators to screen containers entering or leaving their ports and also provides appropriate training. The key aspect of this initiative is that foreign officials are free to screen containers regardless of their destination. In 2008, its goal was to scan over 50 percent of containers in over 75 large ports (NNSA, 2011). By 2011, it had become operational in 34 ports around the world and was working with 18 more ports. Its goal is to scan more than

80 percent of all containers leaving 100 ports by 2016. However, many financial and technological hindrances remain and the DOE encountered difficulties in its efforts to sign agreements with some high priority ports (Cole, 2011).

In an effort to operationalize the SAFE Port Act of 2006 and to achieve greater operational integration, the DHS developed the Secure Freight Initiative (SFI). It blended several inspection programs into three pillars. In addition to the CSI program, an Importer Security Filing Program was mandated. Known as the 10+2, it comprised ten data points concerning the container and its contents including the manufacturer, seller, buyer, importer and the container filling location and two data points concerning the location of the container on the ship and status messages. This information has to be provided 24 hours before the container leaves port. The third pillar, the Global Trade Exchange (GTX), a database to track containers and their content, ran into considerable opposition because it involved the sharing of corporate data by the US government with foreign governments. It was put on hold and remains under study. One goal of the SFI was to test the feasibility of scanning 100 percent of all the containers destined for the USA. The difficulties that arose during its implementation helped alert decision makers to the plethora of potential logistical, technological and financial problems that would result from the application of the 100 percent rule and the possible creation of security gaps, as high-risk containers might not receive the high-level attention they should (Caldwell, 2007; US GAO, 2007; Huizenga, 2008).

International organizations such as the Asia Pacific Economic Cooperation (APEC) and especially the IMO have also sought to enhance the security of global supply chains. The IMO developed the International Ship and Port Facility Security (ISPS) code, a set of security measures and standards, which signatory states agree to implement. The ISPS was adopted in July 2004 as an amendment to the Safety of Life at Sea Convention of 1974 (SOLAS), and signed by all existing members of that convention. Non-compliance of member countries either in their ports or on their vessels endangers future participation in international trade (North, 2009). Additionally, the World Customs Organization (WCO) has developed standards, and offers technical assistance to aid their implementation. In 2002, the USA was successful in convincing the WCO and the Group of Eight (G8) to recognize the CSI framework as the model for the required development of port security initiatives in all 161 member states. However, this WCO resolution retained the freedom for each nation to design and implement their own initiatives along those lines, instead of signing on to the CSI program (Brew, 2003; Banomyong, 2005).

8.8 PROGRAM WEAKNESSES OVERSEAS

Although all of these programs have contributed to port and container security in the USA and elsewhere, they do contain weaknesses. Moving the inspection overseas inevitably raises questions about the integrity, reliability and honesty of the local officials checking suspected containers as well as what might happen during the long voyage. In 2003, ABC News successfully smuggled depleted uranium into the USA, once from Europe, once from Indonesia. The CBP subsequently 'enhanced its ability to screen targeted containers for radioactive emissions by deploying more sensitive technology at its seaports, revising protocols and procedures, and improving training of CBP personnel' (Skinner, 2005). There are also known cases (such as occurred in 2008 in the South Korean Port of Busan) where workers, fearing radiation, did not use the nuclear scanner, so that an estimated two million containers left South Korea without having met official requirements.

Ensuring security in foreign ports is the responsibility of the US Coast Guard, which inspects, or monitors the inspection of, US-bound cargo. However, for years, there was no organized plan to focus on high-risk ports. Since 2008, however, it has attempted to remedy this grave deficiency by 'placing greater emphasis on countries that were not in compliance or that were struggling to comply with International Ship and Port Facility Security (ISPS) Code requirements,' though the effectiveness of its methodology remains unclear. Perhaps not surprisingly, the Coast Guard recently estimated that in up to 15 countries, the contracting governments had failed to audit the ISPS code compliance of its port facilities and that their ports did not adequately control access of personnel and cargo (US GAO, 2010).

In such cases, the Coast Guard 'explains the identified deficiencies and makes recommendations to the country for addressing the deficiencies and provides possible points of contact for assistance' to help the country improve. Its officials also seek the assistance of the local embassy to identify additional resources that might be available. It emphasizes low-cost solutions and shares 'best practices' with the government and other countries via its website. The team then follows up in an attempt to determine what progress has been made and has the power to impose restrictions on ships that have stopped at those ports (US GAO, 2010).

8.9 LIMITATIONS OF CONTAINER INITIATIVES

Balancing the need for security and the need for efficient supply chains is no easy matter, but at its core lies the problem of achieving international cooperation. The US programs all depend on the willingness and ability of foreign governments and organizations to cooperate. If such cooperation is achieved, the results benefit everyone. For example, though the initial equipment and implementation costs of CSI are to be borne by the host nation, they do offer numerous benefits to foreign governments, the shipping industry and international organizations as a whole including increased information and intelligence sharing on a multinational scale, and enhanced communication and coordination between importers, exporters and trade representatives, thus further enhancing supply chain effectiveness. SAFE Ports also codified the need for CBP inspections of foreign ports, their screening processes and other security measures in which these initiatives are implemented. Because of a lack of international inspection methods, the measures developed in SAFE Ports by the CBP have been endorsed by the international bodies to enforce their own maritime security requirements as well (Caldwell, 2007; North, 2009; US GAO, 2010).

Obtaining the cooperation of other states, however, has not always been easy and remains a difficult challenge. The head of DHS, Janet Napolitano, has often called for enhanced international cooperation. In January 2011, for example, she stated that 'Governments must step up co-operation to stop attempts by terrorists to send shipments in the global supply chain.' The implication is clear. The existing arrangements have not yet yielded the kind of global security network that would adequately safeguard supply chains. In addition to the structural problems created by the very nature of the international system that were discussed above, one must consider the additional difficulties that arise from the emphasis by the USA upon the implementation of US security initiatives at foreign ports. Even when governments are willing to cooperate, problems and concerns inevitably arise. These can be assigned to two general categories – those based on perceptions of US intentions and challenges to national sovereignty, and those based on local or national differences.

8.9.1   Perceptions of US Unilateralism

National sovereignty is highly prized and strongly defended by all states but US policy infringes upon sovereignty at several levels. Many countries view the attempt to establish bilateral relations through CSI and to enforce C-TPAT in terms of neo-imperialism, of the USA seeking to impose its will upon weaker states, which are forced to accept for fear of the political and economic consequences if they refuse. Many companies may feel resentful that they must take on the additional costs and measures associated with C-TPAT if they want to ship goods to the USA, feeling that it is not truly an optional program. Some companies may choose to wait until it is actually a mandatory policy, missing out on the additional security and economic benefits of the initiative. With the increasing number of C-TPAT-like initiatives appearing in other countries or trading blocs, such as the European Unions's EU's Authorized Economic Operator (AEO) program, companies with only a small US market may even decide to forgo C-TPAT altogether to join another program, and/or even decrease or eliminate their trade with the USA (Banomyong, 2005; Bichou, 2008; Grillot et al., 2010, p. 81).

The policies that the Coast Guard seeks to implement further enhance this concern with what is often perceived as US neo-imperialism. Many countries have expressed worries over its inspections, which are viewed as burdensome and as just another way to expand US influence. Accordingly, many states including China, Egypt, Brazil, India, Russia and Venezuela have created difficulties to reassessments. Furthermore, the US Coast Guard has taken a rather inflexible position regarding the EU's regulatory and inspection approach (US Customs and Border Protection, 2006; US GAO, 2010), implying that the USA holds the power to accept the validity and integrity of other nations' programs, an implication that is widely resented.

Clearly, the Coast Guard, being the lead agency, faces a difficult challenge in attempting to deal diplomatically and effectively with diverse actors in a range of states. Doing so is obviously a critical and delicate aspect of its role and requires well-trained staff in areas that are not commonly associated with the armed forces. Coast Guard officials recognize that personnel working in the program have unique demands placed on them since they must be not only proficient security inspectors but also culturally and diplomatically sensitive in liaisons with foreign countries. The challenge, however, has been complicated by Coast Guard plans to compress its schedule for completing follow-up visits so that all were to be completed within a two-year time frame and by the Coast Guard personnel rotation policy that moves personnel between different positions every three to four years (US GAO, 2010).

Many around the world also view US maritime policy not only as misguided (the emphasis on terrorism minimizes the resources that foreign ports can spend on such pressing issues as smuggling, theft and safety) but driven by US domestic political considerations (Grillot et al., 2010, p. 83). At another level, several countries have had concerns over the stationing of US Customs agents in their country and the imposition of US standards and practices. Australian officials, for example, objected to being supervised by US authorities and to having to accept US scanning practices even though their regulations and practices already surpassed

ISPS standards and matched those required for CSI. Australian officials expressed 'uncertainty' about the intentions of the USA in using CSI to establish a new global 'security regime.' Accordingly, Australia chose not to participate in CSI. Despite expectations that it would eventually join, as late as the end of 2008, none of its ports were listed as a 'currently operational port' on the CBP website. Additionally, the reliance on bilateral agreements by the USA (for CSI and subsequently SAFE Ports) limits a country's ability to enter into future trade agreements such as existing regional trading blocs or free trade agreements. Feeling that CSI agreements violated fair and genuine competition between EU ports, the European Commission initiated legal proceedings against EU members with CSI agreements (Brew, 2003).

8.9.2   Local and National Differences

The second problem area includes all those issues that arise when dealing with cultural, political, social, economic, environmental or other attributes of unique foreign settings. The economic one is obvious because there are increased costs involved in implementing CSI. There are at least two dimensions to this issue. First, costs vary dramatically across ports depending on the methodology, port management structure (public or private), national customs' policies and the role of commercial terminal operators. For example, in the Port of Rotterdam, the scanning machine was purchased for €14 million, while in Singapore the equipment was purchased for $1.9 million. Adding to the frustration is that many foreign officials have reported a lack of knowledge of the correct security equipment to purchase, based on the needs of their port, as CSI does not specify those types of particulars. Moreover, neither the ISPS code nor CSI deal with how initial and maintenance costs are to be recovered. Furthermore, many ports in developing countries lack sufficient funding to provide even basic physical security through fencing, let alone meet and maintain ISPS standards (Banomyong, 2005; Allen, 2006; Carafano, 2008; US GAO, 2010; Bichou, 2011; Commander Walcott, n.d.).

Thus, the question of the extent to which, and for what purposes, the USA should provide funding arises and extends well beyond whether it should provide funding to poor countries. The UK, for example, believes that British ports, businesses and government agencies should not be responsible for the costs of what is 'essentially a mandatory US domestic security requirement.' At one point, its freight industry was even encouraged by the British International Freight Association to forward all CSI and 24 hour rule-related costs to US importers (Brew, 2003). Other financial considerations involve liability issues. Given that US Customs agents have no authority in the foreign port, and therefore no responsibility, does this mitigate or absolve the responsibility of the USA for failing to prevent the attack? Does the host nation bear all responsibility?

The differences among US ports (that themselves vary dramatically in layout, structure and operations) are even greater when these are compared to ports in other parts of the world. For example, European ports, which rely largely on barge traffic, have very different screening challenges from those of most US ports, which are truck oriented. Officials in Singapore have also expressed concerns over the problems caused by their offshore loading and unloading systems (Grillot et al., 2010, p. 81).

Culture also creates frictions in many ways. Many countries such as Belgium, the Netherlands and Japan have different views on individual privacy and have refused to accede to US demands for expansive background checks of port and other workers (Wilson, 2008; Grillot et al., 2009, 2010). Not only is there no way to ensure that all personnel have been adequately screened but since neither CSI nor C-TPAT has requirements for a universal standardized ID card, it is difficult to assess the quality of even a mandated ID card, even if the officials have received relevant training as required by CSI and C-TPAT (Kumar and Verruso, 2008; Grillot et al., 2009). Since training is handled domestically, it is unclear who has been trained and what levels of expertise have been achieved.

Such differences are aggravated by the different roles played by national security and private security forces. In some ports, the former are primarily responsible, in others the latter. In India, for example, the national force handles security at Kandla, the major port for oil imports, whereas in Mundra, a port that handles much traffic from Pakistan for export, security is handled by a private company (Maheshwari, 2008). Such decisions are made by central governments, usually on the basis of other criteria than the potential threat to the USA.

Such concerns extend to the port's security personnel structure. The CSI regulations do not try to impose a specific structure so great variations are possible. For example, a port facility security officer may be a singular, dedicated position or simply an added responsibility to an existing position that is already overtasked. The same is true for the ISPS code (Bichou, 2008, 2011). Such lack of specificity is perhaps inevitable given the many differences across the world but it may also slow implementation and create administrative duplication and confusion over where responsibility resides.

Foreign governments play a critical role in many other ways. The CSI and CBP teams may supervise some security or scanning measures, but foreign officials are responsible for most of the evaluation, especially for the physical and perimeter security. Unfortunately, corruption of various forms is often commonplace as evidenced by smuggling and other illegal activities that often characterize the supply chain and can obviously influence the decision to validate a foreign port or a shipper participating in the C-TPAT program (Grillot et al., 2009).

Cultural differences, even when both sides are genuinely striving to cooperate, can also play a role. Westerners tend to express themselves in a direct, straightforward manner but many other peoples communicate through context and are reluctant to give a direct or negative response. Thus, a foreign official may simply tell a CBP agent seeking to learn if a particular measure is operational, what he thinks the US official wants to hear. A similar situation applies to inter-business communications when an American company is seeking to verify compliance within its supply chain.

The communication problem also extends to the need for public–private cooperation, a cornerstone of both CSI and C-TPAT. For some states, this may be an unusual arrangement so that the two groups may not be used to communicating with each other. For example, in Trinidad and Tobago, owners and operators have not been adequately informed of the need to remain compliant, and may not maintain the security measures following initial certification. Additionally, there are many cases where local businesses, and even local governmental officials, have complained about what they regard as imposed inefficiencies and costs from CSI and C-TPAT regulations. At least some of these complaints result from a failure of the businesses requesting C-TPAT certification to communicate the requirements effectively to their supply chain partners and of a similar failure by the host governments in their relations with the officials and businesses actually operating in the ports (Allen, 2006; Kumar and Verruso, 2008; Grillot et al., 2009; North, 2009; Commander Walcott, n.d.).

8.10 CONCLUSIONS

Clearly, achieving a high level of maritime security remains a work in progress. Although the situation has improved greatly since 9/11, the difficulties in integrating and coordinating programs run by different agencies whose effectiveness requires the strong support of the private sector and foreign governments is, under the most favorable circumstances, no easy matter. Essentially, two basic sets of issues have to be resolved if the US efforts to achieve security in its supply chains is to be achieved in a balanced manner. The first involves the domestic dimension of the policies that have been implemented. The second is the international dimension.

On the domestic side, the large number of projects, programs and policies that have been implemented since 9/11 may be viewed by the DHS as providing a coherent, layered approach to maritime security. There is no doubt that there is a degree of overlap and redundancy and that important issues have not yet been dealt with effectively. These are well known and have been summarized as follows: (1) workforce planning and administration; (2) measuring performance; (3) logistical and other operational difficulties; (4) technology and infrastructure; (5) use and ownership of data; and (6) consistency with accepted risk management principles (US GAO, 2008).

Although the USA can accomplish much through appropriate domestic policies and actions, dealing with other weaknesses listed by the GAO (and even some of those listed above) can be remedied only through the willing cooperation of other states. For example, much valuable data is generated and collected by foreign ports but UK privacy legislation has prevented their customs from sharing information on cargo containers with the CBP. For the systematic and effective transfer of information, a new international agreement between the USA and the EU is required. Similarly, as noted earlier, the 'Resource responsibility' of the USA toward the security of foreign ports remains unclear. Finally, the GAO identified 'Reciprocity and trade concerns' as a major issue for foreign states to demand reciprocity of 100 percent scanning. Moreover, the European Commission has voiced concern that meeting US demands for 100 percent scanning would divert resources away from strengthening EU security and the WCO has argued that the 100 percent mandate would amount to an unfair non-tariff trade barrier and disrupt the international trading system. Finally, the GAO also listed 'Host nation examination practices' as a major weakness.

In other words, a variety of security gaps remains in certified compliant ports around the world. Despite all the programs, it is not at all clear that regulations have been implemented thoroughly and completely, or are operating correctly, in many foreign ports. Potential confusion in the international community over competing program requirements, along with incomplete or training, inadequate personnel checks and identification, insufficient funding and staffing, prohibitive national policies, and differing infrastructure and environmental conditions combine to create a lack of efficiency, transparency and reliability for security level at many ports.

The USA has taken some actions and made some modifications to US programs in order to address particular concerns and problems reported in foreign ports or by foreign officials. This includes the sharing of best, low-cost, security practices, and training methods, by US Customs with foreign officials and port operators to help them find affordable ways to meet at least the ISPS standards, the partnering of US Customs with other US agencies and with regional blocs such as APEC and Organization of American States (OAS) for joint assessment visits to help reduce the US 'footprint' in foreign states. The CBP has also considered restructuring the CSI teams from a country to a regional basis partly in order to increase the geographic and cultural knowledge of team managers and to promote a manager's consistent relationship with several countries. On paper, CBP officials are to recommend to countries an implementation strategy based upon the readiness of that particular foreign government to implement CSI, yet it is difficult to determine the extent to which the strategy promoted by CBP teams has followed this guideline or been effective. Despite these improvements, many of the other issues discussed above have not received the consideration they deserve. Often official statements simply state that they should be given consideration 'at some point in the future' (US Customs and Border Protection, 2006).

The implication for maritime cargo security of the present situation is very serious – countries may increasingly choose not to participate in the US programs, may create various competing initiatives of their own or cherry-pick which aspects they feel should be fully implemented in their ports. The result would be, at best, a lack of confidence in the level of security of any port, even if they were technically certified by a particular program. Such a situation would create diplomatic and economic confusion, and leave the container shipping industry open to a wide selection of gaps that could be exploited by terrorists to attack the USA or another country with a WMD.

The situation of the poorest nations deserves particular attention because if their fears are realized and existing programs contribute to a widening gap between them and the advanced countries, there is a real possibility that the result would be to create new perceived grievances in many countries, and thereby facilitate the creation of new security threats (Allen, 2006). On the other hand, if security regulations are not carefully implemented in developed countries, this might lead to costly delays and drive exporters to use less secure ports in some of the lesser developed regions, which would make those shipments easier for terrorists to penetrate (Carafano, 2008).

Such possibilities can only be avoided through the wise application of a new paradigm. It is clear that any attempt to enhance maritime security must involve close consultation and cooperation with many foreign countries. Achieving such cooperation is seldom easy for, as noted above, international politics is characterized by a system of autonomous states, each pursuing its own interests. It is further complicated by widespread hypocrisy and the application of double standards. The USA has not been immune from such practices, but the new administration does not share its predecessor's aversion to a multilateral approach. In the area of maritime security, the USA should shift from a US-centric approach to a global approach that emphasizes the benefits for the development of poorer nations, the integration and efficiency of the international shipping industry, and develop an overarching system of initiatives that provides security against a variety of security threats, including but not limited to terrorism.

For such an approach to work, a common set of standards that are applied uniformly is required so that a level of confidence can exist between countries. Mutual recognition arrangements with other countries can provide an important first step toward that goal. For example, the CBP has successfully developed a formal understanding whereby the actions or decisions of a customs administration are recognized and accepted by customs everywhere. Similar agreements could be reached with the EU, which has developed and implemented a set of regulations to ensure that the ISPS standards are adhered to by its member countries. In this manner, the USA should move toward increased international consensus when developing practices with the intention of including them in a universal global framework. The ability for all the stakeholders in maritime cargo trade to reap the benefits of enhanced security measures without exorbitant costs or redundancy in implementation and operationalization is crucial for the promotion of a secure and efficient international trading system.

Such an approach is, at its core, not consonant with the strategy that underlies the present US security paradigm. Since 9/11, the USA, and to a significant degree its coalition partners, have essentially implemented a counter-terrorism strategy based on pre-emption that seeks to capture or kill terrorists and punish those countries that provide support of any sort. However, it has become clear that the logistical requirements and the associated costs of such a strategy cannot be sustained much longer though deterrence will always remain an important foreign policy tool. However, the approach outlined is based on the development and implementation of a new strategic vision for national security based on identifying and implementing new rule sets for acceptable global behavior in maritime security by an ever-increasing number of states. The initiatives and programs that are part of the US approach to maritime security must not only treat the symptoms by attempting to mitigate terrorist threats before they reach the homeland but also pay more attention to the disease by establishing new rule sets that like-minded states can not only agree on but will dedicate resources to enforce. The goal should be to create a new global system based on shared interests in securing the maritime domain from terrorism and other unlawful or hostile acts. This will not happen quickly or easily but the USA is not the only nation that recognizes the vital importance of maritime security and is willing to work to achieve it. An effective global maritime security framework that coordinates free trade and security will enlist the assistance of like-minded states while recognizing sovereignty, strengthening economies and enhancing international partnerships.

NOTES

*   This chapter draws upon some of my previously published work, especially 'Transportation security: issues and challenges' (2009) as well as excellent seminar papers written by Mr Steve Olson and Ms Courtney Schultz who also did additional research on this topic.
1.   National Strategy for Maritime Security, http://www.ise.gov/sites/default/files/0509%20 National%20Strategy%20for%20Maritime%20Security.pdf, p. 20.

REFERENCES

Allen, N.H. (2006), 'The Container Security Initiative costs, implications and relevance to developing countries', *Public Administration and Development*, **26**, 439–47.

Banomyong, R. (2005), 'The impact of port and trade security initiatives on maritime supply-chain mangement', *Maritime Policy Management*, **32** (1), 3–13.

Bemis, R. (2002), 'Statement before the Committee on Government Reform', Subcommittee on National Security Affairs and International Relations, 18 November.

Bichou, K. (2008), *Security and Risk-based Models in Shipping and Ports: Review and Critical Analysis*, Paris: Organisation for Economic Co-operation and Development and International Transport Forum, December.

Bichou, K. (2011), 'Assessing the impact of procedural security on container port efficiency', *Maritime Economics and Logistics*, **13** (1), 1–28.

Brew, N. (2003), *Ripples from 9/11: The US Container Security Initiative and its Implications for Australia*, Melbourne: Information and Research Services, Department of the Parliamentary Library, 13 May.

Caldwell, S.L. (2007), *Maritime Security: The SAFE Port Act: Status and Implementation One Year Later*, Washington, DC: Government Accountability Office.

Carafano, J.J. (2008), 'A second look at container security: lessons from Hong Kong', Web Memo, The Heritage Foundation, Washington, DC, 30 January.

Cole, J. (2011), 'Installation of Megaports Initiative completed: AIT', *Taipei Times*, 23 February.

Commander Walcott. (n.d.), *The Status of ISPS Implementation in Trinidad and Tobago*, PowerPoint Presntation, Marine Ship Safety and Port Facility Security Unit.

Congressional Research Service (2005), *Port and Maritime Security: Background and Issues for Congress*, Report for Congress, Washington, DC: Library of Congress, 27 May.

Container Security Initiative 2006–11 Strategic Plan (2006), US Customs and Border Protection Office of Policy and Planning and Office of International Affairs Container Security Division.

Fritelli, J.F. (2003), *Port and Maritime Security: Background and Issues*, Hauppauge, NY: Nova Publishers.

Giermanski, J. (2011), 'What DHS has failed to fix is fixable', *The Maritime Executive*, 10 January.

Greenberg, M.D., P. Chalk, H.H. Willis, I. Khilko and D.S. Ortiz. (2006), *Maritime Terrorism: Risk and Liability*, Washington, DC: RAND Center for Terrorism Risk Management Policy.

Grillot, S.R., R.J. Cruise and V.J. D'erman (2009), 'National and global efforts to enhance containerized freight security', *Journal of Homeland Security and Emergency Management*, **6** (1), 1–31.

Grillot, S.R., R.J. Cruise and V.J. D'erman (2010), *Protecting Our Ports: Domestic and International Politics of Containerized Freight Security*, New York: Ashgate Publishing.

Harrald, J.R. (2005), 'Sea trade and security: an assessment of the post-911 reaction', *Journal of International Affairs*, **59** (1), 157–78.

Henrikson, A.C. (2005), 'An interagency approach to U.S. port security', *Strategic Insights*, **IV** (2).

Huizenga, D. (2008), Testimony on NNSA's Megaports Initiative and its Role in the Secure Freight Initiative (SFI) before the Senate Commerce, Science, and Transportation Subcommittee, National Nuclear Security Administration, Washington, DC, 12 June.

ITA (International Trade Administration) (2005), http://www.ita.doc.gov/td/industry/otea/usfth/aggregate (accessed 2010).

Kumar, S. and J. Verruso (2008), 'Risk assessment for the security of inbound containers at U.S. ports: a failure, mode, effects, and criticality analysis approach', *Transportation Journal*, Fall, 26–41.

Lorenz, A.J. (2007), 'Al Qaeda's maritime threat', 15 April, available at http://www.maritimeterrorism.com (accessed 2010).

Maheshwari, D.V. (2008), 'Port security in Pvt hands: a cause for concern, say many', *Express India*, 31 July.

NNSA (National Nuclear Security Administration (2011), *Megaports Initiative*, available at http://www.nnsa.energy.gov (accessed 25 February 2011).

North, J.L. (2009), 'The ins and outs of modern ports: rethinking container security', *South Carolina Journal of International Law and Business*, **5**, 191–208.

Skinner, R.L. (2005), Testimony Before the Committee on Commerce, Science, and Transportation, US Senate, Washington, DC.

Szyliowicz, J. (2009), 'Transportation security: issues and challenges', in M. Tahmisoglu and C. Ozen (eds), *Transportation Security Against Terrorism*, NATO Science for Peace series, Amsterdam: IOS Press, pp. 13–26.

US Bureau of Transportation Statistics (2008), *Transportation Statistics Annual Report*, Washington, DC.

US Customs and Border Protection (2006), *Container Security Initiative: 2006–2011 Strategic Plan*, Washington, DC: Department of Homeland Security.

US DHS (2005), *National Strategy for Maritime Security*, Washington, DC: Department of Homeland Security, September.

US Department of State (2010), *Quadrennial Diplomacy and Development Review: Overview*, May, available at http://www.state.gov/s/dmr/qddr (accesse 2010).

US GAO (2007), *Maritime Security: The SAFE Port Act: Status and Implementation One Year Later*, Washington, DC: Government Accoutability Office, 30 October.

US GAO (2008), *Supply Chain Security: CBP Works with International Entities to Promote Global Customs Security Standad and Initiatives, but Challenges Remain*, Washington, DC: Government Accountability Office, 15 August.

US GAO (2010), *Maritime Security: Responses to Questions for the Record*, Washington, DC: Government Accountability Office.

US GAO (2011a), *Transportation Worker Identification Credential: Internal Control Weaknesses Need to Be Corrected to Help Achieve Security Objectives*, Washington, DC: Government Accountability Office, 10 May.

US GAO (2011b), *Maritime Security. DHS and Sciences and Technology: Additional Steps Needed to Ensure Test and Evaluation Requirements are Met*, Washington, DC: Government Accountability Office, 15 June.

US GAO (2011c), *Maritime Security: Federal Agencies have Taken Actions to Address Risks Posed by Seafarers, but Efforts can be Strengthened*, Washington, DC: Government Accountability Office, 14 January.

US GAO (2013), *Card Reader Pilot Results are Unreliable; Security Benefits Need to Be Reassessed*, Washington, DC: Government Accountability Office, 8 May.

Wilson, R.M. (2008), 'An overview of U.S. initiatives and technologies to secure shipping containers at overseas ports', *Journal of Applied Security Research*, **3** (2), 241–67.

Wrightson, M.T. (2005), *Maritime Security: Enhancements Made, but Implementation and Sustainability Remain Key Challenges*, Washington, DC: Government Accountability Office, 17 May.

9. Maritime security in Canada

Mary R. Brooks

9.1 INTRODUCTION: A HISTORY OF TRANSPORTATION SECURITY REGULATION IN CANADA

In the early years of Canadian policy-making, the country's shipping policy was a product of the British Empire in that it reflected Britain's pro-shipping stance as opposed to Canada's pro-trade stance (McDorman, 1984). Canada adopted the legislation, rules and regulations of British maritime tradition through the British Commonwealth Merchant Shipping Agreement, 1931, which called upon Canada to reserve its domestic shipping to 'British' (Commonwealth) ships. This Agreement, signed the day before the Statute of Westminster, 1931, remained the critical shipping policy until the 1970s when Canada developed a Maritime Code that never received Royal Assent, and therefore did not become law. It was not until the Coasting Trade Act, 1992 that Canada removed the term 'British ship' from Canadian shipping legislation, and access to domestic shipping via flag of registration or waiver issued by the Canadian Transportation Agency was implemented.

Until the Coasting Trade Act, 1992 and the Canada Shipping Act, 2001 established shipping-specific policies, Canada's attitude towards maritime security can be discerned from its policy statements on security in the broader transportation context. Since 1967, Canada's policies on transportation have generally focused on consistent and persistent themes of balancing economic performance with social needs like access for the disabled (Waters, 2006). The Royal Commission on Transportation of 1959–62 effectively defined transportation policy in Canada; its recommendations were implemented in the National Transportation Act, 1967. At this time, the foci of national public interest were rail regulation and rate-making, with the legislation intended to substitute competition for regulation, but failing to go far enough (House of Commons, 1985, p. 3) or for that matter to address security. Transport Canada's 1985 *Freedom to Move* policy document (Transport Canada, 1985) also contained no mention of security, and so the Standing Committee on Transport (House of Commons, 1985) noted the insufficient focus on safety under a section entitled 'Transportation safety and security'; while the word security may have appeared in the title, it was not to be found in the substance. In summary, the Standing Committee called upon the government to ensure that transportation safety be included in the policy objectives in amending legislation, but the word security did not make it into either of the Standing Committee's Recommendations 42 and 43 or into the purpose clause (3 (1)) of the National Transportation Act, 1987, which sought 'a safe [new addition], economic, efficient and adequate network'.

In 1993, the National Transportation Act Review Commission reported to the Minister of Transport on its five-year review of the 1987 Act. Again, a deregulatory focus did not see security issues as worthy of printer's ink. Revisions included in the Canada Transportation Act, 1996 and the Canada Marine Act, 1998 were focused on further deregulation and the unwinding of subsidies in favour of new public management principles. The serious debt and deficit situation facing the Canadian government in 1993 had clarified the critical issue for the country: the need to get Canada's fiscal house in order was paramount. The purpose clause (now appearing as clause 5(1)) remained mostly unchanged in its initial wording, still seeking a safe network, but with greater emphasis on market forces and with access for the disabled now holding greater priority. 'It is declared that a competitive, economic and efficient national transportation system accessible to persons with disabilities and that makes the best use of all available modes of transportation at the lowest total cost . . . the national transportation system meets the *highest practicable safety standards*' (Canada Transportation Act, 1996, emphasis added).

By 2001, the task of a five-year review of the Canada Transportation Act, 1996 fell to the Canada Transportation Act Review Panel and its report, *Vision and Balance*, was released in June 2001. This document captured the need for reform of Canada's transportation industry very eloquently, with passion and enthusiasm for making solid progress in support of improving industry competitiveness through market forces. It posited a 'compass for the journey' but its guiding principles did not note any need for changes to security programmes or planning, and unfortunate timing sidelined its recommendations. Before any substantive discussion on revising the regulatory and legislative agenda could occur, the terrorist acts of 9/11 took place, violently redirecting Canadian priorities from the domestic regulation of the industry to a more global need to ensure Canada's trade interests were not jeopardized by the USA's security agenda, discussed in the next section.

By the time the 2006 revisions were made to the Canada Transportation Act, security had become a critical priority; section 5 has been revised to read:

5. It is declared that a competitive, economic and efficient national transportation system accessible to persons with disabilities that meets *the highest practicable safety and security standards* [emphasis added] and contributes to a sustainable environment and makes the best use of all modes of transportation at the lowest total cost is essential to serve the needs of its users, advance the well-being of Canadians and enable competitiveness and economic growth in both urban and rural areas throughout Canada. Those objectives are most likely to be achieved when . . .

(b) regulation and strategic public intervention are used to achieve economic, safety, *security* [emphasis added], environmental or social outcomes that cannot be achieved satisfactorily by competition and market forces and do not unduly favour, or reduce the inherent advantages of, any particular mode of transportation; . . . (Canada Transportation Act, 2006)

While marine transportation regulation in Canada began as a result of the country's historical ties to Great Britain, its colonial master, its path to current times has been more broadly influenced by its proximity to and relationship with its closest trading partner and ally, the USA. The next section explores the impacts of Canada's relationship with the USA on the development of a subset of transportation regulation – Canada's maritime and port security regulatory regime.

9.2   THE INFLUENCE OF AMERICAN POLICY ON CANADA'S MARITIME SECURITY

Underlying all of these revisions to the policy framework governing transportation was the basic tenet that as a nation of traders, Canada could not afford to jeopardize its trading interests by interrupting the flow of trade significantly. Canada's largest trading partner is the USA, accounting for more than 50 per cent of its total export sales. Of all the products traded between Canada and the USA since the Second World War, none has been as important as auto parts, and so the first 'free trade' agreement was the Automotive Products Agreement (or Auto Pact), signed in 1965. By the turn of the millennium, the largest trade flow in the world was that between the province of Ontario, Canada, and the state of Michigan, USA, and one-third of all Canada–USA trade passed over the Ambassador Bridge between Windsor, Ontario, and Detroit, Michigan. That mutual dependence as trading partners continues today, although not at the levels seen in 2000. Trade data show that the US share of Canadian trade rose from 80 per cent in 1993 to 84 per cent in 2004 and then fell to 64.5 per cent in 2011; on the other hand, Canada's share of US trade was 22 per cent in 1993, 24 per cent in 2004 and fell to 19 per cent by 2011 (Government of Canada, 2012). As of 2008, Canada ceased to be the USA's largest partner, losing that position to China.

US military policy has been a dominant influence on Canada's security arrangements and decision-making since the Second World War. The concept of Fortress North America emerged when large parts of Western Europe fell quickly to the German blitzkrieg; the resulting fear that the rest of the world might fall as well inspired the two governments to consider the necessity of a joint plan to defend the continent. The Permanent Joint Board of Defense was established in 1940, well in advance of the Japanese bombing of Pearl Harbor. After the war, numerous examples of Canada–US security cooperation were realized: the formation of the North American Air Defense Command (NORAD) in 1957; the development of US Customs pre-clearance at Canadian airports since the 1970s; and the 1995 Shared Border Accord (intended to streamline procedures, promote trade and address smuggling and illegal entry) to name a few. A timeline of selected pre-2002 security initiatives is found in Table 9.1.

> Perhaps nothing signals the closeness of the Canada–US relationship more strongly than the ironic fact that on 11 September 2001, it was a Canadian at the helm of NORAD when the military jets were scrambled at the time of the attacks on the US. (Brooks, 2008, p. 159)

After the tragic events of 9/11, the nature of the border became a significant discussion point between the two countries, with proposals for hardening the border front and centre in American minds (Flynn, 2003). The two countries over the next several years signed an even longer list of agreements than found in Table 9.1, with each agreement taking the commitments further and generating greater clarity on the extent of cooperation. A very detailed review of these may be found in appendices 7.1 and 7.2 of Brooks (2008) for those seeking to understand the minutiae of the transportation and security aspects of the NAFTA relationship, and particularly the key components of the Security and Prosperity Partnership between the three NAFTA leaders in 2005–07.

On 4 February 2011, US President Barack Obama and Canadian Prime Minister Stephen Harper released their 'Beyond the border: a shared vision for perimeter security and economic competitiveness', the most recent of these agreements. After a stalled, tripartite Security and Prosperity Partnership, the bilateral vision expressed renewed interest in refining and retuning the Canada–US relationship in security, trade and transportation:

> [W]e intend to pursue a perimeter approach to security, working together within, at, and away from the borders of our two countries to enhance our security and accelerate the legitimate flow of people, goods, and services between our two countries. We intend to do so in partnership, and in ways that support economic competitiveness, job creation, and prosperity. (The White House, 2011)

Table 9.1   A timeline of Canada–US security cooperation prior to 2002

Date	Key event/activity
1940	Permanent Joint Board of Defense established
1957	Formation of the North American Air Defense Command
1952	The first informal US Customs pre-clearance facility established at Toronto airport at the request of American Airlines
1974	US Customs pre-clearance facilities formalized by the passage of the Air Transport Preclearance Act, 1974
1987	The Canada–US Trade Agreement is signed (no substantive security or maritime features are included)
1992	The North American Free Trade Agreement (NAFTA) is signed with effect 1 January 1994 (no substantive security or maritime features are included)
1995	The Canada/United States of America Accord on Our Shared Border is signed. The objectives of the Accord are to promote trade, streamline processes for commercial goods and legitimate travellers and enhance protection against drug smuggling and the illegal entry
1999	Canada–US Partnership is launched to promote bilateral dialogue on border issues and identify emergent ones
October 2000	Canada–US Transborder Working Group established; jointly managed by Transport Canada and the Federal Highway Administration, the Group focuses on border transportation management
11 September 2011	Terrorist attacks in New York and Washington redirect the nature of the Canada–US and NAFTA relationships to focus on security rather than trade promotion and facilitation
12 December 2001	Canada and the USA sign the 30-Point Smart Border Declaration and Action Plan (Department of Foreign Affairs and International Trade, 2004)

The 2011 declaration implied that negotiations between the two countries would provide a framework for joint threat assessment, intelligence gathering and information sharing, as well as a commitment to cross-border law enforcement targeting transnational crime. In addition to enabling the Canadian government to make key investments in US border infrastructure, including a second bridge between Windsor and Detroit, a key feature of the integrated relationship is the establishment of Integrated Border Enforcement Teams (IBETs) of Canadians and Americans to share information and resources across five core agencies. Although IBETs have been at work since 1996, recent activities have included US Customs and Border Protection teams in Canadian ports and the joint enforcement teams of the Shiprider programme on the Great Lakes. Canadian and US maritime security efforts have become even more integrated.

After a discussion of Canada's port and shipping traffic and an assessment of the impact of port governance reform on maritime security, this chapter will discuss the specifics of Canada's maritime and port security organization and execution before drawing conclusions on the strengths and weaknesses of current security initiatives.

9.3   AN OVERVIEW OF VESSEL AND PORT TRAFFIC IN CANADA

Now that the security mindset of Canadians has been established, it is important to return to the role of trade in security policy. Canada's trade with the world accounted for C$447 billion in 2011, and trade represents about 30 per cent of gross domestic product (GDP), significantly less than in 2000 when Canada's trade dependence exceeded 40 per cent of GDP. While domestic and transborder marine traffic make up the majority of vessel movements at Canadian ports, as opposed to overseas movements (Table 9.2), they are not the majority of cargo tonnes transported. Domestic tonnage in 2010 constituted 25.9 per cent of total tonnes handled and US cargoes added another 22.9 per cent, with other international cargoes making up the remaining 51.3 per cent (Statistics Canada, 2010, table 1). Vessels flying a multitude of flags call at Canadian ports, with foreign flag vessels carrying the majority of Canada–US volume.

Much of Canada's trade is carried by sea. Canada's maritime trade with the USA in 2010 totalled 102.9 million tonnes of a total 333.6 million tonnes of maritime traffic. Of Canada's non-US trade in 2011, 64.5 per cent by value was carried by the marine mode (Transport Canada, 2012a, table EC7). By value, non-US trade's single largest commodity exported is agricultural products including grain, followed by coal and wood pulp. On the import side, crude petroleum is the largest marine import (Transport Canada, 2012a, table M29). While the number of Canadian-registered, ocean-going merchant vessels is small, its flag is flown by a significant number of bulk carriers operating in the transborder St Lawrence Seaway/Great Lakes system. Canada has long pursued a policy of engagement in the work of the International Maritime Organization (IMO), including active participation in the IMO's maritime security initiatives.

Canada has three types of ports (not including private facilities): Canada Port Authority (CPA) ports, local and regional ports, and remote

Table 9.2   International shipping: vessel capacity (gross tonnes), cargo tonnage transported and number of movements by flag of registry

Flag of registry	Total vessel capacity (millions gt)		Tonnage transported (million tonnes)		Movements (number)	
	2001	2010	2001	2010	2001	2010
Transborder traffic						
Canada	88	58	54	40	11,293	8689
USA	53	29	11	9	11,841	8532
Other (flag)	285	316	43	54	10,853	8135
Sub-total transborder	426	404	108	103	33,987	25,356
Overseas traffic						
Canada	1	1	0	1	102	116
USA	1	1	0	0	32	33
Liberia	36	54	18	25	1099	1235
Bahamas	46	22	12	13	1426	791
Panama	89	113	45	61	2513	2835
Norway	23	22	10	7	836	726
Greece	26	26	15	18	582	423
Cyprus	14	16	7	9	655	653
Japan	8	2	2	1	178	32
Philippines	6	1	3	1	257	49
Hong Kong	16	40	8	22	506	1099
Malta and Gozo	11	13	6	8	471	485
South Korea	1	7	1	3	56	122
Denmark	4	3	1	1	127	101
UK	10	11	3	4	254	242
Singapore	11	13	5	7	322	325
People's Republic of China	2	7	1	3	82	147
Other (flag)	91	108	40	48	4978	4058
Sub-total overseas	396	459	179	231	14,476	13,472
Total traffic	821	862	287	334	48,463	38,828

Source: Calculated from data found in Statistics Canada (2010), *Shipping in Canada*, cat 54–05, table 14.

ports. About 50 per cent of Canada's international traffic is handled at CPA ports (the top 15 ports by volume handled being found in Table 9.3). As already noted, the majority of Canada's trade in tonnage terms is bulk cargo, and a significant share of that is transferred at privately owned facilities that do not come under the regulatory jurisdiction of CPAs. To

Table 9.3   Top 15 ports in Canada in 2010 and percentage of domestic traffic

Port	Total handled (thousand tonnes)	Percentage domestic (%)	Port share of tonnes handled (%)	Port status
1. Metro Vancouver	104,743	9.9	23.3	CPA
2. Saint John	30,588	13.2	6.8	CPA
3. Come-By-Chance	27,070	39.2	6.0	LR
4. Port Hawkesbury	26,317	1.7	5.8	LR
5. Montréal/Contrecoeur	24,775	19.6	5.5	CPA
6. Sept-Îles/Pointe-Noire	24,613	8.0	5.5	CPA
7. Québec/Lévis	24,580	18.2	5.5	CPA
8. Port-Cartier	17,903	21.0	4.0	CPA
9. Prince Rupert	14,994	0.0	3.3	CPA
10. Newfoundland Offshore	14,020	85.9	3.1	Private
11. Hamilton	11,402	45.5	2.5	CPA
12. Halifax	10,196	25.8	2.3	CPA
13. Nanticoke	7386	15.9	1.6	D
14. Thunder Bay	6751	72.1	1.5	CPA
15. Sorel	6187	51.0	1.4	LR
Sub-total of top 15 ports	351,524	19.8	78.1	
Other ports	98,506	47.6	21.9	
Grand total	450,030	25.9	100.0	

Notes: CPA = Canada Port Authority; LR = local/regional port; P = private;
D = deproclaimed.

Source: Calculated from data found in Statistics Canada, *Shipping in Canada*, cat 54-205, table 13.

illustrate, the third and tenth largest 'ports' in Canada are the refinery at Come-by-Chance and the offshore oil platforms of Newfoundland and Labrador (Table 9.3).

On the other hand, container trade being relatively high value and low density is a minor player in tonnage terms but a significant player in value terms. Its importance from an economic perspective is due to its role in both job creation at the ports and contribution to port revenue. For many security analysts, the container is seen as an ideal venue for the importation of a 'bomb in a box' and so security assessments have tended to focus here. We shall return to this traffic in a later section.

9.4 HAS THE DEVOLUTION OF PORT GOVERNANCE BEEN A CRITICAL SECURITY ISSUE?

Canada is a coastal nation, and the significant number of harbours, bays and inlets makes managing or monitoring the 'port' infrastructure very important for the country's security. Canada established its first independent (from British) ports policy in 1936 with the creation of the National Harbours Board (NHB), a Crown Corporation reporting to the federal government. By the early 1980s, there were 15 ports under the control of the NHB but management systems were bureaucratic and control was centralized as the NHB reported to the Minister of Transport. In addition to the NHB ports, there were nine local harbour commissions, each governed by the Harbour Commissions Act of 1964 but incorporated and operated under its own private Act; their activities were managed by a board of both federal and municipal appointees (Gratwick and Elliott, 1992). There was a third group of 'ports', the more than 500 small ports and government wharves administered directly by Transport Canada, where the Minister of Public Works had responsibility for major repairs and investment. Furthermore, there were more than 2000 public harbours and government wharves that were transferred in 1973 to the Department of the Environment. In summary, there was a strong history of government ownership and control, and therefore a history of government responsibility for port security.

In 1981, the first wave of governance reform saw legislation (The Canada Port Corporation Act, 1982) introduced that would move port governance onto a more commercialized path. However, execution of the reform was less than satisfactory with responsibility and accountability still considerably influenced by the Minister of Transport (Brooks, 2007). As the global regulatory environment changed in the early 1990s with a move towards the principles of new public management, the pressure for further port reform grew as Canada's dire fiscal situation became very obvious. The transportation system needed not only to be safe, reliable and efficient but also affordable. The decision was made to withdraw from government operation of transportation infrastructure while retaining ownership and the government introduced the Canada Marine Act, 1998, which did not allow CPA ports to be agents of the Crown in their financial matters. Transport Canada also set in motion the process of removing all but remote ports from Transport Canada's non-CPA inventory. (For further understanding of the history of this governance change and its impact on the current port regulatory environment in Canada, see Brooks, 2004, 2007.)

As part of its reform of port governance, the federal government established a hierarchy of who might 'acquire' a privatized port. First priority was decentralization, for example, transfer to another federal government department. If no department wanted responsibility for the port, then provinces were given the nod before municipal or other public bodies. Only if none of these government agencies expressed an interest could the port be transferred to a private entity. As a result of this 'acquisition' hierarchy, most local and regional ports have either been transferred to other federal government departments, to the provinces or to municipalities. All three local/regional ports in the top 15 (Table 9.3) load and unload bulk commodities only. Port security today is a landlord function with national regulation, compliance and enforcement (Brooks, 2004).

The Standing Senate Committee on National Security and Defence (2007, p. 18) concluded that all is not rosy with maritime security in Canadian ports in the post-devolution era:

> From the point of view of security, the devolution of seaports and airports to local authorities has failed. Security forces at seaports and airports are understaffed and ill-prepared to deal with organized crime and terrorism. There is a need for specialized police in unique environments – and seaports and airports clearly qualify as unique environments. The Netherlands has about 420 police permanently stationed at the Port of Rotterdam alone. There are only 24 RCMP officers assigned to Canada's 19 ports, and every one of them is posted to Halifax, Montreal or Vancouver.

While terrorism was part of the remit, the Senate's focus was predominantly on organized crime activity in Canadian ports.

9.5   THE REGULATION OF MARINE AND PORT SECURITY IN CANADA

Not unlike other countries, Canada adopted the current global regulatory regime for ports and port security, the IMO's International Ship and Port Facility Security (ISPS) code, which came into force on 1 July 2004. The ISPS code, which imposes measures on ships, ports and terminal operators, required Transport Canada to certify that Canadian ports met the code at the time of its implementation. Canada went even further than required, however, enforcing the ISPS code not only with ships of the size or type designated by SOLAS, but also 'non-SOLAS' vessels – those under the SOLAS minimum limit of 500 gross tons down to 100 gross tons, any vessel that carries more than 12 passengers regardless of tonnage and all working barges carrying dangerous cargo whenever they are on an international voyage. Practically, this means that Canada applies ISPS code standards to all foreign-going merchant ships, cruise ships and ferries and adopts the widest interpretation of what structures (including oil rigs and offshore platforms) are included under its ISPS code oversight. Moreover, Canada has also incorporated many of the non-mandatory Part B elements (for elaboration, see Hossain et al., 2009). Canada and the USA also have a bilateral arrangement for the recognition of each other's ship security documentation.

In order to do more to ensure Canada's trading interests were met, the Canadian government also made security grants available to help each port secure its premises, introduce or enhance existing security requirements for personnel, add security cameras, update perimeter fencing and so on. These grants reimbursed up to 75 per cent of the eligible costs of security enhancements incurred after 1 April 2004 and before 30 November 2009. In total, four rounds of funding amounted to $C108.6 million over 1112 projects by 293 recipients (Transport Canada, 2010). There has been no publicly available assessment, and no rumours of a government-led one, to assess whether these security enhancements were effective in raising the security bar.

Furthermore, all containerships calling at US ports are required as part of the Container Security Initiative (CSI) to declare the contents of all containers on the ship's manifest 24 hours prior to loading via the Automated Targeting System to the US Department of Homeland Security (DHS). Halifax, Montréal and Vancouver are CSI ports with US Customs and Border Protection (CBP) agents working to secure cargoes bound for the USA. In fact, these three Canadian container ports were the first to join the CSI in the fall of 2001. The extent of information sharing between CBP officials and the Canada Border Services Agency (CBSA) is a key factor in the joint security efforts by both countries against terrorism, drug and human smuggling. Canada has chosen to replicate many US efforts to secure its interests in the area of cargo notification. Furthermore, Canada has established a cargo programme, Partners in Protection, comparable to the US Customs Trade Partnership Against Terrorism (C-TPAT) initiative that is supposed to fast-track containerized cargo at border crossings, and enhanced the impact of the ISPS code by adopting measures for trans-border movements instituted by other international organizations, like the World Customs Organization (WCO, 2005), the International Labour Organization and the International Standards Organization (Hossain et al., 2009).

In their study of US companies, Brooks and Button (2006) found that the security costs that cargo interests bear account for less than 1 per cent of the total costs of shipping a container and given the high value container cargo represents, cargo owners are in a position to endorse container security measures for their own benefit. Furthermore, large corporations seeking to control their supply chain efforts (retailers like Wal-Mart, Canadian Tire and Home Depot or contract manufacturers like Nike and Dell) have become highly involved in their supply chains, providing oversight scrutiny across the globe; they actively monitor their suppliers. Brooks and Button (2007) concluded that suppliers of first mile or last mile links – those involving collection and distribution – are often the weakest link in the supply chain and are landside and off-terminal, as opposed to facilities under the scrutiny of marine and port security agencies.

By 2007, according to the Office of the Auditor General of Canada (2007, p. 23), the CBSA was 'one of only three [Australia being the third] border agencies in the world using advance automated targeting tools to risk-score incoming shipments'. Targeting was also happening in the US ports of Seattle, Washington and Newark, New Jersey on containers destined for land transport into Canada (CBSA, 2008). The automated risk assessment tool for marine cargo, TITAN, which was introduced in 2004, was audited by the Auditor General in 2007 and found wanting; about 90 per cent of Automated Commercial Information supplied was being processed but risk management protocols on those supplying poor quality information to the system were poor and the offenders were not being subjected to additional monitoring (Office of the Auditor General of Canada, 2007, p. 22). Furthermore, the Auditor General identified that the risk assessment reviews were too infrequent, being only adjusted every two to three years (section 5.71). Perhaps most important to note is that the CBSA (2008) report focused on health risks, counterfeit goods including pharmaceuticals and other illegal activities including terrorist threats. At least, there was recognition that staffing issues and the lack of a single lead agency were continuing to plague CBSA activities.

By 2012, many small companies were choosing to outsource supply chain management to third-party logistics suppliers as Beyond the Border initiatives were being implemented and new air cargo screening protocols were being developed for implementation in 2013. Public Safety Canada (2012) reported on the Canadian government's prevent-detect-deny-respond strategy in response to rising fundamentalist terrorism; the strategy has a much broader remit than just maritime security and secures alignment even more closely with the US Department of Justice initiatives and efforts that focus on the financing of terrorism. Co-location of five agencies' activities in Marine Security Operations Centres is one element of the strategy implementation. Thus, in the last two years, security has been quietly tightened as government emphasizes the registration of companies for security programmes and focuses on separating 'known' from 'unknown' shippers. In the future, it is highly likely that those who are not registered as 'trusted' will find access and oversight increasingly draining any competitive advantage they may have had.

9.6 ORGANIZATION OF THE MARITIME SECURITY FUNCTION IN CANADA

Transport Canada's Marine Transportation Security Regulations and associated programmes are intended to protect the country and its citizens from marine-related security risks and 'preserve the efficiency of Canada's marine transportation system against unlawful interference, terrorist attacks or use as a means to attack our allies' (Transport Canada, 2012b). The organizational structure for Transport Canada's departmental initiatives is partly illustrated in Figure 9.1.

Transport Canada has been a key agency in many efforts aimed at improving marine security in Canada, including efforts to improve transportation security clearances for transportation workers, alterations to the scanning of cargo containers and their contents on arrival in Canada, waterside security and so on. To take container scanning as an example, two types of scanning equipment are operated: the CBSA employs a number of Vehicle and Cargo Inspection Systems units for the purpose of assessing risk for every arriving container by screening the information supplied by carriers 24 hours before the container is loaded in the port of origin. By arrangement with the terminals, every arriving container is driven through a radiation detection portal before being stacked in the yard or loaded for onward surface transport.

In the aftermath of 9/11, the Interdepartmental Marine Security Working Group (IMSWG) was established to ensure a 'whole-of-government' approach to Canada's marine security. The IMSWG, chaired by Transport Canada and comprising 17 federal departments and agencies, 'coordinates

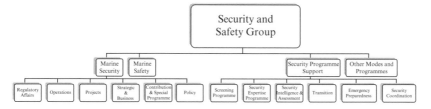

Figure 9.1 Organization chart for Transport Canada's Security and Safety Group

federal responses to marine security issues, analyzes Canada's marine system for gaps, and addresses those gaps' (Transport Canada, 2012a, p. 73). In 2011, the IMSWG completed the Maritime Security Strategic Framework, which serves as a reference point for all departments and agencies with maritime security responsibilities in five activities (marine domain awareness, safeguarding, responsiveness, resilience and collaboration) by documenting action items and next steps in Canada's marine security activities.

Building on Transport Canada's efforts, and those of the IMSWG, are a number of other interdepartmental initiatives. For example, Canada's domain awareness activities include coastal watch programmes and an air surveillance programme that conducts patrols within and outside Canada's 200 nautical mile coastal zone. The Canadian Coast Guard is responsible for the shore-based components required to operate the patrols. Cruise shipping in Canadian waters has grown greatly in recent years and specific measures have been developed for this industry. Even 'tall ships' are subject to special security arrangements in accordance with ISPS code standards (Transport Canada, 2012a, pp. 73–6).

9.7 ASSESSMENT OF MARITIME SECURITY ACTIVITIES IN CANADA

Canada's maritime security policy cannot be isolated from that of the USA in the broader transportation context or from Canada's role as a global supplier of raw materials and a key importer of manufactured goods. Of course, such multimodal security sharing within Transport Canada is only part of the story. In addition to the IMSWG, there are bilateral information-sharing and joint programmes through the Shared Border Accord and the Beyond the Border Working Group. For example, the two countries have launched a pilot project at the Port of Prince Rupert in British Columbia to facilitate a 'cleared once, accepted twice' situation for perimeter security (CBSA, 2012).

Integrated security arrangements have made considerable progress. Proximity to the USA focused the Canadian mindset on security through the first five critical years after 9/11, and by 2006-07, Canada had put in place most security programmes aligned with US interests. The challenge of dealing with the inclusion of Mexico via the Security and Prosperity Partnership diluted efforts for the last years of the Bush Presidency; the Beyond the Border Agreement has restored focus to the bilateral relationship.

The strength of the current relationship contributes to ensuring that the security bureaucracy meets both Canadian needs for free-flowing trade and US demands for security above all else. Cooperation is manifest on several levels. At the lighter end, Transport Canada's marine security website has hotlinks to the US DHS, US Coast Guard, CBP and the Transportation Security Administration. The focus on trade flow streamlining has oriented Canadians towards expedient resolution of issues, with a single-minded determination to ensure US security needs are met, even if the Canadian private sector appetite for further security improvements has waned in the face of the global economic crisis.

It is difficult to judge maritime security in Canada at a very detailed level. As noted by Presidia Security Consulting (2011, p. 32), 'public information from enforcement agencies on interdiction and investigative techniques is frequently vague (for good reason)'. Likewise, there is little interest in, to use a Canadian expression, 'airing dirty laundry in public'. That said, there has been the relatively transparent process of Senate reports, reports by the Office of the Auditor General of Canada and the legislative history. Judging by the legislation before the House of Commons over the last four years, it can be concluded that interest in pure security in Canada has been much more focused on closing the obvious legal loopholes in legislation dealing with financial and immigration matters. Human smuggling and drug trafficking rely on an open banking system and refugee laws that favour the politically disadvantaged. There has been a concerted effort in Canada's recent legislative agenda to pass laws that enhance the likelihood of success in enforcement and prosecution, such as the Protecting Canada's Immigration System Act, 2012, which received Royal Assent on 28 June, and Bill S-7, Combating Terrorism Act, 2013, which received Royal Assent on 25 April 2013.

Among the weaknesses of the current security relationship is the sheer size of the DHS. While Canada has opted to try and coordinate its security arrangements via a 17-unit interdepartmental working group, the USA has put its primary federal security agencies under the DHS roof. Each approach has its disadvantages in dealing with the complexities of the relationships arising from the usual issues of interdepartmental and international coordination. This makes the likelihood of future progress slow, particularly since the global economic crisis refocused interest on trade and economic development.

> The administrative burden on transborder flows needs streamlining. The 'age of terrorism' is a given for the foreseeable future; industry sees security as a competitive necessity. From a transportation network perspective, the system needs to be evaluated continentally, not nationally, if a secure and efficient transportation network for the twenty-first century is to be realized. (Brooks, 2008, p. 206)

In the five years since these words were written, the Bush Adminstration has been replaced by the Obama Administration, Mexico's drug problems have become significantly more noticeable, the Security and Prosperity Partnership has evaporated and the Canada–US security relationship has been revitalized with a greater emphasis on cooperation in the security arena. This is good news, and has been strengthened even further by Royal Assent to the Combating Terrorism Act (on 25 April 2013). Even though very little is published on Canada's maritime security efforts, what can be concluded is that maritime security in Canada has, in the last few years, become even more tightly aligned with that of its major trading partner and continental neighbour.

ACKNOWLEDGEMENT

This research is based on a number of studies in which the author was one of a team of researchers. These studies were funded by several government agencies as well as the Canada–US Fulbright Foundation, which supported the author to study maritime security in the North American context at George Mason University in 2005, a key period in the formulation of the current regulations in both countries. This chapter updates earlier research to October 2012 and was self-funded. Thank you to Janet Lord for being the second set of eyes on the editing of this chapter.

REFERENCES

Brooks, M.R. (2004), 'The governance structure of ports', *Review of Network Economics: Special Issue on the Industrial Organization of Shipping and Ports*, **3** (2), 169–84.

Brooks, M.R. (2007), 'Port devolution and governance in Canada', in M.R. Brooks and K. Cullinane (eds), *Devolution, Port Performance and Port Governance*, *Research in Transport Economics*, Vol. 17, Oxford: Elsevier, pp. 237–58.

Brooks, M.R. (2008), *North American Freight Transportation: The Road to Security and Prosperity*, Cheltenham, UK and Northampton, MA, USA: Edward Elgar.

Brooks, M.R. and K.J. Button (2006), 'Market structures and shipping security', *Maritime Economics and Logistics*, **8** (1), 100–20.

Brooks, M.R. and K.J. Button (2007), 'Maritime container security: a cargo interest perspective', in K. Bichou, M. Bell and A. Evans (eds), *Port, Maritime and Supply Chain Security: Frameworks, Models and Applications*, London: Informa Publications, pp. 221–36.

CBSA (Canada Border Services Agency) (2008), *Pre-arrival Targeting Evaluation Study*, Ottawa: CBSA, available at http://cbsa-asfc.gc.ca/agency-agence/reports-rapports/ae-ve/2008/target-ciblage-eng.html (accessed 26 April 2013).

CBSA (Canada Border Services Agency) (2012), 'Canada and the U.S. announce prosperity-enhancing Beyond the Border pilot project', available at http://www.cbsa-asfc.gc.ca/media/release-communique/2012/2012-10-21-eng.html (accessed 21 October 2012).

Canada Transportation Act Review Panel (2001), *Vision and Balance*, Ottawa: Minister of Public Works and Government Services Canada.

Department of Foreign Affairs and International Trade (2004), *Smart Border Action Plan Status Report*, Ottawa: Department of Foreign Affairs and International Trade, 17 December.

Flynn, S. (2003), 'The false conundrum: continental integration versus homeland security', in P. Andreas and T.J. Biersteker (eds), *The Rebordering of North America: Integration and Exclusion in a New Security Context*, New York and London: Routledge, pp. 110–27.

Government of Canada (2012), *Trade Data Online*, available at http://www.ic.gc.ca/eic/site/tdo-dcd.nsf/eng/home (accessed 1 October 2012).

Gratwick, J. and W. Elliott (1992), 'Canadian ports: evolving policy and practice', in D. VanderZwaag (ed.), *Canadian Ocean Law and Policy*, Toronto: Butterworths, pp. 237–60.

Hossain, K., H.M. Kindred and M.R. Brooks (2009), 'The challenge of maritime security against terrorism: a dialogue between the European Union and Canada', in T. Koivurova, A. Chircop, E. Frnckx, E.J. Molenaar and D.L.Van der Zwaag (eds), *Understanding and Strengthening European Union–Canada Relations in the Law of the Sea and Ocean Governance*, Rovaniemi, Lapland: University of Lapland Printing Centre, pp. 351–86.

House of Commons (1985), *6th Report Standing Committee on Transport*, December, London.

McDorman, T.L. (1984), 'Shipping policy as a British export product: the Canadian case', *Maritime Policy and Management*, **11** (1), 1–13.

National Transportation Act Review Commission (1993), *Competition in Transportation: Policy and Legislation in Review*, Ottawa: Minister of Supply and Services Canada.

Office of the Auditor General of Canada (2007), *Report of the Auditor General of Canada to the House of Commons, Chapter 5: Keeping the Border Open and Secure – Canada Border Services Agency*, October, available at http://www.oag-bvg.gc.ca/internet/English/parl_oag_200710_05_e_23829.html (accessed 25 April 2013).

Presidia Security Consulting (2011), *A Study of the Vulnerability of Marine Port Operations to Organized Crime*, Ottawa: Public Safety Canada.

Public Safety Canada (2012), *Building Resilience Against Terrorism: Canada's Counter-terrorism Strategy*, available at http://www.publicsafety.gc.ca/prg/ns/_fl/2012-cts-eng.pdf (accessed 26 April 2013).

Standing Senate Committee on National Security and Defence (2007), *Canadian Security Guide Book. An Update of Security Problems in Search of Solutions. SEAPORTS.* Ottawa: Standing Senate on National Security and Defence, 39th Parliament, 1st Session, March, available at http://www.parl.gc.ca/Content/SEN/Committee/391/defe/rep/Seaports-e.pdf (accessed 26 April 2013).

Statistics Canada (2010), *Shipping in Canada* (54-205-X), available at http://www.statcan.gc.ca/pub/54-205-x/54-205-x2008000-eng.pdf (accessed October 2013).

The White House Office of the Press Secretary (2011), *Beyond the Border: A Shared Vision for Perimeter Security and Economic Competitiveness: A Declaration by* the President of the United States of America and the Prime Minister of Canada,* 4 February, Washington, DC.

Transport Canada (1985), *Freedom to Move: A Framework for Transportation Reform*, Ottawa, July.

Transport Canada (2010), *Audit of the Marine Security Contribution Program*, January, available at http://www.tc.gc.ca/eng/corporate-services/aas-audit-780. htm (accessed 25 October 2012).

Transport Canada (2012a), *Transportation in Canada 2011 Annual Report*, Ottawa: Transport Canada.

Transport Canada (2012b), *Marine Security*, available at http://www.tc.gc.ca/eng/ marinesecurity/menu.htm (accessed 2 October 2012).

Waters, W.G. (2006), 'Canada's statement on national transport policy', *Proceedings Canadian Transportation Research Forum*, **41**, 793–807.

WCO (World Customs Organization) (2005), *Framework of Standards to Facilitate and Secure Global Trade*, June, available at http://www.wcoomd.org/ie/En/ en.html (accessed 10 August 2006).

10. Maritime and cargo security failures: European cases

Mark Rowbotham

10.1 INTRODUCTION

The events of 9/11 may seem distant in 2013, but they precipitated a global chain of legislation that has necessitated a significant review of maritime security, from a pure marine angle with relation to vessel operations and to port operations, and this has required a complete review on the part of shipping lines and ports concerning the security of the marine sector in general. However, marine cargo security is still very much an issue, and to date the International Maritime Organization (IMO) has not implemented specific rules or codes concerning ways to tighten up security concerning the maritime movement of cargoes. To this extent, cargo security is still the responsibility of both the shipper and the shipping line, and there are no specific global standards concerning the maintenance of a global marine cargo security regime. Even the issue of container scanning has been seen as a controversial issue, and despite statements by P&I (Protection & Indemnity) Clubs concerning the need for vigilance concerning container weights and specific information concerning the carriage of dangerous goods by container, no firm action has been taken by international maritime authorities to address these issues. In the USA, some 80 per cent of incoming sea containers are scanned, and techniques are being sought to increase this to 100 per cent. However, elsewhere in the world, import controls, especially the ENS/EXS electronic system used by the European Union (EU) customs computer for all incoming containers, rely on container manifests for the accurate information needed to clear the container through customs on arrival at the EU seaport in question.

This chapter highlights a number of recent issues concerning the issue of cargo security, including the isolation of a radioactive container at the port of Genoa in 2010–11 containing an unknown cargo, and the mass pilferage of the contents of several containers washed ashore on the South Devon coast in January 2007 as a result of the foundering of the container vessel *MSC Napoli* in the western part of the English Channel en route to the Mediterranean from northern EU ports. The other case quoted and examined is that of the inferno aboard the container vessel *Hyundai Fortune* while transiting the Gulf of Aden in March 2006. In all these cases, there was a clear lapse in security in terms of the reporting of information concerning the cargoes, and, in the case of the *MSC Napoli*, a clear failure to ensure that pilferage of the contents of several containers would and could not take place.

On February 2011, the UK Freight Journal *International Freighting Weekly* (*IFW*) published a report concerning the case of a container located at an isolated part of the Port of Genoa, which was found to be highly radioactive and which could not be moved. It reported that 'dirty bomb' fears were increasing at the Italian port of Genoa as the authorities attempted to establish the contents of a highly radioactive container, and work out how to deal with it.

The container had been at the port's Voltri Terminal since July 2010, but the situation, described by container scanning expert Joe Alioto as 'an ecological nightmare', was reported to be reaching crisis point with fears that the box could be a terrorist weapon and that opening it could trigger an explosive device. At the time of reporting, the authorities were deciding whether to open the container by remote-controlled robot or remove it from the port by barge. By July 2011, it appeared that this situation had still not been fully resolved, although some time later, the offending container was finally removed and neutralized.

The container is believed to have originated from the company Sun Metal Casting in Ajman in the United Arab Emirates (UAE), and was supposed to be carrying 18 tonnes of copper destined for a customer located to the north of Genoa. It was exported through the Red Sea port of Jeddah and was trans-shipped via the Italian port of Gioia Tauro to Genoa, where it sat on the dockside for several days before a technical check found it to be highly radioactive. As a result of this check, it was isolated by other containers filled with stones and water. It was understood that further tests concluded that the box contained a small but powerful source of radiation, in the form of Cobalt-60, although it could not be concluded what the source or origin of such radioactive material was. In any case, nobody was prepared to open the container owing to the risk of major contamination.

The UK online journal *IFW*, now part of the publication *Lloyd's Loading List*, reported that Joe Alioto, Vice President of Sales at VeriTainer, which manufactures container scanning systems, said that it was likely that the container had been tampered with between Adjman and Jeddah, although this could not be confirmed. 'This is a security and ecological disaster,' he is reported to have said. 'The container is very nearly glowing with

Cobalt-60; its contents are unknown and there is no game plan for its disposal. I wouldn't go near it.'

The situation has again highlighted the ongoing debate over container scanning. The box could just as easily have been trans-shipped to New York or any other major city port, said Alioto. 'In fact, 97% of containers arriving in the US are unscanned, then they remain on our docks, exposing 67 million Americans to the threat of a nuclear-radiation event until they are finally scanned when they leave the port. Many ports are surrounded by heavily populated areas, and detonating a nuclear or dirty bomb at a container terminal would be devastating.' This statement flies in the face of the claim that 80 per cent of imported containers are scanned at US ports on arrival.

It was announced in early August 2011 that the radiation scare at the port of Genoa had finally ended after more than a year, by using a robot to open the suspect container and reach the Cobalt-60 material inside. The Mediterranean Shipping Company (MSC) container, which originated in Ajman in the UAE, arrived at the Italian port in July 2010. It was supposed to be carrying a consignment of copper and it was not until it had been on the quayside at Genoa's Voltri Terminal for several days that checks detected the presence of Cobalt-60. This prompted fears that it could be a terrorist weapon and opening it could trigger a 'dirty bomb'. For the following month, the box remained barricaded by other containers filled with stones and water while the authorities considered what to do next. The opening of the box involved more than 100 people, including fire and nuclear response teams. The Cobalt-60 was placed in a container made of lead for transport to a disposal site. An investigation has been carried out into why the Cobalt-60 capsule was in the sea container in the first place. Augusto Russo, of the Genoese fire team specializing in nuclear, chemical and biological emergencies, said that if anyone had handled it without precautions, they would probably now be dead.

Joe Alioto said that the episode highlighted dangers inherent in the supply chain. As reported on several marine freight websites, he stated that the problem would have been avoided altogether if a system was in place to routinely scan containers for radiation at country of origin, using crane-mounted scanning. He said, 'There is virtually no infrastructure whatsoever in place to do anything about it. This is something really bad waiting to happen,' he added. His comments perhaps reinforce the chronic situation that has arisen with regard to overall global maritime vigilance concerning the carriage of cargoes by sea.

Alioto's claim and his overall comments highlight the major concerns shared by many on the (lack of) controls over cargoes arriving at many of the world's major ports, and, for that matter, the similar lack of controls exercised over containers exported from these ports. Indeed, there are distinct concerns that present security regimes implemented by the IMO in the form of the International Ship and Port Security (ISPS) code that have been designed to increase security levels at seaports have done nothing to deal with cargo security itself, and only cover security regimes on both vessels and in the ports in general.

10.2   THE ISPS CODE

The ISPS code as implemented by the IMO applies to ships on international voyages (including passenger ships, cargo ships of 500 gross tonnes (gt) and upwards and mobile offshore drilling units) and the port facilities serving such ships.

Contracting governments are the national governments of countries that have a coastline as defined by the United Nations Convention of the Law of the Sea (UNCLOS) and that therefore have a vested interest in maritime security, especially from a national point of view. They are also the governments that signed and ratified the agreement that set out and initiated the ISPS code, and therefore bind themselves to ensuring that all the provisions of the ISPS code are implemented.

However, the code does not specify particular measures that each port and ship must take to ensure the safety of the facility against terrorism because of the many different types and sizes of these facilities. Instead, it outlines 'a standardised, consistent framework for evaluating risk, enabling governments to offset changes in threat with changes in vulnerability for ships and port facilities'. Specific actions that are taken to minimize or neutralize security threats are therefore the responsibility and decision of the master of the vessel or his security officer, or the port security officer in the case of a port being threatened. In the case of Somali piracy, the ISPS code allows the shipping company to make its own decisions as to how any of its vessels may take appropriate action to avoid being attacked by pirates, as well as allowing the master to make such provisions as he deems necessary to ensure that his vessel is adequately defended against piracy actions.

There are three categories of Security Levels. These are:

- Level 1 – Normal
- Level 2 – Medium (Heightened)
- Level 3 – High (Exceptional).

Under normal circumstances, Security Level 1 is the main level to be expected, but in the case of security alerts, either Level 2 or Level 3 will be applied. There are therefore different requirements imposed by the ISPS code to account for these different levels of risk.

In many ways, the ISPS code has achieved a means of ensuring that ships and ports undertake security measures that in reality they should have done some years prior to the 9/11 terrorist attacks on New York. Whereas aviation has long had a stringent set of security measures, the maritime sector has been remarkably slow in coming to terms with security threats, and indeed it has been possible for many years for spectators to stand on quaysides 'watching the boats come in'. Now, with the emphasis more on vessel and port security, there are fewer opportunities for the average person to gain access to ports or quaysides, especially where their motives may not be fully ascertained. Not that most people will be considered to be a threat, but in cases where amateur photographers have been accustomed to gaining automatic access to various points in or close to a port, this is becoming less likely. In a way, it is a shame as there are many people who have an interest in ships without being involved in the maritime profession, and who wish to photograph vessels close up. This pastime is becoming increasingly limited. However, on the other side of the coin, there is a need for increased levels of maritime security, bearing in mind the present state of international uncertainty and insecurity at large. Sooner or later, it would have been necessary for all ports and vessels to review their potential risks and respective levels of security. With the implementation of the ISPS code, this review of security has now become necessary, and indeed is now a major part of both port and vessel operations. It has also required a much greater level of overall organization within the daily activities of any port and vessels, and has in reality imposed a much greater level of discipline on both port and vessel operators.

10.3   THE ENTRY SUMMARY DECLARATION SYSTEM

At the beginning of 2011, the EU implemented a regime to ensure that cargoes shipped by sea from around the world into EU ports would have their information submitted to the EU Customs Computer in advance of the container being loaded aboard ship, by means of the Entry Summary Declaration (ENS), in a similar fashion to the Customs-Trade Partnership Against Terrorism (C-TPAT) initiative implemented by the US authorities. This initiative is called the Import Control System (ICS), and the system works in such a way that information concerning all cargoes being shipped to the EU must be entered into the EU Customs Computer at least 24 hours before the computer is despatched to the port of loading and loaded aboard vessel.

In each non-EU load port, the transmission must be carried out no later than 24 hours prior to the start of loading to the vessel bound for an EU port. To comply with this regulation, the shipping line requires complete and correct shipping instructions. The documentation closing times follow the same timelines as other 'advance manifest' 24-hour rule locations such as the USA, Canada or Mexico. They are stipulated in the marine carrier's booking confirmation.

Transmission of ENS is obligatory for all cargo discharged in an EU port (including trans-shipment cargo) as well as Foreign Cargo Remaining on Board (FROB), that is, cargo that is discharged in a port outside the EU after the vessel has called at an EU port.

In many cases, the advance notification that is issued at the port of loading needs to be given by the ship operator, carrier or his representative, such as the ship's agent. At present, there is no distinction within the regulations as to whether, in the case of a chartered vessel, the charterer or the owner is considered to be the operator/carrier for the purposes of submission of the required declarations. However, it is expected that the charterer will be defined as the operator/carrier under a time charter, and the owner will be the operator/carrier under a voyage charter party. In containerized shipping, a freight forwarder, or Non-Vessel Operating Common Carrier (NVOCC), will normally issue the advance notice, although this can also be carried out by the shipping agency at the port of loading. However, in the case of submission by a freight forwarder or NVOCC, this submission can only be carried out with the ship operator's full knowledge and consent. In the case of combined transport operations where trucks are driven on to a Ro-Ro ferry, it is the duty of the haulage company, its representative or the truck driver to submit the advance notification prior to arrival at the port of loading. With regard to vessel-sharing arrangements such as slot carrier agreements in the container trade, the declaration is to be issued by the carrier issuing the Bill of Lading rather than the ship operator.

If the information is submitted by a nominated third party, such as an agent or freight forwarder, the ship operator will still be held responsible if notice is not delivered in advance or on time, and this delay may result in a penalty being imposed. However, the third party will still be liable for the accuracy of the information provided. Regardless of who provides the advance cargo declaration, the responsible party must also provide their Economic Operator Registration and Identification Number (EORI), which is essentially the trader's VAT number plus an additional set of digits, in the case of the UK '000'. For example, if a UK-based trader's VAT number is 123 456 789, their EORI will be 123 456 789 000. The use of an EORI has been mandatory within the EU since 1 July 2009. Once advance notice of the cargo movement has been submitted, a confirmation will be issued containing a unique 18-digit number called a Movement Reference Number (MRN), used hitherto for Community transit movements. The entire system is electronic, and therefore the person giving notice to customs requires a computer system that can interface with the national customs system. However, at the present time there is no system that is common throughout the EU capable of handling the new declarations, and for the present each Member State retains its own national system.

The information submitted in the various declarations is used by customs to conduct a risk assessment of the cargo from a viewpoint of security and safety. As a result of this assessment, the cargo will then be classed as either risk type A, B or C, which in turn determines how the customs authority will respond. For example, if the customs office identifies a serious safety and security risk in relation to cargo to be loaded onto a deep sea container ship and classifies it as risk type A, it will issue a 'Do Not Load' (DNL) or 'Customs Hold' message preventing the carrier from shipping the cargo. 'Do Not Load' is the message returned by the EU customs office of first entry in receipt of the ENS in the place of an MRN. It means that analysis has been carried out on the declaration and that an unacceptable risk exists concerning the goods covered by the ENS declaration. This risk level may be further compounded by a lack of information entered on the cargo manifest with relation to details of the cargo. In the same way that the USA and Canada outlawed the terms FAK (Freight of All Kinds) and 'Said to Contain . . .', the ENS system allows for a similar level of controls applied to scrutiny of the Entry Declaration, hence the risk assessment carried out by the relevant EU customs authority on each declaration.

The shipper is therefore required to submit an accurate and detailed set of shipping instructions to the carrier or their agent in order to facilitate an ENS. The required data elements for the ENS are:

- Full name and address of shipper and consignee.
- Full name and address of notify party where goods are carried under a negotiable 'to order' Bill of Lading (B/L).
- Container number.
- Acceptable goods description (general terms, for example, 'consolidated cargo', 'general cargo', 'Freight of All Kinds', 'Said to Contain', cannot be accepted).
- Minimally, the first four digits of the Harmonized System (HS) Commodity Code, although the six-digit HS Code is recommended.

- Marks and numbers of packages.
- Cargo gross weight (in kilograms).
- Seal number.
- UN Dangerous Goods Code and International Movement of Dangerous Goods (IMDG by sea) Classification Code, where applicable.
- Method of payment for transport charges in case of 'Freight Prepaid' (CFR, CIF, CPT, CIP), for example, payment in cash, payment by cheque, electronic credit transfer and so on.

The ENS will be sent to the customs office of the first port of entry (first port of call) in the EU, and this customs office will carry out a security risk assessment.

In the event that a risk is identified, subsequent ports of arrival and ports of loading will be informed:

- Risk Type A = Do Not Load.
- Risk Type B = Interception of a suspicious shipment at the first port of entry.
- Risk Type C = Interception of a suspicious shipment at the port of discharge.

In addition to submitting an ENS, an operator must also advise the national customs authority of a vessel's arrival by the submission of an Arrival Notification (AN) by a means acceptable to the customs office in that particular Member State. The AN may comprise a list of MRNs relating to the vessel, or what is termed an 'Entry Key', which consists of information about the vessel and the cargo (for example, mode of transport, the vessel's IMO number, expected date of arrival).

There are certain drawbacks with the new ENS system. Firstly, each national customs authority in the EU still retains its own national control system, which, as explained earlier, may not be compatible with those of other national customs authorities within the EU. This implies that information submitted in the form of an ENS to one customs authority cannot necessarily be transmitted to other customs authorities, especially in the case of the diversion of a vessel from one EU port to another port in another EU Member State, owing to a perceived lack of compatibility in systems used by each authority.

Secondly, the information provided for each cargo as contained within the ENS is only transmitted to the customs authority and not to any other national organization. This means that any information deemed as being sensitive or prejudicial to national security may not necessarily be passed to other security authorities, such as other government departments, for example, Defence or Interior. In this sense, the effectiveness of such information may be reduced, as it cannot be disseminated amongst the parties that ultimately may still have an interest in it, and thus leading to the risk of prejudicing national security interests.

In itself, this is not a problem insofar as the information provided is vetted by the EU Customs Computer and will be authorized for entry into the EU on a prima facie basis, that is, its face value. However, there is an increasing incidence of scams and fraudulent activities concerning the issue of fraudulent and false Bills of Lading concerning non-existent cargoes and either fictitious containers or containers that are in reality nowhere near their purported route and that do not contain the supposed cargo. This trend casts grave doubt on the effectiveness of such a regime, especially where no official verification is made of the actual cargo inside the container by means of physical examination, or even a detailed scrutiny of the Load List referring to the cargo stuffed inside the container, assuming that such a Load List for the container actually exists in the first place. It is unfortunate that the days of cargo being physically scrutinized as it is stuffed into the container no longer exist. It has been common practice for the carrier or their agent to rely on the shipper to provide information concerning the containerized cargo for the purposes of the creation of the container manifest, hence the common usage of the term 'Said to Contain . . .', which under the regimes of both ENS and C-TPAT is no longer allowed. However, although this term is no longer allowed and absolute details of the cargo must be submitted to the customs computers, there is still no attempt by port or other national authorities to verify the exact details and accuracy of the cargoes being shipped by container, hence the alarming case of the radioactive container sitting isolated at the Port of Genoa. This may appear to be an isolated case, but it demonstrates and illustrates the alarming ease by which cargoes may be shipped across the oceans without adequate scrutiny and enter a country without a significant degree of vetting. In short, the information submitted through the ENS system may not necessarily equate with the actual cargo occupying the container.

10.4 MULTIMODALISM AND SHIPPER AWARENESS

The concept and principle of multimodalism has in many ways contributed to this challenge. The principle of multimodalism enables a container to be loaded at the premises of the shipper, transported to the port of loading and loaded aboard vessel, shipped across the ocean to the port of destination, unloaded from the vessel and transported directly to the importer with hardly any controls along the way. The resulting movement is a direct door-to-door shipment, and the International Terms of Delivery (INCOTERMs) have been amended over the years to allow for and facilitate such movements. International controls, including customs checks, have been kept to a minimum, and in reality the trader, be it the exporter or importer, has been given the task of self-regulation when it comes to monitoring and controlling such movements, with reliance for accurate export and import declarations placed on the shipper and the recipient by the customs authorities. At one time, there was a significant presence of customs officers at all seaports, and their job was to monitor and control the movement of all import and export cargoes through the ports. Today, this presence has been removed, to the extent that in the UK, with the merger of HM Customs & Excise with HM Inland Revenue a few years ago to form HM Revenue & Customs, the border element of the customs function was removed from HM Revenue & Customs and transferred to the Home Office as part of the new UK Border Agency. However, the overall remit of the UK Border Agency, by nature of its masters, is to deal with the movement of people and less with the movement of cargo. Indeed, there is rarely a presence by UK Border Agency personnel at ports with regard to the inward and outward movement of cargoes, and any checks on port activities are generally conducted on an ad hoc basis based on random checks or intelligence reports. This implies that there are no other checks made on cargo movements while such cargo is in transit. Hence, the relative ease by which a radioactive container could enter a European seaport.

It is appreciated that in an era of increasing use of information technology, there is increasing reliance on the international trader to regulate and control affairs. Indeed, the recent initiatives of the Authorized Economic Operator (AEO) and its equivalents elsewhere in the world have done much to implement international supply chain controls and audit trails, customs authorities in all the major countries subscribing to such initiatives place increasing levels of reliance on traders to ensure that they can comply with these customs initiatives. The purpose of the AEO initiative is to ensure that only traders with a history of customs compliance and adherence to international supply chain audit trails through other initiatives such as ISO 28000/28001 can be authorized to use the AEO facility, thus enabling these traders to use fast-track abbreviated customs clearance regimes for import and export control procedures.

However, neither AEO nor ISO 28000/28001 can substitute the need for physical checks and examinations of cargoes in transit. It has been admitted that 100 per cent scanning of containers in many ports, including those in the USA and Rotterdam, is well-nigh impossible, as it could lead to severe congestion of the port systems that are designed for the rapid transit of containerized cargoes through the ports for the purposes of loading aboard vessel or unloading from the vessel and transfer inland to the importer. It is also recognized that in the process of scanning a container by X-ray machine, should any prohibited cargoes be discovered, that container will have to be isolated and fully examined to determine the nature of such cargoes. This procedure takes time, and risks delaying other container movements, although in general containers found to contain prohibited cargoes will be moved aside and isolated for further scrutiny and examination.

However, such scanning techniques are still based on random checks and do not cover all containers transported aboard vessels. As the size of container vessels increases, so too does the capacity of containers transported aboard such vessels. Presently, the maximum capacity of the largest container vessels on the high seas is 14,000 Twenty-foot Equivalent Units (TEUs), but the Danish shipping company Maersk Line placed an order in 2011 for several 18,000-TEU container vessels, and other shipping lines are set to follow. As the number of containers aboard vessel increases, so too does the risk of uncontrolled cargo being stuffed into such containers, also increasing the risk of disaster or at very least the risk of a major breach of security and even safety. It is already accepted that many ship masters do not know the details of more than 30 per cent of their cargoes, a figure quoted to the author by HM Coastguards at CNIS Dover in 2005, and the increasing size of container ships will no doubt decrease this figure yet further. It is already evident that the cargo manifest for most major container ships can only be stored as a zip file, given the sheer volume of information for all the containers aboard each vessel contained in the vessel's cargo manifest. Given that the ship master may know little information concerning the contents of all the containers onboard vessel, then there is little guarantee that information concerning these containers is known by any other party involved in the shipment of these cargoes. Although there are detailed stowage plans prepared for the loading of every container vessel, these plans refer to the containers themselves and their respective weights rather than their contents, unless it is already known that some of these containers are filled with dangerous or hazardous cargoes that are known to the shipping agents and have already been declared as such. In such cases, both ports and shipping lines make specific provisions for the shipment of dangerous or hazardous (HAZMAT) cargoes, and containers of this nature are generally isolated away from other cargoes at the port or from other hazardous cargoes once loaded aboard vessel as a matter of course. However, such practices generally apply to Full Container Loads (FCLs) where the cargoes are deemed to be of a dangerous or hazardous nature and are supported by the appropriate documentation, including Dangerous Goods (DG) Notes. In the case of Less-than Container Loads (LCLs), which are generally of a consolidated or groupage nature, where several cargoes belonging to a variety of traders are stuffed into a single container, there is more risk that the full details of all, the cargoes inside the container, may not be known or properly declared. The C-TPAT and ENS initiatives have outlawed the use of the term 'Freight of All Kinds (FAK)', which has been commonly used as information on a container manifest, but this does not necessarily mean that, even considering the C-TPAT or ENS initiatives, the trader will ensure that the most accurate information concerning a consolidated or groupage cargo will be submitted in advance to the US, Canadian or EU Customs Computers. It is naturally the disposition or intention of the trader to ensure that just enough advance information is submitted to the customs computer to enable the container to be cleared for loading aboard vessel without the possibility of raising the perceived risk as far as the submitted information is concerned. In this respect, there may still be an element of economy with the truth on the part of the trader concerning the details of the cargo being stuffed into the container in order to ensure that the customs computer will allow the container to be loaded aboard vessel. Indeed, it is more than likely that the more unscrupulous traders will ensure that they do not include information concerning the cargo that is likely to arouse suspicion and trigger a refusal by the computer to authorize loading of the container aboard vessel. It is this flaw that ultimately will lead to a breach in cargo security, and could even jeopardize national or maritime security.

Cargo security has without any doubt become a major issue in the shipping world, especially as failures to ensure the security of containerized cargoes have led in the past few years to some particularly high-profile disasters, which have resulted in major enquiries into the safety of the transportation of containers by sea. The disasters concerned involve the container vessels *Hyundai Fortune*, *MSC Napoli*, *Annabella*, *Husky Racer* and several others, and have led to profound questions being asked in many places as to the accountability of shippers, shipping lines and container terminals in the carriage of containerized cargoes aboard ship. The case of the container vessel *Hyundai Fortune* in particular reinforces the need to establish a regime requiring the master of a commercial vessel to be fully aware of all of his cargoes, especially in the case of container vessels, and to be able to report this information in advance of entering national territorial waters.

10.5   EXAMPLES OF CARGO SECURITY FAILURES

The *Hyundai Fortune* (64,054 gt) was a container ship with a container capacity of 5551 TEU, registered to the shipping line Hyundai Merchant Marine. She had a speed of 25 knots, and was mainly used on the Far East to European container routes, and had been built in September 1996 by Hyundai Heavy Industries at Ulsan, South Korea, and sailed under the Panamanian flag. On 21 March 2006, the vessel was on its way from ports in China and Singapore through the Gulf of Aden, about 60 miles south of the coast of Yemen, and was sailing west towards the Red Sea and the Suez Canal on the way to ports in Europe. Just after mid-day, an explosion of unknown origin ripped through the lower cargo area and hull of the vessel aft of the accommodation area, sending between 60 and 90 containers falling into the ocean. The explosion caused massive clouds of smoke and a tremendous blaze, which spread through the stern of the vessel, including the accommodation area in the vessel's superstructure and the exhaust outlets. As a result of the fire, secondary explosions occurred in seven containers above deck, which, it was discovered later, were full of fireworks. This fact was not known to the vessel's master at the time of the disaster, but was only discovered later as a result of extensive investigations into the vessel's cargo. It was also ascertained that as many as one third of the vessel's complement of containers were damaged by the inferno. Every container aft of the accommodation area was either incinerated or lost at sea. It has been conjectured that the latter, larger explosions that crippled the vessel were caused by the detonation of the fireworks as a result of the heat resulting from the initial blaze. In this case, the requirements set out in the IMDG Code had clearly not been obeyed insofar as the containers, which were filled with pyrotechnics (classed under Category 1 (Explosives) of the IMDG code), were not stowed as far away from the accommodation quarters as possible (a major precondition of the loading of such classes of dangerous goods), and this breach of essential regulations could be used to bring severe liability to bear on the shipping line or its agents.

Photographs of the blazing ship showed that a large chunk of the hull had been blown out below deck and above the waterline on the port side. After efforts to contain the fire failed, all 27 crew members abandoned ship and were rescued by the Dutch destroyer *HNLMS De Zeven Provinciën*. The *De Zeven Provinciën* was performing maritime security operations in the area as part of the naval exercise 'Operation Enduring Freedom'. One sailor from the stricken container ship was evacuated to the French aircraft carrier *Charles de Gaulle* with non-life-threatening injuries. On 23 March 2006, firefighting tugs began to arrive on the scene. With its engine room burned and completely flooded, the listing *Hyundai Fortune* continued to burn for several days.

The law of General Average was declared and it appears at least one third of the containers were damaged by the blaze. Every container aft of the superstructure was either incinerated or lost at sea. Most of the containers forward of the superstructure were left intact, although after the ship lost power, any cargo in the refrigerated containers had likely spoiled. For the benefit of those readers who do not understand marine insurance, General Average is the principle whereby the owners of cargoes onboard a stricken vessel will be asked to contribute towards any cargo lost as a result of the ship being damaged, damage to the cargo itself or the cargo being jettisoned overboard so as to prevent the risk of damage or danger to the vessel.

The combined cost of the ship and lost cargo was estimated at over US$300 million. The hull was eventually towed to Salalah, Oman, and the sound and undamaged containers were offloaded for transport by other vessels to Europe. The empty hull then lay off the UAE coast awaiting its fate, thought at the time to be the ship breakers in Pakistan or India. However, she was eventually rebuilt, and presently operates with MSC as the *MSC Fortunate*, perhaps an apt name for the vessel. It would appear that vessels, like cats, have nine lives. Hyundai Merchant Marine and other slot charter companies suffered massive losses as a result of the incident.

The main element of the issue concerns the knowledge of the cargo by the master of the vessel. It would appear that the containers holding the fireworks were all in close proximity to each other. Under the rules of stowage aboard vessel, any containers known to contain hazardous or dangerous cargoes must not be stowed together in a place close to the management of the ship or its accommodation area. They must be stowed well apart from each other, away from the areas of accommodation, and their presence must be known and understood by the vessel's master, as in accordance with the SOLAS regulations it is the master who must ensure that all steps are taken to reduce the risk of spillage or destruction or the risk of threat to other cargoes or even the vessel itself, while the cargo is in transit. In the case of the need to report the vessel's impending arrival at a port or even the vessel's presence in limited waterways such as the Strait of Dover or the Storebaelt (Denmark), the risk of disaster is increased where the master of the vessel is not aware of certain cargoes aboard vessel, especially those of a hazardous or dangerous nature. If such a disaster had occurred in areas of water more limited than the Gulf of Aden, such as the Strait of Dover, the results would have been even more catastrophic, especially as there would have been no specific report issued to the UK or French maritime authorities concerning the hazardous nature of the cargoes aboard vessel. Previous incidents in the Strait of Dover have reflected similar circumstances, where a collision occurred between two vessels, and the resulting fire aboard one of the vessels resulted in the release of toxic vapours. One of the contributory factors of this fire was that certain containers of hazardous chemicals had been stowed in the forward area of one of the vessels, and these containers were damaged in the collision. The possibility of absence of knowledge of these cargoes by the master of one of the vessels may have contributed to a lack of information reported to HM Coastguards at Dover, coupled with a failure by one of the vessels to adhere to its correct separation lane.

It was later reported that the cause of the fire may not have been the containerized deck cargo of pyrotechnics, but a more likely cause could be attributed to an explosion elsewhere in the vessel, possibly the engine room. It was established that the formulae for the production of fireworks are very stable, and only a series of packing, handling or other mistakes could possibly lead to their ignition onboard a vessel. A more plausible explanation is that the explosion occurred in or close to the engine room, causing a huge fire that subsequently spread to the cargo above deck and ignited it. The fireworks are classified by the IMDG Code as Class 1, which refer to explosives of any kind, and must pass a thermal stability test as part of the classification process.

A major cause for concern focuses around why containers full of pyrotechnics were allowed to be stowed directly behind the vessel's accommodation quarters. One of the IMO's regulations (http://www.imo.org) states that no cargo, which is deemed as being hazardous or dangerous under the IMDG Code, must be stowed anywhere near the accommodation quarters, and furthermore, must be stowed on open deck away from any other dangerous or hazardous goods. It is therefore imperative that the authority responsible for the stowage of all cargoes aboard vessel must be absolutely sure as to the nature and type of cargoes being loaded aboard vessel, and must equally ensure that no unnecessary risk is presented to the vessel as a result of the loading procedures, thus directly implying that the loading authority must take all necessary steps to ensure that all hazardous or dangerous cargoes are stowed as far away from the vessel's accommodation quarters as possible, in order to avoid peril to the vessel or its crew in the event of leakage or other accident. The aft part of a ship, with its machinery and power plants, is the most likely place for fires to start, and thus it is the last place where hazardous or dangerous cargoes should be stowed.

As a result of the *Hyundai Fortune* inferno, Hyundai Marine placed a global moratorium on the transport of all shipments of pyrotechnics.

However, the London-based container insurers TT Club expressed concern that with shipping lines refusing potentially unstable cargoes, shippers would attempt to avoid the moratorium by deliberately mis-declaring the contents of containers, thus putting ships and crews in danger.

The vessel *MSC Napoli* (53,409 gt) was a UK-flagged container ship that was deliberately broken up by salvors after she ran into difficulties in the English Channel on 18 January 2007. The ship was built in 1991 and had a capacity of 4688 TEU of containers on a deadweight of 62,277 tonnes. She was built by Samsung Heavy Industries, Koje Shipyard, owned by Metvale Ltd, a British Virgin Islands Brass Plate single entity company, managed by Zodiac Maritime Agencies and was under charter to the MSC. In 2001, then named *CMA CGM Normandie*, she was en route from Port Klang in Malaysia to the Indonesian capital, Jakarta, when she ran aground on a reef at full speed in the Singapore Strait and remained stuck for several weeks. She was repaired by the Hyundai-Vinashin Shipyard in Khánh Hoa Province, Vietnam, which included the welding of more than 3000 tonnes of metal onto the hull.

While en route from Belgium to Portugal and South Africa, on 18 January 2007, during European Windstorm Kyrill, severe gale force winds and huge waves caused serious damage to the hull of *MSC Napoli*, with a crack developing in one side as well as a flooded engine room. The ship was at the time some 50 miles (80 km) off the coast of The Lizard, Cornwall. At around 10:30 GMT, the crew of the stricken vessel sent out a distress call. Not long afterwards, the captain of the vessel ordered the crew to abandon ship into one of the lifeboats, and they were adrift at sea for several hours before all 26 crew were rescued. They were picked up from their lifeboat by Sea King helicopters of the Royal Navy's Fleet Air Arm and taken to the Royal Naval Air Station (RNAS) Culdrose in Cornwall. During the difficult rescue, one helicopter broke two winch lines, making it even harder to rescue the seamen. Furthermore, the rough seas and gale force winds gave the men acute seasickness, and in some cases several suffered from dehydration due to overheating and constant vomiting.

On 19 January, the ship was taken under tow by the salvage tug *Abeille Bourbon*, which was later joined by the tug *Abeille Liberté*. It was decided to tow the vessel to the safe haven of Portland Harbour, Dorset, some 140 miles distant, the closer ports of Falmouth, Cornwall, and Plymouth, Devon, being rejected in addition to others in France, although the Falmouth harbour master Captain Mark Sansom said that he had confirmed that the *MSC Napoli* could have been accommodated in Falmouth Bay. The flotilla proceeded up the English Channel with the *MSC Napoli* increasing its list and with strong winds forecast refuge was taken in Lyme Bay. Lyme Bay is described as relatively sheltered from northwest, west and southwest winds, common at this time of year. The ship's deteriorating condition raised doubts as to its ability to withstand the rigours of the journey to Portland. The decision was taken by Robin Middleton, the Secretary of State's Representative in Maritime Salvage and Intervention (SOSREP) at the time, who was leading the MCA's salvage response team, to deliberately beach the ship in Lyme Bay. Mr Middleton said that the environmental sensitivities in the Lyme Bay area were fully assessed before the decision to beach the *MSC Napoli* was made. The chosen beaching location was at Branscombe, around one mile off the Devon coast, near the coastal town of Sidmouth. This area of the coastline where the *MSC Napoli* was beached is a part of Britain's first natural World Heritage Site, the so-called 'Jurassic Coast'. In the winter months, Lyme Bay hosts large numbers of wintering seabirds while the sea bed was the habitat for a variety of endangered species of marine life. Brian Greenslade, the leader of Devon County Council, confirmed that the council would be holding a public inquiry into the beaching. The move came amid questions about the decision to take the *Napoli* to an area of protected World Heritage Site coastline.

Of the 41,773 tonnes of cargo onboard, 1684 tonnes were of products classified as dangerous by the IMO under the IMDG Code. Some 103 containers fell into the sea. Oil spilt five miles to the northeast, which affected some seabirds. The ship *BSAD Argonaute* proceeded to the spill area with anti-pollution personnel and equipment. After containers from the wreck began to be washed up at Branscombe, around 200 people ventured onto the beach to scavenge the flotsam, despite warnings from the police that those failing to notify the Receiver of Wrecks of goods salvaged risked fines. Scavenged goods include several BMW R1200RT motorcycles, empty wine casks, nappies, perfume and car parts. After initially tolerating what was seen as a 'salvage' free-for-all, by 23 January the police had branded the activity of scavengers as 'despicable', closed the beach and announced that they would use powers not previously used for 100 years in order to force people to return goods they had salvaged without informing the authorities, pointing out that under the Merchant Shipping Act 1995 such actions constituted an offence equivalent to theft.

Over the course of the week, from 22 January, an attempt to remove the oil and other hazardous materials from the *Napoli* was made. However, the fuel oil became very viscous in cold weather, and needed to be warmed up before it could be pumped onto the tugs. On 23 January 2007, further details of the forthcoming salvage operation of both the ship and its cargo were released, The main point of concern being the threat of an oil spill, some seabirds had already been affected and recovered along the Jurassic coast.

Aside from the main salvage operation of the *MSC Napoli*, a local salvage company was appointed and tasked with clearing up the beach and removing the containers and flotsam. The earlier scavenging of the washed up containers and cargo created a difference of opinion among many people, some claiming it had made the clean-up of the beach harder as wreckers had forced open some sealed containers and sifted through the contents, leaving the unwanted items strewn across the beach. It was, however, claimed by others that by removing the flotsam they had in fact contributed to the clean-up of Branscombe beach. Items from the *Napoli* began to make landfall all along the south coast of England as far east as the Isle of Wight.

The issue of wreckage or collecting the flotsam from the beach caused a great deal of discussion and gained much media attention, as the local population and the authorities became increasingly concerned at the level of scavenging taking place from Branscombe beach and elsewhere along the coast. Eventually, the Maritime & Coastguard Agency (MCA) invoked powers under the Merchant Shipping Act 1995, and stated that people taking goods would now be asked to deliver the items from the beach to the acting Receiver of Wrecks. This effectively meant that no further items could legally be removed from the beach. Following this announcement, and for safety reasons while the beach clean-up operation progressed, the police (Devon and Cornwall Constabulary) together with the support of the National Trust (the owners of the beach) and the Coastguard set up road blocks to effectively close the beach. At the same time the salvage firm erected fences on the beach to prevent public access.

On 9 July 2007, the *MSC Napoli* was successfully refloated, but was immediately re-beached as a 3 m gash was found in the vessel's hull. The decision was made to break the ship up on Branscombe beach. This was attempted using explosives after a previous attempt to use the spring tides failed to break the ship apart. The *MSC Napoli* remained in one piece having survived two attempts to break the ship in two with the explosives. With the report that only her deck plates on the main deck were holding the vessel together around the bridge structure of the vessel, two tugs at either end of the ship tried to pull the ship apart. On 20 July 2007, the ship was finally split in two by means of a third explosion. In August 2007, the bow section of the ship's hull was taken to the Harland & Wolff shipyard in Belfast, Northern Ireland, for disposal and recycling. HM Coastguard placed a 500 m exclusion zone around the wreckage while it was anchored in Belfast Lough, while awaiting entry to the yard. The stern section was cut up in situ, with work starting in May 2008 and taking some five months to complete. The total cost of salvaging the vessel was estimated at some £50 million.

The Marine Accident Investigation Branch (MAIB) (http://www.maib. gov.uk) conducted an investigation into the *MSC Napoli* accident, and a report on the investigation was publicized at the end of April 2008. The MAIB said that a review of safety rules governing container ship design and a code of practice covering operations was urgently needed to prevent further losses. It concluded that the container shipping industry had been allowed to expand rapidly – from 12 million to 140 million containers a year since 1983 – without proper safety oversight. The report stated: 'The commercial advantages of containerisation ... such as speed and quick turnarounds appear to have become the focus of the industry at the expense of the safe operation of its vessels.' The MAIB found that a loophole in safety regulations meant that the buckling strength of the hull near the engine room had not been tested. It also found that the loading of the vessel had contributed to the stresses on the hull. The MAIB condemned the widespread practice in the industry of failing to properly load containers, either to save time or to avoid taxes. 'Container shipping is the only sector of the industry in which the weight of a cargo is not known' (MAIB report into the foundering of the container vessel *MSC Napoli*, April 2008).

The MAIB report went on to say that the container shipping industry is sacrificing safety and risking an environmental disaster to reduce costs and meet tight delivery schedules. Another 22 ships were found to have design flaws similar to those of the *MSC Napoli*, which was deliberately grounded a mile off Sidmouth after her hull cracked in heavy seas. The MAIB found that the ship was carrying many overloaded containers and had been travelling too fast for the conditions. It should be pointed out that a 20-foot container is designed to carry a load of approximately 10 tonnes, and a 40-foot container is designed to carry a load of approximately 25 tonnes of cargo. It would appear, therefore, that these weights had, in many cases, been exceeded in order to maximize the revenue potential per container. At the Maritime Rescue and Co-ordination Centre (MRCC) at Portland, where all of the containers from the ship were taken, some 600 containers were opened and weighed by the authorities. Around half were found to have a wrongly declared weight, 137 containers (23 per cent) revealed a weight discrepancy of 3 tonnes or more and a smaller but significant percentage showed an enormous discrepancy between declared weight and actual weight of 20 tonnes. It was further discovered that 7 per cent of the deckload of containers had not been stowed in the position shown on the cargo plan. It must be pointed out that this was the first time that a large cargo of containers had been opened by the authorities in the more than 50 years of carrying containers by sea, and that the findings were truly worrying for the transport of goods in containers by sea.

The mis-declared weights of the containers also caused substantial damage to four areas of the dock estate of the former naval dockyard at Portland, producing higher levels of damage to the dock infrastructure than was predicted. Portland was just 40 miles east of Branscombe and was the logical base from which to receive the 2318 salvaged containers. The prime objective of the four areas was to ensure that all undamaged cargo was quickly separated from the damaged cargo and forwarded promptly to their destinations. However, the 600 damaged containers were treated in a separate 'hospital' area, where they were opened, and an assessment made as to what was salvageable. Some 40 per cent of water damaged cargo was able to be recycled, with water damaged paper and cardboard sent to newspaper recyclers, and the distorted metal containers and their heavily damaged high value contents such as cars and motorcycles were partly cut up on site before being sent to metal salvage companies for recycling. The remaining 60 per cent of damaged cargo had been contaminated by oil and other substances and was not recyclable.

The problems of the loss of containers on feeder ships have been highlighted by the cases of *Husky Racer* and *Annabella*. The voyage from Rotterdam and Antwerp to Helsinki by the container feeder vessel *Annabella*, owned by Peter Dohle of Germany, in February 2007, resulted in the collapse of a stack of seven 30-foot containers stowed in *Annabella*'s number 3 hold. Fortunately, little damage was done and no one suffered injuries, but the outcome could have been catastrophic given that the top three containers in the stack were carrying Butylene Gas (IMDG Class 2.1, UN 1012). Furthermore, the *Annabella* had been built to an open-hatch design in order to facilitate the handling of loose or bulk cargo, and number 3 hold was an open hold. The MAIB report on the collapse of cargo containers on the shortsea container feeder vessel *Annabella* concluded: 'Evidence obtained during this and other MAIB investigations into container shipping accidents suggests that in reality, the safety of ships, crews and the environment is being compromised by the overriding desire to maintain established schedules or optimise port turn-round times.' It is therefore apparent that the weight limits stated earlier in the text concerning both 20-foot and 40-foot boxes are flagrantly abused. But then, in many cases, the shipper may have no idea whatsoever concerning the acceptable weight limits per container, as in many cases the exporter does not take responsibility for loading the box. The issue of container weighing is very much subject to much controversy as there is still the question as to whether such weighing of loaded containers should be mandatory or not.

This MAIB report on the *Annabella* was thorough, various specific failings were identified and recommendations were directed to those involved, including the ship manager and the charterer. However, the terminal operators and the software suppliers were also found wanting in certain areas. It had been found that the electronic loading procedure in Rotterdam had failed to recognize 30-foot containers, and was only pro-grammed to recognize 20-foot and 40-foot containers. It therefore over-rode the 30-foot container type, and classified these containers as 40-foot boxes, which they were not. The net result was that the 30-foot containers were loaded into the vessel's cells in the cargo hold, and several 40-foot boxes were loaded on top of them. The resulting weight of the 40-foot boxes could not be withstood by the 30-foot containers beneath them and, as a result, the whole stack of containers collapsed while the vessel was sailing through the Baltic Sea en route to Helsinki. The subsequent report attributed the accident to the negligence on the part of the loading authori-ties at Rotterdam in their failure to ensure that the loading procedures had taken into account the stowage of 30-foot containers, which were consid-ered a non-standard type as regards container shipping, which normally accounts for a mixture of 20-foot and 40-foot containers.

The loss of 18 containers overboard on the feeder *Husky Racer* owned by Dr Peters KG of Germany in the port of Bremerhaven on 2 October 2009 were attributable to mis-declared container weights. The stack col-lapse happened shortly after the ship had berthed at Bremerhaven while work began on unlashing the bottom two tiers in the container stacks on deck. This ship was of 950 TEU capacity and on charter to Maersk Line, and the stack collapse happened while in port, but could just as easily have happened at sea as heavy mis-declared weights stowed above empty boxes on a feeder ship cavorting and pitching, yawing and rolling in a winter North Sea gale is an instant recipe for disaster. The Maritime Research Institute of Netherlands (MARIN) recently reported in January 2010 on a four-year study on badly declared weights and this study has some inter-esting recommendations on the stowage of containers. The Lashing@Sea project (http://www.marin.nl) on poor stowage and lashing highlights the frequency of overweight or poorly weighed containers on container ships from the data supplied by eight shipowners, and the Dutch government has now made several recommendations to the IMO:

- The MARIN report recommends that in order to improve the ability of crews to reduce excessive container loads, the crew need more assistance in the stow plan to reduce excessive ship movement. Container ships must not be ordered off berths by terminal manage-ment before the crew have concluded their lashing of the container stacks, even when the terminal lashing gang are satisfied with their lashing work.

- Crews have reported countless incidents where the container has been loaded by the terminal in the right stack but in the wrong vertical position. The project verified these issues relating to the safety of container stacks when containers were not loaded in accordance with load plans. Mis-declared container weights with actual weight being three times the declared weight will seriously affect the dynamic stability of the vessel, especially when placed above a stack with empty containers on the bottom.
- The collapse of badly stowed containers on large container ships where the stacks are tightly packed together is much more common than previously thought. On most big container ships, many stacks are just not visible, being completely surrounded by stacks of the same height. When collapses occur, loss of cargo results and damage is often done to surrounding stacks of containers, resulting in an expensive operation to salvage the remains of containers and their cargoes when the ship reaches port.
- The Dutch government and MARIN welcome the recent guidelines of the International Chamber of Shipping/World Shipping Council aimed at improving safety at sea by ensuring containers are properly packed, labelled (especially for hazardous cargo), weighed and stowed.

CONCLUSIONS

The cases of the above vessels reinforce the need to establish a regime requiring the master of a commercial vessel to be fully aware of all of his cargoes, especially in the case of container vessels, and to be able to report this information in advance of entering national territorial waters. The main element of the issue concerns the knowledge of the cargo by the master of the vessel. Under the rules of stowage aboard vessel, any containers known to contain hazardous or dangerous cargoes must not be stowed together, nor must they be stored in a place close to the management of the ship or its accommodation area. They must be stowed well apart from each other, away from the areas of accommodation, and their presence must be known and understood by the vessel's master, as in accordance with the SOLAS regulations it is the master who must ensure that all steps are taken to reduce the risk of spillage or destruction or the risk of threat to other cargoes or even the vessel itself, while the cargo is in transit. Furthermore, the master and chief officer must be fully aware of the exact nature of the cargoes aboard vessel, in order to take any necessary precautions to avoid the risks associated with the carriage of these goods as required by the SOLAS Convention, the ISM Code and the MARPOL regulations. In the case of the need to report the vessel's impending arrival at a port or even the vessel's presence in limited waterways such as the Strait of Dover or the Storebaelt (Denmark), the risk of disaster is increased where the master of the vessel is not aware of certain cargoes aboard vessel, especially those of a hazardous or dangerous nature. If such a disaster had occurred in areas of water more limited than the Gulf of Aden, such as the Strait of Dover, the results would have been even more catastrophic, especially as there would have been no specific report issued to the UK or French maritime authorities concerning the hazardous nature of the cargoes aboard vessel.

Vessel reporting must be based on the risk posed by the vessel and its cargo to the maritime environment and the region that it is approaching. The higher the risk, the greater the need for a robust mandatory vessel reporting system imposed by either a national or a supranational government. A simple dissemination of existing known information concerning a vessel or its whereabouts is insufficient. There is the need for commercial vessels to physically report into a national authority prior to entering national territorial waters and state its sailing plan, its cargo and its intended port of destination. In this way, decisions can be taken earlier concerning how to handle, monitor and control the vessel's movements prior to its entry into port, as well as making adequate provision for its safe arrival at port and security concerning the unloading or discharge of its cargo. Although provisions are presently made for the arrival of the vessel at port by the shipping agents, these provisions are made upon the level of knowledge available concerning the cargo of the vessel, and do not necessarily account for the actual details of the cargo, which may not always be known by all parties concerned, details that may compromise the safety and security of the vessel and its cargo, as exemplified by the disaster onboard the *Hyundai Fortune* in March 2006.

Despite all the various global initiatives that rely on electronic means to transmit information with relation to maritime security, especially security concerning cargo movements, there is still a need for extensive physical checks to be carried out on maritime cargoes before and during transit. There is a definite need for customs officers to be located at ports to make such physical checks on cargoes prior to loading aboard vessel. Computer controls are only as good as the information submitted to the computer in the first place regardless of its accuracy or otherwise, whereas physical checks ensure greater levels of security. In many ways, the concept of multimodalism has led to the compromise of marine security, given its assumption that the trader can be relied on to submit accurate information concerning the cargo at all times. However, this premise cannot be assumed, and in many ways is very dangerous. The nature of international trade relies on a series of physical controls to ensure compliance and security, and this cannot be compromised in any way. Present trends in terms of the reduction in physical checks by customs authorities on cargoes in transit lay wide open the risk of future incidents such as that encountered at the Port of Genoa, and indeed also increase the risk of terrorism activity directed at shipping movements, especially the movement of containerized cargoes. Despite initiatives such as C-TPAT, ENS, AEO and the ISPS code, the issue of marine cargo security remains paramount and has yet to be properly resolved, as none of these aforementioned initiatives fully provide a solution to the problem of total transparency and accountability in terms of the issue of cargo security and accuracy of information. We live in a world of increasing levels of political and physical uncertainty, and the maritime sector is especially vulnerable to increasing levels of threat from a variety of sources. In many respects, the level of awareness of procedures and compliances in the international maritime sector is not necessarily fully perceived by international traders, who in many cases are simply concerned with selling goods and being paid, and pay little attention to how these goods are shipped from one place to another. It is this lack of knowledge concerning international transport, logistics and the supply chain that can inevitably lead to breaches in security and at worst disaster. To this extent, greater degrees of training and education in terms of transport and logistics procedures and compliances are required, and the emphasis must ultimately be placed on directing these towards shippers and traders involved in the international movement of goods. Without this, we may be heading towards increasingly troubled times and indeed troubled waters. We may indeed have missed the boat.

11. Maritime security in Nigeria

Frank Ojadi

11.1 INTRODUCTION

The Federal Republic of Nigeria has an area of 923,769 square kilometres (km) (made up of 909,890 square km of land area and 13,879 square km of water area). The coast of Nigeria is a belt of mangrove swamps traversed by a network of creeks and rivers and the great Niger Delta that covers 70,000 square km (National Bureau of Statistics, 2009). The country's territorial waters and Exclusive Economic Zone (EEZ) cover 1555 square nautical km and 25,925 square nautical km, respectively. The southeast corner of the EEZ is shared with three neighbours: Cameroon, Equatorial Guinea and Sao Tome and Principe.

11.1.1 Political Structure

The last census of 2006 puts Nigeria's population at approximately 140 million people with a growth rate of about 3 per cent. Nigeria is a federation of 36 states, 774 local governments and a central government. The three arms of the central government (executive, legislative and judicial) are replicated at the state level. Nigeria's constitution demarcates federal and state areas of responsibility but there is constant jostling to attempt to redraw these boundaries, especially in the areas of control of internal security and the country's revenue allocation formula. The central government retains exclusive control over some sectors of the economy including security and defence agencies (the armed forces, police, intelligence, customs, immigration and various paramilitary formations).

The executive branch of the central government is organized in ministries, departments and agencies (MDAs). Ministries are headed by cabinet ministers who are appointed by the president and confirmed by the upper legislative house. There are over 500 departments and agencies. Some departments and agencies are not subordinated to particular ministries and therefore, do not report to the ministers. Others, which are subordinated to ministries, take policy direction from their supervising ministries.

Some agencies are created by statute while others are created by executive order.

All units in the executive wing are subject to legislative oversight and the relevant committees in both chambers of the National Assembly have the power to hold hearings at which the activities of the executive departments can be subjected to examination.

Although the country relies on ocean shipping for the bulk of its international trade, it is difficult to describe Nigeria as a nation with a historical maritime tradition since maritime matters have not often been seen as issues of any great economic importance to the nation.

11.1.2   Policy Making

The highest policy-making body in Nigeria is the Federal Executive Council (FEC), which is chaired by the president and includes all cabinet ministers. At its weekly meetings, it considers memoranda from various MDAs. Its approval is required for any new policy to become effective. For matters that require legislative action, the requisite executive bill cannot be forwarded to the legislature without the approval of the FEC. An agency or department that is supervised by a ministry would normally channel any requirements for FEC approval through the supervising minister. However, instances of mandate conflict (the same piece of bureaucratic turf being assigned to more than one agency) are not uncommon.

11.1.3   Economy

Prior to the discovery of crude oil in the Niger Delta in the late 1950s, Nigeria relied chiefly on agricultural exports for foreign exchange (Davies, 2000). This trend has reversed since the 1970s resulting in Nigeria being a net importer of all sorts of products including petroleum products.

11.1.4   National Security Establishment

The highest security organ in the country is the National Security Council, which is composed of the heads of the armed services, police, internal security and intelligence agencies and the national security adviser to the President. Its meetings are usually chaired by the president. As can be seen from its composition, the council is heavily tilted towards the military and their allies in intelligence and internal security. With the exception of the Navy and the Marine Police, the entire national maritime establishment is made up of civilian agencies.

11.2 EVOLUTION OF MARITIME SECURITY INSTITUTIONS IN NIGERIA

11.2.1 Nigerian Marine Department

The Nigerian Marine Department (NMD) was created in 1914 by the British colonial authorities from the amalgamation of two existing regional maritime agencies. NMD was a quasi-military arm of the British Royal Navy and was responsible for the administration of ports and harbours and coastguard functions (NPA, 2000). In 1955, the colonial administration split the NMD into three separate bodies: the Nigerian Ports Authority (NPA), which became the port operator and regulator, the Inland Waterways Department and the Nigerian Naval Force, the forerunner of the Nigerian Navy. After this restructuring exercise, the NMD ceased to exist.

11.2.2 Nigerian Ports Authority

In 2006, the persistent inefficiencies at the ports (congestion, low productivity, cargo insecurity among others) resulted in the involvement of private sector port operators in the form of concessions of the terminals with NPA assuming the roles of technical regulator, marine services operator and landlord of the port (NPA, 2008).

11.2.3 Nigerian Navy

The Nigerian Naval Force was renamed the Naval Defence Force (NDF) and it commenced operations in 1956. It was later redesignated as the Nigerian Navy and charged with the following responsibilities: the defence of the national territory; the assistance in the enforcement of customs and immigration laws, illegal bunkering, anti-pollution and fishery protection laws. The Navy was responsible for the enforcement of all national and international maritime laws ascribed or acceded to by the government (Ibrahim, 2011a).

On the face of it, the Navy had been entrusted with the responsibility for the national coastguard function and therefore was in a position to challenge any 'usurpers' in the form of other government agencies that attempted to wrest the coastguard function away from them. For over two decades, the Navy's strategic plan was based on a 'trident' strategy of achieving effective coastal defence, sea control and support to the Army through sealift and naval fire support (Ibrahim, 2011b). Its ship acquisition plan was tailored to suit these objectives, and the Navy retained these blue sea aspirations until the unveiling of the 'transformation plan' for the period 2011–20. This plan marked a shift in strategic focus to 'the development of a fleet capable of sustaining effective EEZ presence and response in defence of Nigeria's maritime interests' (Ibrahim, 2011a).

In recent times, whilst the Navy had often been criticized for its failure to put the sea pirates and crude oil thieves out of business, the head of the Navy admitted at legislative public hearings that the Navy 'had always had difficulties patrolling the country's extensive territorial waters and crude oil pipeline network due to the serial neglect of maritime security institutions' (Ibrahim, 2011a). This claim deserves a closer look. Virtually every government agency in Nigeria claims to be underfunded and attributes all its shortcomings to the insufficiency of resources. It is a fact that the Navy is, as in most other African countries, much smaller than the Army and consequently receives a lower level of resource allocation. Whether these resources are sufficient or not is debatable. However, it is important to point out that even if the underfunding claim were true, the Navy's problems and deficiencies also had other causes. For example, the earlier emphasis on a prestigious (and expensive) blue water strategy was obviously aimed at threats other than the single most important maritime problem facing the country – piracy. This, probably more than any other factor, appears to be the principal reason for the Navy's unpreparedness to tackle the piracy scourge. A late reappraisal of priorities has led to a change in strategic focus, and the results of the shift will take some time to appear.

11.2.4 Nigerian Maritime Authority

The Nigerian Maritime Authority (NMA) was initially set up as a regulatory body under the National Shipping Policy Act of 1987. The thrust of its original mandate at inception was aimed at the development of a domestic shipping industry through a higher level of participation by Nigerian companies in the carriage of the country's imports and exports. In August 2006, the NMA and the Joint Maritime Labour Industrial Council (JOMALIC) were merged to form the Nigerian Maritime Administration and Safety Agency (NIMASA) under the Laws of Federal Republic of Nigeria Act 17 of 2007. The Act stipulates that NIMASA is responsible for the execution of all federal legislation on maritime labour, safety and security. Other responsibilities include the provision of national maritime search and rescue services, air and coastal surveillance, control and prevention of marine pollution, and the establishment of the procedures for the implementation of conventions of the International Maritime Organization (IMO) and the International Maritime Labour Organization and other international conventions to which the Federal Republic of Nigeria is a party on marine safety and security, maritime labour and commercial shipping. NIMASA was authorized to collect a levy of 3 per cent of the gross freight earnings on all import and export cargoes, a further half a per cent of all stevedoring charges collected by employers of dock labour and a 2 per cent surcharge on cabotage transport for funding its activities. Thus NIMASA, an entirely civilian outfit, became the lead government agency in the maritime sector of Nigeria, of which some of its responsibilities tend to overlap with those of the Nigerian Navy.

The 9/11 attack on the World Trade Center towers in the USA resulted in a series of changes to maritime security of which the IMO adopted a mandatory International Ship and Port Facility Security (ISPS) code aimed at improving security of ships and port facilities for its member countries. The Nigerian government set up an ad hoc body, the Presidential Implementation Committee on Maritime Safety and Security (PICOMSS), to oversee Nigeria's efforts to achieve compliance with the ISPS code. The government may have felt that a presidential committee provided the quickest route to compliance given the mandatory dateline of July 2004. PICOMSS was not immediately wound up after the July 2004 deadline. Although PICOMSS was set up by the Ministry of Transport, it was later transferred to the office of the National Security Adviser (NSA) under the presidency, of which the government sought to explain that the move was made on national security grounds. This move resulted in PICOMSS assuming higher roles in maritime security such that it went on to acquire surveillance radars and aircraft, Automatic Identification Systems (AIS) antennae (Oyewole, 2011).

In an attempt to strengthen the position of the law on armed robbery and sea piracy, NIMASA and the Navy called for the enactment of a Maritime Security Act. However, a bill for the establishment of the Maritime Security Agency (MARSECA) was submitted to the national legislature in 2009 by the government with one of its stated major objectives being in the field of intelligence gathering, coordination and dissemination. Supervision of the new agency would be entrusted to the NSA who was accountable only to the president. Opposition to the bill from the local maritime industry was vocal and vigorous, resulting in its withdrawal in 2012. Subsequently the government embarked on a partnership with a private company, Global West Vessel Specialist Nigeria Limited (GWSVNL) in the same year. Under the terms of this partnership, GWSVNL was to supply and maintain a fleet of patrol boats for NIMASA operations for ten years.

From the foregoing, it seems that the Nigerian maritime security establishment is characterized by a multiplicity of agencies and insufficiently demarcated agency borders. Inter-agency coordination has often been complicated by the fact that the agencies involved in a given issue are not always answerable to the same authority. For example, the Nigerian Customs Service takes its orders from the Ministry of Finance, the police from the President, the immigration from the Interior Ministry, NIMASA from the Ministry of Transport and the Navy from the Ministry of Defence.

11.2.5   Legal Framework

One of the basic requirements for the successful prosecution of the war on piracy is the domestication of relevant international maritime treaties and conventions to provide a legal framework for trying apprehended pirates as well as dealing with other crimes at sea that are covered by these treaties and conventions. Nigeria, as at 2012, has yet to set up such a legal framework, meaning that captured pirates cannot be prosecuted in the country. This is surprising for a country with a serious piracy problem. Furthermore, a number of international treaties and conventions on maritime issues to which she is a party are yet to be ratified. These lapses are yet to be explained by the government.

11.3   MAJOR MARITIME PROBLEMS FACING NIGERIA

These problems include:

- piracy and armed attacks on shipping
- maritime accidents
- cargo and ship insecurity within ports
- illegal unreported and unregulated exploitation of maritime resources
- trafficking of drugs and narcotics and items under absolute ban for importation such as fire arms and other conventional weapons
- trafficking in human beings
- maritime pollution
- theft of crude oil and vandalization of oil and gas production infrastructure
- smuggling.

The problems cannot be isolated from the external and internal events that occur around Nigeria. The internal socio-economic situation in Nigeria may have largely given rise to the state of insecurity within the country and its immediate regions. Simmering discontent in the Niger Delta region over perceived decades of neglect and gross inequities in the distribution of oil revenues and the toll extracted from the inhabitants of the area by the ravages of environmental degradation associated with oil exploitation broke out into open conflict in the early 1990s. Huge oil revenues accruing to the country over the years seem to have had very little impact on the poverty in the delta. Also, the struggle in the delta achieved an appreciable level of resonance with many other groups in the country who saw themselves as disadvantaged and excluded from the distribution of the national wealth.

The initial targets of the various militant groups were the international oil companies operating in the delta (especially the kidnapping of expatriate personnel for ransom) but this has since escalated to include oil installations and merchant vessels and personnel. In addition to the militants whose struggle had a political character, there were also organized crime gangs in the delta engaged in piracy and attacks on shipping, crude oil theft and smuggling of weapons and persons. It is estimated that as much as 70 per cent of illegal arms in West Africa are held in Nigeria in the hands of groups and persons outside the forces of law and order (Abdullahi, 2010). The trafficking of arms and the proliferation of light weapons seem to have influenced the rise of armed robbery and politically motivated religious insurrections such as the Boko Haram insurgence in the northeastern parts of the country.

In 2012, the Nigerian President identified threats to the nation's territorial waters to include poaching, piracy, pipeline vandalism, coastal insecurity, illegal bunkering, non-payment of statutory levies and charges, illegal entry of ships, illegal importation of arms and hard drugs and other sundry crimes. The United Nations (UN) Office on Drugs and Crimes estimated that West Africa was a transit point for about one third of all the cocaine consumed in Europe (Ploch, 2011). Although local addiction levels have traditionally been low, more cases are being reported, especially among the affluent urban segment of the population.

The illegal exploitation of marine resources goes largely unnoticed and unchecked. Estimates of the value of fish caught illegally off the coast of West Africa run into billions of US dollars each year (Baker, 2011). The theft of crude oil has direct consequences on Nigeria's economy since the country relies largely on oil revenue for economic development. Estimates of the value of crude oil stolen annually range from $US1 billion to $6 billion ('Oil theft as organized crime', *This Day* newspaper). The government in 2012 published an estimate of US$7 billion ('Nigeria's fiscal challenge', *This Day* newspaper). Whatever may be the true figure, the fact remains that the scale of the theft is scandalously high and the country can ill afford losses on that scale.

African ports are currently rated as the least efficient in the world, with dwell times that are nearly quadruple those of Asian ports (Pálsson et al., 2007). Nigeria has made some progress in improving port efficiency and port security. On the heels of 9/11 came the mandate to implement the ISPS code. Before 2006, NPA had the sole mandate to secure the seaports and the approach channels. Incidents of theft and vandalization of cargo at the ports were many. However, after the concessioning of the ports, the private terminal operators in almost all the ports have adopted the ISPS code by installing perimeter fencing to secure the terminals, installation of terminal gates with security gadgets of which access is limited to card-carrying personnel, installation of closed circuit television (CCTV) cameras and the engagement of private security outfits in addition to the conventional security operatives, to mention a few. Incidents of theft and pilferage of cargo at the ports and on vessels at anchor particularly in the Lagos ports complex seem to have reduced.

According to the International Maritime Bureau (IMB) of the International Chamber of Commerce, pirates/robbers are often violent and have attacked, hijacked and robbed vessels and kidnapped crews along the coast, rivers, anchorages, ports and surrounding waters. Tables 11.1, 11.2 and 11.3 show a summary based on IMB annual reports of the numbers of attacks on shipping reported in West and Central African waters between 2004 and 2012. These figures paint a fairly accurate picture of the piracy situation in the sub-region and in Nigeria in particular.

One important feature of piracy in this region is the absence of Somalia-type havens at which hijacked ships and their crews can be held while negotiating ransom payments. For this reason, these pirates do not hold ships for longer than is necessary to rob the ships and their crews. Attacks off Nigeria accounted for 30 per cent of all attacks in West and Central African waters and 2.9 per cent of the global total between 1993 and 2003. For the following decade (2003–12) the figures rose sharply to 55 per cent and 7.6 per cent, respectively, indicating a significant worsening of the situation. Nigerian waters have sometimes been described as 'the most dangerous marine environment in the world' (Delano, 2009). As illustrated in Table 11.2 for the period 2004–12, boardings accounted for 93 per cent of all attacks off Nigeria against 7 per cent for hijackings. Table 11.3 shows that the bulk of the attacks took place while the vessels were either anchored (52 per cent) or steaming (32 per cent). The fact that 14 per cent of the attacks occurred while vessels were at berth can only be seen as a reflection of an elevated level of insecurity within port premises in the country.

Table 11.1   Locations of actual and attempted attacks on ships in West and Central African waters, 2003–12

	2003	2004	2005	2006	2007	2008	2009	2010	2011	2012*	Total
Angola	3	0	0	4	1	2	0	0	1	0	11
Benin	1	0	0	0	0	0	1	0	20	1	23
Cameroun	2	4	2	1	0	2	3	5	0	0	19
Congo	0	0	0	3	0	1	0	1	3	2	10
DR Congo	0	0	0	0	4	1	2	3	4	2	16
Equatorial Guinea	0	0	0	0	0	1	0	0	0	0	1
Gabon	0	0	0	0	0	0	0	0	0	0	0
Gambia	0	0	0	0	0	0	0	0	0	0	0
Ghana	3	5	3	3	1	7	3	0	2	2	29
Guinea	4	5	1	4	2	0	5	6	5	0	32
Guinea Bissau	0	0	0	0	0	0	1	0	0	0	1
Ivory Coast	2	4	3	1	0	3	2	4	1	3	23
Liberia	1	2	0	0	1	1	0	1	0	0	6
Nigeria	39	28	16	12	42	40	29	19	10	17	252
Senegal	8	5	0	0	0	0	0	0	0	0	13
Sierra Leone	0	3	0	2	2	0	0	0	1	0	8
Togo	1	0	0	1	0	1	2	0	6	5	16
Total West and Central Africa	64	56	25	31	53	59	48	39	53	32	460
Total World	445	329	276	239	263	293	410	445	439	177	3316

Note: *The data for 2012 cover only the period January to June 2012.

Source: Adapted from ICC, *International Maritime Bureau, Piracy and Armed Robbery Against Ships Annual Reports* (2004–12).

Although accurate figures are not available, it has been estimated that thousands of litres of waste are dumped illegally off the coast of Africa every year (Baker, 2011). The littoral states have neither the technical capability to detect the dumping nor the enforcement capability to apprehend the dumpers.

West Africa is believed to be a major entry point for trafficking in cigarettes and counterfeit anti-malaria drugs. Corruption-riddled enforcement regimes make it easy for the traffickers to escape detection, arrest and prosecution.

That the Gulf of Guinea plays a significant role in the supply of oil to most of the key western economies suggests the desire of these nations to secure the security of supply. The need to secure the West African source of oil and international trade routes in the region may have

Table 11.2   Nigeria: actual and attempted attacks on ships, 2004–12

		2004	2005	2006	2007	2008	2009	2010	2011	2012*	Total
Actual	Boarded	22	15	8	35	27	21	13	5	7	153
	Hijacked	0	0	1	1	3	1	0	2	3	11
	Detained	0	0	0	0	0	0	0	0	0	0
Subtotal		22	15	9	36	30	22	13	7	10	164
Attempted	Fired upon	1	1	0	1	5	3	4	2	6	23
	Attempted boarding	5	0	3	5	5	3	2	1	1	25
Subtotal		6	1	3	6	10	6	6	3	7	48
Grand Total		28	16	12	42	40	28	19	10	17	212

Note: *The data for 2012 cover only the period January to June 2012.

Source: Adapted from ICC, *International Maritime Bureau, Piracy and Armed Robbery Against Ships Annual Reports* (2004–12).

Table 11.3   Nigeria: status of ships during actual attacks, 2004–12

	2004	2005	2006	2007	2008	2009	2010	2011	2012*	Total
Berthed	3	0	0	5	8	5	2	0	0	23
Anchored	14	14	4	19	14	11	4	2	3	85
Steaming	5	1	4	9	8	6	7	5	7	52
Not stated	0	0	1	3	0	0	0	0	0	4
Total	22	15	9	36	30	22	13	7	10	164

Note: *The data for 2012 cover only the period January to June 2012.

Source: Adapted from ICC, *International Maritime Bureau, Piracy and Armed Robbery Against Ships Annual Reports* (2004–12).

fuelled a couple of initiatives designed to pressure the West African states to take very seriously the issue of maritime security. Such initiatives include the UN Security Council resolution condemning all acts of piracy and armed robbery committed off the coast of the Gulf States, and the call on all member states of the region to cooperate in the fight against piracy. The actions of some international bodies and/or agencies culminated in the introduction of the initiatives described in the following section.

11.4 GULF OF GUINEA ENERGY SECURITY STRATEGY

This programme started in 2005 as a joint effort involving Nigeria, the UK and the USA and with a focus on the security problems in the Niger Delta. This focus was subsequently widened to include the development of strategies aimed at countering criminal activities and achieving maritime domain awareness in West and Central Africa.

11.4.1 African Partnership Station

The US government created the US Africa Command (AFRICOM) in February 2007 to promote US national security objectives in Africa and its surrounding waters. AFRICOM is headquartered in Stuttgart, Germany, because most of the African countries were not in favour of hosting the Command. The African Partnership Station (APS) was launched by the AFRICOM. APS has been described as a floating university that moves from one port to another, offering a host of programmes on maritime topics onboard US Navy ships to countries in West and Central Africa.

11.4.2 Regional Initiatives

Africa consists of 53 states of which 38 are littoral states. Most of the littoral states have very little control over their maritime domains, lacking the vessels, surveillance systems and trained manpower for effective monitoring of their waters. Table 11.4 depicts the personnel strength of the defence forces of some of the littoral states. Consequently, some of these waters

Table 11.4 Comparison of personnel strength of Army and Navy of five Gulf of Guinea States

Country	Army	Navy
Nigeria	62,000	8000
Cote d'Ivoire	6500	900
DR Congo	110,000–120,000	6703
Equatorial Guinea	1100	120
Gambia	800	70

Source: Mugridge (2010). Quoted in *Freedom C Onuoha* (2012), *Piracy and Maritime Security in the Gulf of Guinea: Nigeria as a Microcosm*, http://studies/aljazeera.net/ResourceGallery/media/Documents/2012/6/12/201261294647291734Piracy and Maritime Security in the Gulf of Guinea.pdf.

have become infested with a wide range of criminal activities that the littoral states appear powerless to stop.

The principal continental political grouping, the African Union (AU), launched a number of initiatives including the AU Maritime Transport Charter and the Maritime Transport Plan of Action that was adopted in October 2009 by ministers responsible for maritime transport and endorsed by the heads of state in January 2010. The 2009 meeting also produced the Durban Resolution in which the countries pledged to cooperate in tackling the maritime problems facing the continent (African Union, 2009). The Plan of Action provided a roadmap covering seven key areas: institutional and legal measures; capacity building; strengthening maritime safety and security; enhancement of port performance; strengthening of inter-African and international cooperation; facilitation and financing of maritime transport and ports; and development of maritime transport equipment. Under the Charter, member countries agreed to revise and harmonize their national maritime laws so as to bring them into line with international conventions and treaties to which these countries were party and to share maritime intelligence.

11.4.3 Sub-regional Initiatives

The Maritime Organization of West and Central Africa (MOWCA) came into being in May 1975 with the objective to cooperate and achieve for the sub-region a cost-effective maritime/transit transport service, high in safety and low in pollution, improvement of environmental protection, combating piracy and trafficking in drugs, arms and humans, and setting up search and rescue facilities. The body was made up of 20 littoral and five land-locked member states (Addico, 2008). MOWCA agreed to set up an integrated coastguard network, which would be based on individual national coastguard units and a coordination function for the individual units. The coastguard network was to be divided into four zones of five countries each, with zonal coordination centres located in Dakar (Senegal), Abidjan (Cote d'Ivoire), Lagos (Nigeria) and Pointe Noire (Gabon), and two principal coordinating centres in Accra (Ghana) and Luanda (Angola). These regional and sub-regional initiatives were all marked by meetings, discussions, resolutions and grandiose plans, and crowned with agreements and memoranda of understandings signed with fanfare and hope. Unfortunately, the situation on the implementation front was not fully matched with concrete actions. The enthusiasm with which the agreements were signed often failed to manifest in the actualization of the agreed objectives.

After decades of haemorrhaging economic losses and the hardship resulting for millions of people, and despite prodding and assistance from trading and development partners and others in the international community, the fight against piracy in the sub-region could be described as generally inadequate. One question that needs to be asked is: why were all these international, regional and sub-regional initiatives uniformly unsuccessful in achieving their stated goals? The answers lie in a complex interplay of historical, political and socio-economic factors. International efforts were clearly hobbled by an unspoken fear of the return of the colonial master through the back door, which, these countries feared, would be provided by foreign military bases. This explains the deep-seated reluctance of countries on the continent to provide hosting facilities for the US AFRICOM or the US Navy, and the lack of interest on the part of West and Central Africa governments in a Gulf of Aden-style anti-piracy patrol by international naval task forces. Any force that was capable of taking independent action (political or military) without the express permission of the host country was unlikely to be acceptable to the host country. Secondly, African countries have a rather poor record with respect to multilateral cooperative efforts. Such efforts sometimes require, in the interest of the overall good of the grouping, either a subjugation of the national interest or even a minor surrender of sovereignty. These are issues that have always been politically unpalatable to these newly independent countries. Thirdly, it is clear that most of these countries do not have the requisite resources to combat the internal problems facing them, which include large-scale poverty, illiteracy, disease and underdevelopment. Asking the same countries to provide funds for coastguards, surveillance aircraft, coastal radars and the like is a very tall order indeed. Many of the signatories to the MOWCA agreement on coastguards must have been aware of the fact that they were in no position to finance their commitments under the agreement but they still went ahead anyway and signed the agreement. As pointed out by the then head of the Nigerian Navy, 'Some of the MOWCA signatories may be unable to make the requisite investment in platforms, facilities and human resources. Those who can afford to: should they be expected to cover the coastlines of others indefinitely?' (Ibrahim, 2011c). Fourthly, many of the countries have been dogged by domestic political instability and internal strife (tribal/religious conflicts that sometimes degenerate into civil wars). The effort required to stay in power and in control is often capable of consuming the attention of a national leader at the expense of issues that may be regarded as 'external', for example, maritime security. Staying in power and maintaining control (especially while employing less than democratic methods) require a firm grip on the army and the internal security establishment. In such circumstances, the navy, not being in a position to contribute to the maintenance of a leader in power, is bound to remain a poor cousin to the army. There are some littoral states that do not have an effective navy.

Nigeria is, of course, better positioned than her neighbours as far as resources are concerned. But in her case, the combined effect of debilitating corruption, poor planning and poor visioning has largely negated the advantage conferred on her by her abundant natural resources and reduced her effectiveness to almost the same level as that of her resource-poor neighbours.

11.4.4   National initiatives

Initially, the Nigerian government appears to have categorized the uprising in the Niger Delta purely as an internal security threat aimed at the country's main source of revenue. The military were deployed in strength to the area with orders to quell the insurrection. But the delta with its labyrinth of inlets, creeks, rivers, estuaries and mangrove swamp was a guerrilla fighter's paradise and the military may have found it difficult and very challenging compared to dry land warfare.

A change of government in 2007 brought with it a change of strategy. In 2009, a decision was taken to substitute the carrot for the stick with a view to achieving a political solution to the problem. An amnesty deal was reached with the main groups of militants and the level of violence declined appreciably, including attacks on shipping. This can be seen from the data in Tables 11.1, 11.2 and 11.3. As part of the amnesty agreement, the government pledged to draw up a 15-year strategic plan for the development of the delta. It was generally agreed that the amnesty deal was but an essential first step on the road to finding solutions to the problems in the delta.

As noted in several IMB reports, pirates operating off Nigeria have always been armed and have shown a propensity for violence. It was therefore expected that the state, in its fight against piracy, would confront the pirates with armed force. However, the agency charged with this responsibility (NIMASA) is a civilian outfit that had neither the platforms nor the capable armed personnel. In 2010, NIMASA signed a memorandum of understanding with the Nigerian Navy under which the Navy provided platforms for NIMASA operations. This saw the creation of a Maritime Guard Command, made up of NIMASA personnel who had been trained by the Navy and were operating on platforms supplied by the Navy, which was to assist NIMASA in its law enforcement role.

NIMASA went a step further through a public–private partnership with GWSVNL, under which it obtained a second set of platforms. GWSVNL would supply, crew and maintain platforms to be used by NIMASA for maritime patrols. NIMASA, having no air assets of its own, also took steps to obtain intelligence from the air. In 2012, it revived negotiations with the Air Force for the use of their aircraft for maritime surveillance. The Air Force was also to provide training for NIMASA staff on search and rescue techniques.

NIMASA has adopted a three-pronged approach (partnerships with the Navy, Air Force and a private company). It is not clear whether these arrangements are a permanent replacement for the coastguard project or just a stopgap measure. This partnership approach is attractive to NIMASA's partners probably because NIMASA is awash in cash and willing to foot the bills. As for effectiveness and durability, only time will tell. The success of these partnerships will be very much dependent on the diligence and sincerity that the partners devote to their cooperative effort.

A Regional Maritime Awareness Capability (RMAC) system comprising ground-based radars and sensors, and an AIS was installed in Lagos in 2011 with the assistance of the US and UK governments. A similar system had earlier been installed in Bonny Island in the Niger Delta region by the US Navy as part of the APS programme. The RMAC system was to be integrated into the Global Maritime Safety and Security Information System.

From the foregoing, it appears that the responsibility for managing the country's maritime affairs has been divided among a number of agencies. This by itself is neither unusual nor inherently wrong. However, when many agencies are involved in a matter, bureaucratic turf wars, conflicting objectives and the existence of different priorities tend to creep in and undermine the efficiency with which the entire system operates. This may impact on any strategic direction towards the maintenance of effective maritime security.

11.5 FUNDING OF PUBLIC BODIES

The budgeting process of the central government is fairly straightforward. MDAs prepare their own budget proposals for each fiscal year (which corresponds to the calendar year). However, each MDA receives guidelines from the Ministry of Finance. When all the separate budget proposals have been collated, a decision is then made as to projects the anticipated revenues would cover. A final version of the budget is then forwarded to the National Assembly, which invariably makes changes. The bottom line is that an MDA is not very certain of receiving approval in line with its proposals.

Usually, revenue generated by government agencies is paid into a central account from which the legislative appropriations are made. However, some agencies are authorized by law to apply some part of their generated revenue to fund their capital and operational expenses. Such agencies are spared the vagaries of the budgeting process and are considered to be lucky cash cows. NIMASA, the central bank, the customs service and the Inland Revenue Service (IRS) have so far been the beneficiaries of this exemption provision that, according to its proponents, is designed to improve revenue generation, reward efficiency and, in the case of the central bank, guarantee agency independence. There are no known laid down criteria for obtaining an exemption and it seems to depend on the lobbying clout of the agency. Whether or not the exemptions improve agency efficiency has so far not been verified by studies.

Government revenues have been under pressure from two directions: a constantly ballooning bureaucracy and instability in global oil markets. The public sector recurrent budget has grown to dwarf the capital budget resulting in the various ministries and departments being involved in a perennial competition for scarce funds to finance projects and capital acquisitions. Although the control of security agencies is firmly in the hands of the central government, state governments often make significant contributions to federal agencies for operations within their states.

11.6   CONCLUSIONS

Nigeria has for some time been in a situation where she has been grappling with maritime security issues. Success in this endeavour depends in part on the cooperative effort of her neighbours, but not much effort seems to be coming from her neighbours. The countries of West and Central Africa appear to have become trapped in a Catch 22-type quandary, which is, at least in part, of their own making. Pirates and sea robbers, human and drug traffickers, poachers, arms smugglers, oil thieves and a host of organized crime gangs have, for decades, operated with swashbuckling impunity in the waters off these countries, inflicting on their relatively poor economies losses on a scale that even rich developed countries would find difficult to accommodate. These countries lack the resources and capability to undertake the effective patrolling and monitoring of their maritime domain and are consequently not in a position to fully stamp out the criminal activities. But, for reasons that are not usually articulated in public discourse or debated openly, they have shown limited interest in accepting direct assistance from other countries that are willing and able to take the fight to the criminals as has been done off East Africa and in the Gulf of

Aden. Indirect assistance of the type already being given (training, ship calls, joint manoeuvres, funding for seminars and workshops and so on) is important and useful but highly unlikely to bring victory in the near future since its impact on the criminals is also indirect, slow to manifest and lacking in potency. As long as these criminal activities continue to flourish on a large scale, the economic losses sustained by these countries will continue to further degrade their ability to generate and deploy the resources demanded by the fight against crime on their waters. Every dollar lost to the criminals is a dollar that becomes unavailable for the numerous health, education, welfare and infrastructure projects that are crying out for funding in these struggling developing nations, as well as for the fight against maritime crime. And, as pointed out earlier, the failure to create employment, develop infrastructure and welfare services, and improve living standards pushes more people into poverty and enlarges the pool of potential recruits for the criminal gangs.

It should be borne in mind that delay has dangerous potential consequences – the criminals may choose to apply part of the bountiful harvest they are reaping towards upgrading the scope, diversity and sophistication of their offensive capabilities to the detriment of the affected states. Also, when a government appears helpless in the face of an external threat such as that posed by these criminals, there is the risk of severe (and sometimes irreversible) damage being done to public confidence in the ability of that government to protect the interests of the nation. For the reasons outlined above, the governments concerned have a real and urgent need to rethink the level of priority accorded to maritime security matters. Even if doubts had existed before about the seriousness of the problem, it has become indisputable that this vicious circle has to be broken for the good of these countries and their people, and it is up to their leaders to decide on the best way to do so.

In conclusion, it may not be far off the point to state that a comprehensive, long-term national maritime security strategy for Nigeria is still very much a work in progress.

REFERENCES

Abdullahi, B. (2010). '70% of illegal arms in West Africa are in Nigeria – NATFORCE boss', *Daily Trust*, 9 November, quoted in *Freedom C Onuoha, Piracy and Maritime Security in the Gulf of Guinea: Nigeria as a Microcosm*, available at http://studies/aljazeera.net/ResourceGallery/media/Documents/201 2/6/12/201261294647291734Piracy and Maritime Security in the Gulf of Guinea. pdf (accessed 17 July 2012).
Addico, M.T. (2008), 'Maritime security threats and responses in the West

and Central African maritime region/Gulf of Guinea, available at http://www.un.org/Depts/los/consultative_process/documents/9_magnusaddico.pdf (accessed 15 March 2012).

African Union (2009), *Second African Union Conference of Ministers Responsible for Maritime Transport, Durban Resolution on Maritime Safety, Maritime Security and Protection of the Marine Environment in Africa*, available at http://www.au.int/pages/sites/default/files/Durban resolution_1.pdf (accessed 21 August 2012).

Baker, M. (2011), 'Towards an African maritime economy', *US Naval War College Review*, **64** (2), available at http://www.usnwc.edu/getattachment/b49b0607-c0a4-41e-964d-dc37cf03e0b0/Towards-an-African-Maritime-Economy--Empowering (accessed 15 March 2012).

Davies, P.N. (2000), *The Trade Makers: Elder Demspter in West Africa, 1852–1972, 1973–1989*, Krbenhavn, Denmark: International Maritime Economic History Association, pp. 73– 519.

Delano, K.H. (2009), 'The Gulf of Guinea and its strategic center point: how Nigeria will bridge American and African cooperation', Air Command and Staff College, available at http:// www.dtic.mil/cgi_bin/GetTRDoc (accessed 17 March 2012).

Federal Republic of Nigeria (2007), Nigerian Maritime Administration and Safety Agency Act, *Official Gazette* No. 75, Vol. 94, Government Notice No. 48, Act No. 17.

Ibrahim, O.S. (2011a), 'Achieving effective maritime security in the Gulf of Guinea: plans of the Nigerian Navy for offshore patrol vessel development', available at http://www.nigeriannavy.gov.ng (accessed 11 March 2012).

Ibrahim, O.S. (2011b), 'Resource protection and challenges to maritime security: Nigerian Navy perspective', available at http://www.nigeriannavy.gov.ng (accessed 11 March 2012).

Ibrahim, O.S. (2011c), 'Creating an integrated maritime security strategy for Africa', available at http://www.nigeriannavy.gov.ng (accessed 11 March 2012).

ICC (2004), *International Maritime Bureau, Piracy and Armed Robbery Against Ships Annual Report*, 1 January–31 December, available at http://www.icc-ccs.org/prc/piracyreport.php (accessed 18 July 2012).

ICC (2005), *International Maritime Bureau, Piracy and Armed Robbery Against Ships Annual Report*, 1 January–31 December, available at http://www.icc-ccs.org/prc/piracyreport.php (accessed 17 July 2012).

ICC (2006), *International Maritime Bureau, Piracy and Armed Robbery Against Ships Annual Report*, 1 January–31 December, available at http://www.icc-ccs.org/prc/piracyreport.php (accessed 17 July 2012).

ICC (2007), *International Maritime Bureau, Piracy and Armed Robbery Against Ships Annual Report*, 1 January–31 December, available at http://www.icc-ccs.org/prc/piracyreport.php (accessed 25 March 2012).

ICC (2008), *International Maritime Bureau, Piracy and Armed Robbery Against Ships Annual Report*, 1 January–31 December, available at http://www.icc-ccs.org/prc/piracyreport.php (accessed 17 July 2012).

ICC (2009), *International Maritime Bureau, Piracy and Armed Robbery Against Ships Annual Report*, 1 January–31 December, available at http://www.icc-ccs.org/prc/piracyreport.php (accessed 17 July 2012).

ICC (2010), *International Maritime Bureau, Piracy and Armed Robbery Against*

Ships Annual Report, 1 January–31 December, available at http://www.icc-ccs. org/prc/piracyreport.php (accessed 25 March 2012).
ICC (2011), *International Maritime Bureau, Piracy and Armed Robbery Against Ships Annual Report*, 1 January–31 December, available at http://www.icc-ccs. org/prc/piracyreport.php (accessed 16 July 2012).
ICC (2012), *International Maritime Bureau, Piracy and Armed Robbery Against Ships Annual Report*, 1 January–31 December, available at http://www.icc-ccs. org/prc/piracyreport.php (accessed 22 July 2012).
Mugridge, D. (2010), 'Piracy storm brews in West Africa: Gulf of Guinea under maritime siege', *Defence IQ*, 18 August, available at http://www.defenceiq. com/sea/articles/piracy-storm-brews-in-west-africa-gulf-of-guinea-u/ (accessed 17 July 2012).
National Bureau of Statistics (2009), *Annual Abstracts of Statistics*, Federal Republic of Nigeria.
NPA (2000), *NPA Handbook*, in English and French, Lagos: Nigerian Ports Authority, pp. 31–144.
NPA (2008), *Ports Development, Management and Reform in Nigeria*, Lagos: Nigerian Ports Authority.
Oyewole, O.L. (2011), *Assessing the Work of the Nigerian Government on Maritime Security in the Gulf of Guinea*, available at piracy-westafrica.com/uploads/ files/1467/Oyewole_Leke.pdf (accessed 21 August 2012).
Pálsson, G., A. Harding and G. Raballand (2007), *Port and Maritime Transport Challenges in West and Central Africa*, Sub-Saharan Africa Transport Policy Program, SSATP Working Paper No. 84, Washington, DC, available at http:// www.worldbank.org/afr/ssatp (accessed 15 March 2012).
Ploch, L. (2011), 'Africa command: US strategic interests and the role of the US military in Africa', Congressional Research Service, available at http://docsfiles. com/pdf_africa_command_u_s_strategic_interests_and_the_role_of_the_u_s. html (accessed 15 March 2012).

12. Maritime security in Oman

Sigurd Neubauer

12.1 INTRODUCTION: OMAN A SEAFARING NATION

Oman, strategically positioned across Iran, north of Yemen and to the east of Saudi Arabia, has since the days of the ancient Magan civilization, from the fourth millennium BC, sought contact with the nations of the ancient and modern world by taking advantage of its unique geographical position at a junction of sea routes between Arabia, East Africa and Asia. By the eighth century, Omani merchants navigated the perils of the Indian Ocean and sailed to Canton in China and to East Africa. In the first half of the nineteenth century, Oman's ruler, Sultan Sultan Said bin Sultan (1797–1856), sent merchant ships to London and New York and subsequently forged strong commercial and diplomatic ties with both Great Britain and the United States; a strategic alliance maintained by Oman until the present.

In addition to its strategic alliance with Washington and London, Muscat has since the 1970s established a foreign policy doctrine based on neutrality, while avoiding interfering in the internal affairs of any state in the region. Given Oman's precarious location, sharing the Straits of Hormuz with Iran coupled with its close geographical proximity to the Indian Ocean, where Somali pirates operate, maritime security has over the past decade become a key pillar of the country's foreign policy strategy. By closely linking maritime security policies to its overall foreign policy doctrine, this chapter outlines how Oman seeks to counter a range of threat scenarios stemming from Somali piracy to regional tensions over control of the Straits of Hormuz by maintaining friendly relations with all of its neighbors, including with Iran. Consequently, as maritime security remains a national priority, Oman continues to invest significant resources in its defense capabilities while closely tying maritime security to its overall foreign policy strategy.

Oman carries out a number of annual naval exercises with the United States, Great Britain, France, India and Pakistan. Although Oman does not carry out any naval exercises with Tehran, Muscat coordinates counter-piracy operations with the Iranian Navy on an informal basis. By doing so, Muscat seeks to preserve its independence by strengthening maritime security cooperation with its neighbors and partners within both a bilateral and multilateral framework. Over the past number of years, policies to combat Somali piracy have also become a national priority as pirates are increasingly drawing closer to its shore. This chapter also analyses Omani strategies to transform its port efficiencies while examining the government's holistic approach to maritime security. Consequently, this analysis seeks to identify how maritime security issues are defined, agendas established, decisions made, policy formulated and resources allocated. Within that framework, the following issues are also examined:

- Policies implemented to mitigate Straits of Hormuz tensions.
- Efforts taken to overhaul domestic maritime legislation.
- Measures taken to prosecute Somali pirates.
- Measures taken to strengthen port security.
- Measures taken to extend Oman's continental shelf.

The research here was graciously sponsored by the Omani government. The analysis draws heavily on interviews with maritime experts and senior officials from the Ministry of Foreign Affairs and the Ministry of Defense who, given the sensitivity of the subject matter, requested that their comments and insights be used on a not-for attribution basis. Names and affiliated organizations of these individuals have therefore been omitted from the text. However, any mistakes made are entirely my own.

12.2 DOMESTIC STABILITY, POLICY OF INDEPENDENT INTERNATIONALISM

Prompted by a strong historic desire to create economic and cultural ties with the outside world, Omanis throughout the millennia developed a culture of tolerance while fiercely maintaining its unique cultural heritage as a seafaring nation. In sink with its historic tradition of tolerance, while preserving its independence and distinct national character, Oman's modern day foreign policy doctrine can arguably be described as 'independent internationalism.'

Under the reign of His Majesty Sultan Qaboos bin Said (1940–), Muscat's stated foreign policy objective centers on maintaining friendly relations with its immediate neighbors, while avoiding interfering in the internal affairs of any state in the region. A neutral foreign policy, coupled with Qaboos's strong emphasis on socio-economic developments has brought remarkable prosperity to his nation. According to a 2010 United Nations Development Programme report examining overall progress made in 135 countries over the past 40 years, Oman ranks first in health, education and income followed by oil-rich Saudi Arabia listed as number five (Khali, 2011).

Politically, Oman remains stable as the country has been able to skirt large-scale political disruptions witnessed across the Middle East and North Africa; Qaboos is widely regarded for having ushered in a 'new era' of prosperity, security and stability, often described by his countrymen as the 'Omani Renaissance' (Neubauer, 2011).

On a strategic note, Oman has arguably been able to secure its rapid economic growth, prompted by oil riches, by maintaining friendly and cordial relations with all of its neighbors, including with Iran.

Since assuming power in 1970, through a bloodless palace coup, the Shah of Iran Mohammad Reza Pahlavi and King Hussain of Jordan were the only regional leaders to support the young British-educated prince in his quest for the throne; Qaboos apparently never forgot and has since forged strong political ties with Tehran. Presently, however, Oman enjoys friendly relations with all countries of the region.

As a testimony to its effective policy of neutrality, Muscat successfully mediated the release of 15 British Navy personnel captured at gunpoint by Iranian forces in 2007 (Friedman, 2011). Similarly, again drawing upon its friendly relations with Iran, Oman mediated the release of three US hikers, accused by Tehran of 'espionage' in 2011. As Iran is growing increasingly isolated, both regionally and internationally, an 'Omani channel' to the West can arguably also serve Tehran's interests.

As an apparent testimony to the country's success in maintaining friendly relations with all of its immediate neighbors, Oman's three land borders are secure, including with Yemen. Without the support of its neighbors, Muscat believes that stability cannot be achieved. Aside from its friendly relations with Iran, the Sultanate enjoys a strategic alliance with the members of the Gulf Cooperation Council (GCC), which comprises Bahrain, Oman, Kuwait, Qatar, Saudi Arabia and the United Arab Emirates (UAE). Additionally, Oman remains a staunch US ally and enjoys close defense cooperation with the United Kingdom in particular (International Institute for Strategic Studies, 2012).

Oman also lies at the mouth of the Arabian Gulf, and its territorial waters meet Iran's as the two countries share the strategic Strait of Hormuz; a 21-nautical mile chokepoint at its narrowest. In an effort to mitigate risk presented by great power politics over access and control of the Strait of Hormuz, while maintaining its independence and national interests, Oman's foreign policy objective of neutrality and non-interference also seems to serve as an overall guide to its maritime security policies.

12.3 SEA THREATS AND LIMITS TO OMANI TOLERANCE

Despite its stable and secure land borders, prompted by its foreign policy doctrine of neutrality, Oman's precious location leaves the Sultanate's security and prosperity vulnerable to a host of threat scenarios, all stemming from the sea. From the south, Somali pirates not only threaten international shipping off the coast of Africa but emboldened pirates are increasingly drawing nearer Omani territorial waters. In August 2011, pirates, disguised as fishermen, entered southern Omani territorial waters and hijacked a chemical oil tanker with 21 Indian sailors onboard near the Port of Salalah. The ship, later en route to Somalia, was ultimately successfully intercepted by a Dutch Navy ship (Reuters, 2011). Similarly, in May 2012, pirates hijacked a Liberian-flagged oil tanker off the coast of Oman (BBC, 2012). Consequently, the International Maritime Board (IMB) listed Oman in a high-risk zone of pirate activity as at least four vessels were attacked close to its geographic vicinity, while over a dozen attempted pirate attacks were reported in 2012, according to the agency (Oman Coast, 2012).

Aside from piracy, Oman fears that political instability in Somalia and elsewhere could prompt waves of illegal immigration, ultimately testing its Navy and Coast Guard (CG). The country's 3165-kilometer coastline also remains vulnerable to smuggling and illegal fishing, officials stress.

As tensions between the international community and Iran over Tehran's controversial nuclear program continue to escalate, Iranian threats to close the Strait of Hormuz would not only threaten global energy supplies, as some 35 percent of all crude oil carried by ship passes through, but effectively violate Omani territorial waters.

Building on Muscat's close relations with Tehran, Omani officials express confidence in their ability to ultimately persuade Iran from closing the Strait as Iranian ships will no longer be able to access the Indian Ocean. Unlike the UAE and Saudi Arabia, which over the past couple of years have invested significant resources in building alternate pipelines as part of an effort to circumvent the Strait of Hormuz, Iranian ships are solely reliant on the narrow passage to enter the sea, officials reason.

Aside from friendly relations with Iran, Omani officials stress that 'none of its neighbors' receive 'preferential treatment,' apparently in a bid to balance its relations between Tehran, the GCC and the international community at large. Omani officials also say, in the event Iran attempts to block the Strait, it remains 'doubtful' whether that threat can be actualized due to the heavily patrolled waterway by the US Navy and its British, French and GCC counterparts. Nonetheless, Muscat officials stress, privately, that a 'Western' war with Iran and threats presented by piracy present limits to 'Omani tolerance,' as its economic interests would be severely hurt.

12.4   MARITIME SECURITY, A NATIONAL PRIORITY

Given the various threats to the country's security and prosperity, maritime security is addressed at the national level. Operationally, maritime security responsibilities are divided between the Royal Oman Navy (RNO) and the CG, responding directly to the Royal Oman Police (RPO). Counter piracy operations are also supported by the Royal Air Force Oman (RAFO).

Within Oman's territorial waters, the CG is responsible for the country's maritime security policies. Beyond Oman's 12 nautical miles, the RNO resumes that responsibility. Aside from combating piracy, the RNO is also responsible for protecting fisheries and other resources.

Throughout Oman's defense establishment, operational decisions are all made by the various service commanders but ultimate authority rests with the country's ruler, His Majesty Sultan Qaboos, who is the Commander in Chief. At the rank of Marshal, Qaboos oversees each branch of the country's military. Similarly, the Inspector General of the RPO responds directly to the Sultan, and traditionally hails from the Royal Grade Brigade. Aside from the Office of the Public Prosecutor, Oman does not have a civilian component to its defense establishment.

As part of an effort to streamline maritime security policies and interagency intelligence cooperation, the government is currently setting up a committee comprised of a representative from the following agencies: the RNO, the ROP, the RAFO, Ministry of Transport and Communications (MOTC) and Palace Affairs (responsible for the interior). The new interagency task force will also be responsible for identifying how maritime security issues are defined, agendas established, decisions made, policy formulated and resources allocated.

As the country is seeking to reform its maritime security decision-making process, in tandem with overhauling its present maritime legislation, Oman's maritime budgetary process is also expected to be reformed. Under current legislation, the ROP receives its annual budget from the Ministry of Finance and subsequently allocates funding to the CG. However, the CG enjoys additional discretionary resources for combating piracy and illegal infiltration. While the ROP has signed various customs agreements with the GCC, under the 2004 landmark anti-terrorism treaty, the CG also enjoys a certain degree of autonomy as it operates according to its own code.

12.5 MARITIME SECURITY POLICIES

Under the reign of Qaboos, the RNO has since the 1970s transformed itself into a modern entity, enjoying close security cooperation with the United Kingdom in particular. Citing historic ties, officials acknowledge, 'Britain continues to understand Omani maritime needs well, and vice versa.' Consequently, as recent as 2007, the RNO placed an order of three Kareef Class Corvettes with British Aerospace Electronic Systems (Naval Technology.com, 2012). However, although British companies are often awarded major contracts, officials stress that all defense contract awards are merit based. Additionally, many of the RNO's premier officer corps received their education in Britain.

Sizable relative to its small population (3.02 million), the RNO is made up of 4200 well-trained personnel (International Institute for Strategic Studies, 2012). By comparison, the country's CG, responsible for enforcing much of the country's maritime security policies, employs a staff of 400.

Although Oman lacks warfighting experience, its Navy and Armed Forces maintains a good state of readiness (International Institute for Strategic Studies, 2012). Primarily focusing on territorial defense, and as part of an effort to respond to increasing threat scenarios presented by sea, Oman is believed to have increased its annual defense budget from 57.5 billion USD in 2010 to 66.6 billion USD in 2011. Drawing on its strong alliance with Washington and London, Muscat 'has ensured a steady flow of new equipment . . . to maintain military effectiveness' (International Institute for Strategic Studies, 2012). Additionally, responding to regional unrest prompted by the 'Arab Spring,' the GCC initially pledged a 10 billion USD aid package to Oman in a bid to help create another 10,000 public sector jobs, mostly meant to staff its military and security forces (Neubauer, 2011). However, at the present stage, officials say, 'it remains unclear whether the funding will be granted.'

12.6 REGIONAL DIPLOMACY MANIFESTED BY MARITIME SECURITY COOPERATION

Extending Oman's foreign policy doctrine of neutrality at sea, the RNO conducts annual bilateral exercises with its GCC partners, India, Pakistan and with the United States. Additionally, Oman also conducts annual multilateral exercises with the GCC, the United States, Britain and France.

Similarly, while building on its Joint GCC Defense Treaty, the RNO participates in an annual multilateral exercise; rotating each year into the territorial waters of one of its partners. Although the theme of the GCC naval exercise varies from year to year, it takes six years before the drill in question returns to the host country. When it comes to missile firing tests, due to the Gulf's narrow waterways, each of the GCC participants conducts testing in the Arabian Sea, typically ranging between 80 to 100 miles off the coast of Oman. The RNO also conducts a separate annual bilateral exercise with both its Indian and Pakistani counterparts, each year alternating between each other's territorial waters.

In addition to the RNO's annual bilateral 'Magic Carpet' exercise with the US Navy, Oman also commits herself to a yearly multilateral '*Khanjar Hadd*' ('sharp dagger') drill; drawing participation from the navies of Britain, France and the United States. Aside from testing operational capabilities, a central component to Oman's various naval exercises is forging strong relationships in a bid to enhance the nation's foreign policy doctrine of 'independent internationalism.'

Although the RNO aims to send one ship from each class to each of its exercises, the exact ship participation depends on availability and previous commitments, officials say.

While details of the RNO's overall budget remains classified, officials reveal that funding for its various annual naval exercises are derived from the RNO's training budget, which also covers resources allocated for RNO staff training seminars abroad and at home.

12.7   LIMITED NAVAL COOPERATION WITH IRAN, EXTENSIVE INTELLIGENCE COOPERATION WITH GCC AND INTERNATIONAL PARTNERS

While Oman does not conduct any drills with the Iranian Navy, the two countries coordinate counter-piracy efforts and its navies occasionally dock at each others ports. However, counter-piracy coordination is solely conducted with the Iranian Navy, and not with Iran's Revolutionary Guards. Aside from its 'informal' piracy coordination with Iran, officials stress, Muscat has not signed any intelligence cooperation agreements with Tehran (Times of Oman, 2013). Formal bilateral naval cooperation is strictly limited, for example, a junior Omani officer dispatched to Tehran to study Farsi while his Iranian counterpart is sent to Muscat to learn

Arabic. In the Strait of Hormuz, Oman and Iran 'operate independently' of one another, Omani officials stress.

Meanwhile, in September 2012, the RNO, along with its GCC counterparts, participated in a US-led naval exercise, known as International Mine Countermeasures Exercise (IMCMEX-12), focusing on clearing mines that Tehran, or guerrilla groups, might deploy to disrupt tanker traffic, notably in the Strait of Hormuz (United States Department of State, 2012).

In a bid to prevent extremist groups from threatening the prosperity and stability of the Arabian Gulf and the Middle East at large, in 2002 the leaders of the GCC countries adopted a security strategy for combating terrorism-related radicalism. The very same year, the GCC issued what became known as the 'Muscat Declaration,' a commitment to fight terrorism. On 4 May 2004, the GCC leaders convened again, this time in Kuwait, where they signed an extensive counter terrorism agreement.

Under the new GCC anti-terrorism treaty, the parties agreed to conduct annual joint naval exercises and share intelligence on threats ranging from piracy, terrorism at sea and smuggling, to issues pertaining to illegal immigration. At a subsequent GCC summit in the Saudi Arabian capital, a new agreement focusing on transportation security was reached in 2006. Under the 'Riyadh Memorandum of Understanding,' GCC port officials would be able to inspect all ships docking in its ports while its intelligence services could monitor and share intelligence on any suspicious vessel operating in any of the territorial waters of the GCC countries. As part of the 'Riyadh Agreement,' a permanent secretariat, with an information center and a permanent security committee, was established in Muscat.

Oman has also signed intelligence cooperation treaties with the United States, Britain, France, India and Pakistan. Oman has not signed any intelligence cooperation agreements with Iran. (In 1974, during the reign of the Shah of Iran, the two countries signed a joint bilateral patrolling agreement but the treaty in question has not been in place since the Islamic Revolution of 1979.)

Building on the 2004 GCC anti-terrorism treaty, Oman, the UAE and Saudi Arabia signed the 'Djibouti Code of Conduct,' at an anti-piracy summit in Djibouti in January 2009. According to the International Maritime Organization (IMO) document, the signatories commit to abide by United Nations (UN) Security Council Resolutions 1816 (2008), 1838 (2008), 1846 (2008) and 1851 (2008) and of UN General Assembly Resolution 63/111, which fall within the competence of the IMO and all international anti-piracy agreements (International Maritime Organization, 2009).

Accordingly, all signatories of the Djibouti Code,

Commit themselves towards sharing and reporting relevant information through a system of national focal points and information centres; interdicting ships suspected of engaging in acts of piracy or armed robbery against ships; ensuring that persons committing or attempting to commit acts of piracy or armed robbery against ships are apprehended and prosecuted; and facilitating proper care, treatment, and repatriation for seafarers, fishermen, other shipboard personnel and passengers subject to acts of piracy or armed robbery against ships, particularly those who have been subjected to violence. (International Maritime Organization, 2009)

The IMO document continues,

(a) the investigation, arrest and prosecution of persons, who are reasonably suspected of having committed acts of piracy and armed robbery against ships, including those inciting or intentionally facilitating such acts;
(b) the interdiction and seizure of suspect ships and property on board such ships;
(c) the rescue of ships, persons and property subject to piracy and armed robbery and the facilitation of proper care, treatment and repatriation of seafarers, fishermen, other shipboard personnel and passengers subject to such acts, particularly those who have been subjected to violence; and
(d) the conduct of shared operations – both among signatory States and with navies from countries outside the region – such as nominating law enforcement or other authorised officials to embark on patrol ships or aircraft of another signatory. (International Maritime Organization, 2009)

12.8   MITIGATING HORMUZ TENSIONS

As a testimony the potentially disastrous consequences tensions in the Strait of Hormuz could have on Omani interests, the *Financial Times* reported on a 'mysterious incident' that involved a Japanese oil tanker passing through Omani territorial waters in July 2010. Shortly after midnight, the ship 'reported a flash, quickly followed by what sounded and felt like an explosion. The double hull, holding about 2 m barrels of crude oil, withstood the explosion but damage was visible inside . . . Mystery still surrounds the incident. According to Mitsui OSK Lines, owners of the vessel, there seemed to have been an "attack from external source".' Following the incident, 'Tehran quickly distanced itself from the blast, saying it must have been accidental.' The cause of the incident remains a mystery (Blas, 2012).

In a bid to mitigate risk stemming from the strategic water passage and the potentially disastrous effect an international war with Iran could have on the region and on Omani commercial interests in particular, the government recently constructed a new port, Al Duqm, with a strategic location in the Arabian Sea. The new port also provides dockyard facilities and ship maintenance services, potentially becoming a major regional transport hub.

While Al Duqm will be accessible by ground transportation, talks are ongoing between Oman and its GCC allies on potentially constructing a pipeline transferring energy resources to Duqm, and from there to world markets.

12.9 TRANSFORMING PORT EFFICIENCIES, OVERHAULING MARITIME LEGISLATION

Aside from Al Duqm, Oman has commercial and industrial maritime ports strategically positioned from the Port of Salalah in the south to Port Sohar and the Port of Shinas in its northeast, and the Sultan Qaboos Port (SQP) in Muscat. Within the vicinity of the Strait of Hormuz, but inside the Gulf, the Port of Khasab is strategically positioned.

Over the past three decades, Oman's port sector has grown dynamically and the country has taken a series of subsequent steps to establish herself as a regional transportation hub. Accordingly, the government appears to be changing from a port-driven port policy toward a deeper strategic national approach on how to fully utilize its various ports' potential. As a case in point, following a Royal Decree, Muscat's SQP will be transformed from an industrial port into a cruise hub. Meanwhile, all cargo operations will be transferred to the Port of Sohar, the country's largest in overall tonnage, located in the northeastern Batinah region.

At the backdrop of the government's strategic vision to increase the overall efficiency of all of its ports, the GCC states are planning to construct a joint rail line running from Kuwait along the Gulf coast to Muscat. Given the potential economic magnitude of the 1940-kilometer regional network, Oman is projecting that the GCC project will significantly boost growth at its various ports over the next decade.

While Oman is overhauling its national port strategy, the country is also in the midst of renewing its maritime legislation in a bid to streamline regulations and increase its overall competitiveness; a new legal framework is expected by the end of 2013.

Since signing on to the Ship and Port Facility Security (ISPS) code of the IMO in 2002 and having implemented its code in 2004, Oman remains on the IMO's white list (Standards of Training, Certification and Watchkeeping, STCW). As Oman seeks to upgrade its various port facilities while complying with international regulations and standards, the MOTC is implementing a series of recommendations brought forth by the IMO. (The report and its findings remains an internal document, unavailable to the public.) Moreover, the MOTC is contemplating standardizing security regulations for all the ports while seeking to maintain business-friendly practices.

Enjoying a public–private partnership, all Omani ports, each operating by a Royal Decree and a concession agreement, lease their operation to a privately held management company. Under the present legislation, Omani ports are structured according to the European 'landlord model,' where the government owns the ports while providing a concession agreement to port management companies. The government continues to be responsible for covering the port's external security-related costs; inside the port, the operating management company covers security costs. Moreover, each port management company acts as port authority, leasing out land while granting concessions to specialised stevedoring and other port service companies. Oman is currently consulting Dutch and Belgian ports on respective legislation covering issues ranging from security to 'landlord' best practices. In sink with its national port strategy overhaul, all of Oman's port security standards and practices are currently being evaluated, port executives say.

12.10   PORT SECURITY PRACTICES

The government is responsible for the port's external security while the MOTC carries the costs for fencing and gates. Within each port, a private security company is hired to maintain daily security procedures. As part of a 24/7 security scheme, all ships docking at Omani ports are susceptible to random inspections all year around. While the CG patrols the waters outside the port, the ROP is responsible for the ports' external security on shore.

As a testimony to strict Omani security regulations, a ROP commander is assigned to each port, and his rank ranges from colonel to major, depending on the size of the port. Given that some of its ports are positioned 'between areas of tensions,' the ROP has issued strict visitor regulations as part of an effort to protect ships and secure its cargo. Consequently, the ROP is responsible for security standards and practices while providing security guidelines to the company responsible for managing each Omani port. The ROP is also responsible for implementing and executing various customs agreements, falling under the GCC anti-terrorism treaty of 2004.

12.11   ANTI-TERRORISM PROCEDURES

Prior to implementing the ISPS code, two annual drills simulating terrorist attacks were carried out at each port. However, since 2008, one annual exercise has been held at each port, involving all agencies ranging from ROP, CG, MOTC, Ministry of the Environment to local and national hospitals. At each port exercise, port officials from the other Omani ports may join as observers.

Aside from anti-terrorism drills, following the previously specified multi-agency principle of participation, each port also carries out annual oil spilling exercises, spearheaded by the Ministry of the Environment. During both the anti-terrorism and oil spill exercises, only one part of the port is sealed off while the remaining part continues to be operational. Throughout the year, Oman's ports remain open, 24/7, with the exception of the first eight hours of the festival of Eid and on the last eight hours of the holiday in question, counting 16 hours total annually.

12.12   OMAN'S HOLISTIC APPROACH TO MARITIME SECURITY POLICIES, AIMS TO EXTEND THE CONTINENTAL SHELF

As a testimony to Oman's visionary commitment to overhauling its various maritime security policies, while remaining firmly committed to regional peace and stability, Muscat is currently working on extending its continental shelf with an additional 150 nautical miles. Following its June 2010 UN petition, Oman is crafting a policy centering on its ability to (responsibly) govern the additional 150 nautical miles. Muscat expects to submit its full application to the UN within the next three to five years; the project is spearheaded by Ambassador Salim Bin-Alawi, a former RNO Admiral, appointed for the task by His Majesty Sultan Qaboos.

In the event that Oman's continental shelf extension request is granted, Oman will be in full control of the natural resources in the seabed of the extended area but not the water above it. Muscat is also assessing what additional RNO resource allocations are needed in terms of manpower and procurement, should its continental shelf request be granted.

While Oman's Exclusive Economic Zone (200 nautical miles) covers approximately 550,000 square kilometers, Muscat is not expecting that any of its neighbors, including India, will object to its continental shelf extension request, officials say. By extending its continental shelf, Oman is also signaling to the international community its firm commitment to fighting piracy as its extended naval presence arguably could help push pirates further into the Indian Ocean. On the other hand, by closely linking its maritime security policies to its overall foreign policy objective of maintaining friendly relations with all of its neighbors, Oman has arguably succeeded in mitigating risks stemming from regional rivalries over control of the Strait of Hormuz to protecting its own interests. Nonetheless, it should be added that maritime security will likely remain a top priority for years to come as Oman's precarious location leaves it vulnerable to a number of threat scenarios stemming from sea.

REFERENCES

BBC (2012), 'Pirates "hijack" oil tanker Smyrni near Oman', available at http://www.bbc.co.uk/news/world-africa-18032948 (accessed 11 May 2012).

Blas, J. (2012), 'Energy: corridor of power', available at http://www.ft.com/intl/cms/s/2/b4f57138-0ca7-11e2-b175-00144feabdc0.html#axzz2BZzdIzgJ (accessed 4 October 2012).

Friedman, U. (2011), 'Oman: the world's hostage negotiator, available at http://blog.foreignpolicy.com/posts/2011/11/14/oman_the_worlds_emerging_hostage_negotiator (accessed 14 November 2011).

International Institute for Strategic Studies (2012), *The Military Balanced*, available at http://www.iiss.org/publications/military-balance/the-military-balance-2012/, p. 342.

International Maritime Organization (2009), *Djibouti Code of Conduct*, updated 2011, available at http://www.imo.org/OurWork/Security/PIU/Pages/DCoC.aspx.

Khali, A. (2011), 'UNDP: Oman leads top of the world's ten long-term developments', available at http://www.english.globalarabnetwork.com/201011057945/Culture/undp-oman-leads-top-of-the-worlds-ten-long-term-developments.html (accessed 5 November 2011).

NavalTechnology.com (2012), *Khareef Class Corvettes, Oman*, available at http://www.naval-technology.com/projects/khareef-class/.

Neubauer, S. (2011), 'How the Arab Spring skirted Oman', available at http://www.huffingtonpost.com/sigurd-neubauer/oman-arab-spring_b_1144473.html (accessed 13 December 2011).

Oman Coast (2012), *Pirates of the Arabian Sea*, available at http://omancoast.blogspot.com/2012/08/pirates-of-arabian-sea.html (accessed 10 August 2012).

Reuters (2011), 'Somali pirates hijack Indian ship with 21 crew off Oman', available at http://www.reuters.com/article/2011/08/20/india-hijack-idUSL4E7JK05T20110820 (accessed 20 August 2011).

Times of Oman (2013), 'Iran's navy foils piracy attempt', available at http://www.timesofoman.com/News/Article-7311.aspx (accessed 29 January 2013).

United States Department of State (2012), *Senior Administration Officials Preview of the U.S.-GCC Strategic Cooperation Forum*, available at http://www.state.gov/r/pa/prs/ps/2012/09/198424.htm (accessed 28 September 2012).

13. Container security at Indian dry ports

Girish Gujar and Hong Yan

13.1 BACKGROUND

The fact that container security is a critical factor in global supply chains is universally accepted. However, the methodology to measure it and the means to reduce associated risks is widely disputed. The disagreements become even more stringent when the tangible costs and time factors rise sharply without any clearly perceivable benefits of risk reduction. The responsibility and liability for container security failure complicates the issue even further. Globally at present, the majority of the containers are stuffed/de-stuffed at the dry ports located further away from gateway sea ports. The authority to permit the stuffing and allow transportation of a container lies with Customs who also set the standards of security at a dry port.

Customs could be rigorous in ensuring that the dry ports religiously adhere to the set rules for container security. However, our research reveals that this is not done in the interest of commerce. This chapter evaluates container security at 26 Indian dry ports located in five different regions to see what impact stringent container inspections by Customs will have on associated risks, either with or without apportioning liability of the dry port operator (DPO). We conclude that container security by itself is unlikely to be enhanced in the absence of suitable security policies in place that unambiguously and firmly saddle the DPO with commensurate liability for container security failure.

13.2 CONTAINER SECURITY

Container security has yet to find a universally accepted definition. The concept is subjective and can indirectly be defined as retention of safety and security of the containerized cargo as declared in the cargo manifest (in terms of value, quantity and quality) by maintaining the integrity of the container seal or container security device (CSD). The maritime transport industry understands and accepts the security strategic decisions of national governments, particularly the USA, that preventing and detecting the possible containerized transportation of unlawful and hazardous material is the number one container security priority but it is unable to build a consensus about the methodology to achieve the stated objectives. For example: What specific thing must a CSD do? What specific events must be captured and recorded? Should it record the opening of just one door on the container or must it be able to capture either door opening? Is capturing entry through the doors enough or must it detect entry into the container through the walls, ceiling or floor? Does the device have to detect conditions other than entry intrusion?

The USA recently announced the formation of a new organization, the International Container Standards Organization (ICSO), for the stated purpose of establishing 'global standards' for CSDs. While there may be legitimate differences of opinion regarding the security value of container seals, the function and operational requirements of container seals are clearly defined and well understood in the USA and internationally, by both industry and governments. It would appear that the ICSO wants to establish what those functional requirements should be.

It has often been suggested by numerous scholars of this subject that container security would be the most vulnerable at a foreign seaport/dry port that does not participate in the Container Security Initiative (CSI). Indian dry ports do not participate in the CSI. Each year an estimated eight million containers arrive and depart from Indian seaports. There are several stakeholders involved in the movement of these containers. Despite all efforts to reduce security risks, vulnerabilities exist. Our focus is on vulnerabilities in land transportation and at the dry ports. The security agencies of advanced countries use non-intrusive inspection equipment such as radiation portal monitors, gamma ray and X-ray scanners in addition to personal identification detectors for container inspections.

For identification of high-risk containers they also make use of the Automated Targeting System (ATS), which runs a complex algorithm and assigns a risk score for each container. The outcome depends on the cargo manifest information and intelligence information among other inputs. None of these equipment or procedures are being used at dry ports in India. This is solely due to the fact that the DPO is not liable for third-party liabilities arising out of container security failure. He is only liable for loss of revenue to Customs. In other words, he does not recognize any other losses that may be ancillary to container security failures.

There are three main tenets of container security research; firstly, to identify the potential weak links where the integrity of the container is most vulnerable and the implications of security failure; secondly, to choose a method to strengthen the weak link; and thirdly, to conduct a cost-benefit analysis.

The procedure for stuffing/de-stuffing of containers is more or less the same in most countries of the world; broad inferences that are drawn here for one country could easily be applicable to others too. In addition to the shippers and consignees, the other players in the dry port are Customs authorities who authorize the DPO to stuff and transport the containers to and from the dry ports and the DPO himself, who actually stuffs and transports the container. It should be recognized *ab initio* that Customs are not held responsible for the failure of container security. In order to prevent loss of revenue during inland transit Customs insist that the DPO furnish a bank guarantee for a specific amount equivalent to the value of the cargo handled at the dry port. However in the absence of any third-party liability for container security failure the DPO does not upgrade container transportation security nor is he sufficiently motivated to improve container inspection at the dry port.

13.3 SECURITY INSTRUMENTS: A GLOBAL AND NATIONAL SURVEY

In recent years, maritime security has become a major concern on the international maritime agenda. Various security measures and initiatives have been devised and implemented at the international, national and organizational levels, such as the International Maritime Organization's (IMO) International Ship and Port Security (ISPS) code, the US Customs-Trade Partnership Against Terrorism (C-TPAT), the CSI and others developed by the International Labour Organization (ILO) and the World Customs Organization (WCO). At the same time, it is argued that security improvements resulting from maritime security requirements may also bring about some benefits to service quality and business performance for the organizations. Security improvements have an impact on several aspects of maritime transport. We see that applications of information technology (IT) and other technological solutions are especially encouraged in security initiatives promoted by governmental, regional and international organizations. The presence of IT plays a critical role in success. It also becomes imperative to make radical changes in operating practices to comply with security requirements.

There are dual objectives of this policy: firstly, better control of shipment visibility under maritime transport, either in transit or at ports/dry ports, and secondly, better management of information regarding the shipment. Such security requirements will hardly be complied with if the early reporting of cargo and schedule details is not facilitated by improved IT systems by shippers and shipping lines, or freight forwarders. The Smart and Secure Trade lane initiative, for example, aims at enhancing the control of shipment visibility, while containers are onboard the ships and at ports. The importance of addressing the vulnerability of the world's logistical nodes has generated several globally applied instruments since 2001. As a contextual foundation to assessing the security of Indian dry ports, these instruments and their application are discussed here.

13.3.1 International Ship and Port Security Code

The perceived strategic vulnerability of the global supply chain was the impetus for the drafting of the ISPS code. The ISPS code was adopted by the IMO in December 2002, and was fully effectuated in July 2004. It is presently the most obvious indication of an international recognition of the strategic vulnerability of the global supply chain following the 9/11 terrorist attacks in the USA. The code is based on the IMO's International Convention for the Safety of Life at Sea (SOLAS) 1974 and its subsequent additions regarding Special Measures in Enhancing Maritime Security (chapter XI-2) to SOLAS. In essence, the ISPS code takes a risk management approach to security, implying that in order to determine appropriate security measures, an assessment of the risks needs first to be made in each individual case. The code also provides a standardized and concise framework for evaluating risks and possible responses. Several major Indian dry ports are ISPS compliant.

13.3.2 ISO: 28000-2007 Certificate

The International Organization for Standardization (ISO) has published specification for the ISO 28000-2007 certification aimed at implementing safety management in supply chains. It is a risk-based management system for transport and DPOs. For organizations working in logistics, this certification can be a valuable addition. It supports the management and reduction of security incidents as well as 'just in time' delivery of goods. Very few of the Indian dry ports are ISO 28000 certified.

13.3.3 Container Security Initiative

International trade security and facilitation programmes also include the CSI. This initiative was undertaken by the US Department of Homeland Security Customs and Border Protection (CBP) with efforts focused on establishing working bilateral partnerships with foreign authorities aiming to identify high-risk cargo containers before they are loaded on vessels with destination in the USA. Border security, therefore, is moved from the US territory to the territory of the country of port of origin (CBP, 2012) and leads to the development of port security standards worldwide. India, however, is not included in the CSI although discussions about Indian participation in the programme have been reportedly conducted by US and Indian government officials (personal communication with authors). At present, approximately 86 per cent of maritime containerized cargo that enters US territory originates from or is trans-shipped in CSI ports. The USA would like to implement a 100 per cent container scanning rule. India is, however, unlikely to accede due to an enormous increase in the costs of security.

13.3.4 National Regulatory Competencies in India

An Inter-Ministerial Committee (IMC), acting under the overall control of the Ministry of Commerce, was set up in India in 1992 with the primary aim of facilitating exports by way of encouraging the establishment of dry ports. The IMC is thus the competent authority, licensing the setting up of dry ports. However, the IMC guidelines for setting up and specifying the functions of dry ports are silent when it comes to the law that should apply to dry port operations. The guidelines do state that dry ports would broadly be under the overall control of the local Customs Commissioner, but they fail to give details on the powers and duties of the Commissioner (Customs Act of India, 2012). Thus, by delegating the mechanism for the review of the dry port (who is considered a custodian of the cargo in his charge) conduct and performance to the local Customs Commissioner, the IMC, which had initially licensed the applicant for setting up a dry port, does not play any further role in the functioning of the dry port.

According to the Customs Act of 1962, the jurisdictional Commissioner of Customs is the competent authority for the approval of a physical place as customs area and for the approval/appointment of a custodian (in our case a DPO), under sections 8 and 45, respectively. The General Clauses Act of 1897 (section 16) stipulates that powers vested with an authority, for any appointment, include the power to suspend or dismiss the person so appointed. Hence, the Commissioner of Customs also has the authority to de-notify or take away a custodianship, in the case of non-compliance to the principles of natural justice (Customs Circular F No. 450, 2008). However to date there has not been a single example where such de-notification of dry ports has taken place.

13.4 DRY PORTS IN INDIA

The reliability, safety, time and cost of transportation, both on land and at sea, have morphed global trade and almost uniformly enhanced standards of living. Technological developments in ship design and construction, and the ensuing economies of scale of larger ships, have also promoted trade – particularly of developing countries – by making the transportation of goods over longer distances economically feasible. Economic distances have thus shrunk and this has expanded markets for raw materials and final products, facilitating the industrialization of many countries around the world. Often international ocean transportation and information and communications technologies (ICT) have been referred to as the two basic ingredients of globalization (Haralambides, 2007).

Dry ports have been playing an increasingly important role in the global trading system. Globalization, economic reforms, trade liberalization and the development of land infrastructure have abolished captive hinterlands, thus obliging dry ports to compete for custom. The consequent greater choice in the routing of cargo, and parallel advances in supply chain management techniques, have altered the nature of competition from one between ports and dry ports to one between supply chains. These are some of the reasons that make container security a most critical, relevant and timely issue in supply chain performance (Benacchio et al., 2000).

Usually located near or alongside gateway seaports, industrial areas and/or transportation axes, dry ports perform several important functions (Nozick and Turnquist, 2000; Woxenius et al., 2004). These include (1) cargo aggregation and unitization; (2) in-transit storage; (3) Customs clearance; (4) issuance of bills of lading; (5) relieving congestion at gateway seaports; (6) assistance in inventory management; and (7) deference of import duties payments for goods stored in bonded warehouses (Paul, 2005).

Efficiency in a narrow sense, therefore, would tend to penalize economic agents who, either by necessity or choice, have internalized such externalities, as society expects them to do these days. The approach we take here, as well as in our earlier and forthcoming research, is that the output of a productive agent is a multi-product one, including such intangibles as the benefits deriving from a clean, safe and secure environment. Societal priorities such as these, no matter how desirable they may be in modern societies, cost money and if not properly weighed within a dry port's comprehensive output could lead to lower efficiency assessments for dry ports of higher societal awareness. Some examples of such costs, and disruptions, from India could suffice to exemplify this point.

Through personal interviews of the authors with a number of senior Indian dry port stakeholders, it has become apparent that there is a certain lack of clarity on liability and responsibility issues regarding container security. Among others, this often necessitates the actual examination of all containers, something naturally rather impractical.

According to the manning guidelines of the Central Board of Excise & Customs, dry ports would normally operate with a staff of 10–12 officers. For dry ports having an annual throughput of 10,000 Twenty-foot Equivalent Units (TEUs) or more, it appears that such officers may be insufficiently equipped to undertake a thorough inspection of cargoes and containers, and are thus often obliged to outsource security-related activities. This is one of the reasons why explosive materials and live ammunition have escaped the eye of dry port officials at the Tughlakabad and Ludhiana dry ports, near New Delhi. Ironically, none of the Indian dry ports or for that matter most of the ports have explosives detection equipment or X-ray scanning facilities.

Indian dry ports are both in the public and private domains and permission for their construction is granted by the Ministry of Finance. In granting such permission, the government implicitly expects individual dry ports to develop their own security plans. However, no explicit stipulations are in place on liability and responsibility issues in cases of security breaches. Inspections are random and largely based on documents such as shipping bills and forwarding notes prepared by the shippers themselves. Furthermore, only a small percentage of randomly selected packages are actually opened for physical inspection and verification of actual contents. Due to time, manpower and equipment constraints, the reliability of such examinations is not satisfactory.

13.4.1   Classification of Dry Ports

There are several different kinds of dry ports. Broadly speaking, they could be classified by size, primary mode of connectivity to gateway sea ports and distance from the seaports. We understand that it would lead to erroneous inferences if different classes of dry ports are compared, hence in this chapter, for the sake of simplicity, we have selected 26 dry ports located in five different regions in India.

Essentially, there are three major types of dry ports: gateway terminals, rail terminals and distribution centres. A seaport terminal provides an interface between the maritime and inland systems of freight distribution whereas the rail terminals serve as linkages to gateway port terminals. They could be located very near the gateway ports or quite some distance away. The chief difference between the different types of dry ports is not the distance but the ability to clear sea port with or without Custom clearance.

Table 13.1   Regional location of specified dry ports

North		East		West		South		Central	
Public	Private	Public	Private	Public	Private	Public	Private	Public	Private
7	5	2	1	6	4	8	5	1	1

The DPO transports the container to the dry port without clearing Customs at the gateway ports, furnishing a bond for potential liabilities arising out of leakage of Customs revenues. The movement of containers by rail benefits the shipper by lower cost of transportation per ton-kilometre of cargo transported and also eliminates the delays caused by congestion of road transport. However, the train transportation requires a minimum volume of containers to make a train load, which could result in delays. On the other hand, road transportation accords flexibility but is cost-effective at shorter distances only. It also entails loss of scale benefits.

For the purpose of this study, we collected data by conducting personal interviews with several dry port stakeholders located in five different regions of India (Table 13.1). Half of the 40 dry ports are managed by private operators and the remaining dry ports are under public administration. Only 12 public sector dry ports enjoy a comparative advantage over their private counterparts in that they possess their own rail heads located on their own premises; six of the privately operated dry ports also enjoy this facility. The rest have to transport their containers by road to the nearest rail head, resulting in additional generalized costs.

13.5   LIABILITY OF DRY PORTS IN INDIA

The Inland Way Bill (IWB) is prima facie evidence of receipt of cargo by the DPO from the consignor who is the carrier (shipping line/freight forwarder) in apparent good order and condition, except as otherwise noted with respect to damage sustained by the cargo before arriving at the dry port. The IWB is issued by the DPO for the containers to be carried by it, and the carrier must give it back at the destination at the time of taking delivery. The IWB is issued subject to the conditions and liabilities as specified in the India Railways Act 1989 and, according to the terms stated in it, the consignor must accept responsibility for all particulars furnished in respect of cargo tendered by him for carriage to the gateway port. Furthermore, the IWB goes on to state that the consignor is deemed to have indemnified the dry port against any damage or loss suffered by it by reason of incorrect particulars provided by him in regard to the cargo. Thus, it is obvious that the DPO absolves himself of all liability for ensuring the correctness of the particulars of goods declared. This becomes pertinent if the goods cause any kind of third-party damage.

It can be surmised from the above that the Indian DPO treats the carrier (shipping lines' Non-Vessel Operating Common Carrier (NVOCC) or freight forwarder) as a consignor and enters into a contractual relationship with him to handle and transport containerized cargo to and from the gateway port. The DPO does not recognize the shipper of the goods with whom the carrier has its own contractual relationship. Thus, the shipper cannot move against the DPO for loss or damage to his goods that occurs in the custody of the DPO. Accordingly, the DPO does not automatically indemnify the carrier with regard to any liabilities and responsibilities the latter may have accepted vis-à-vis the shipper.

It is noteworthy that CONCOR's IWB mentions that 'This Inland Way Bill is issued subject to the conditions and liabilities as specified in the Railways Act 1989.' However, the Claims Procedure of CONCOR (n.d.) mentions that in no circumstance would the liability exceed Rs 50 per kg while goods are in custody of CONCOR. This is a contradiction as under the Railways Act 1989, the liability of the railway is not limited to Rs 50 per kg, but the value of goods (Railways Act, 1989, section 103).

In practice, the dry ports have distanced themselves from the railways' procedure. It has been contended before a high court that the Railway Claims Tribunal has no jurisdiction to adjudicate a dispute between a customer who has filed for claim and the DPO as the DPO is not 'Railways'. This view has been upheld by the Delhi High Court.

13.6 CONTAINER SECURITY FAILURE ANALYSIS

In order to understand container security and security failures we adopted a two-pronged strategy. The first was to conduct in-depth interviews with various stakeholders while the second was to collect information about instances where the cargo inside the container did not match with the cargo particulars declared in the manifest, with or without the seals found to be intact.

With the use of the Delphi technique, we constructed a questionnaire covering five dimensions and 25 service items, taking into account the opinions of the various stakeholders. We broadly divide dry port customers into three major groups, depending on the kind of services rendered to them. The questionnaire is further validated with the help of Exploratory Factor Analysis (EFA) and, following this, the service items are reduced to 24.

Table 13.2   Details of respondents

Categories of respondents	No. of respondents
Shipping lines/NVOCC operators	30
Surveyors	30
Consignees/clearing agents/freight forwarders	25
Dry port management personnel	25
Dry port employees	25
Customs officers	30
Dry port security personnel	35
Total	200

Subsequently, data was collected through personal interviews, with the use of structured questionnaires. The questionnaire was administered to 200 specifically selected addressees who patronize dry ports. Respondents were classified in the categories shown in Table 13.2.

During our research, we also collected data with regards to container security failures where the actual cargo stuffed in a container did not match the cargo particulars stated in the manifest. We categorized such failures into three classes, Type 1, II and III, explained in detail in the next section.

The 24 service items of the questionnaire shown below were anchored on a 7-point Likert scale (that is, 7 = strongly agree and 1 = strongly disagree). These service items reveal the differences between the expectations and perceptions of the respondents. The average dimension scores of expectations and perceptions are tabulated, with the difference between the two scores revealing the gaps. The total of the products of weights (allotted by respondents according to their own perceived significance) and the average dimension scores divided by five gives the weighted CONSEC score, shown in Table 13.3. The groupings of the service items, under their respective dimensions, are summarized below.

Equipment:

1. adequacy of the quantity of equipment
2. achievement of objectives/targets
3. appropriateness of maintenance programmes
4. regularity of equipment upgrades
5. functionality of IT and surveillance systems.

Table 13.3   CONSEC score of dry ports

Dry port	CONSEC score	Dry port	CONSEC score
1	−0.78	14	−0.09
2	−0.50	15	−0.39
3	−0.34	16	−0.77
4	−0.04	17	−0.57
5	−0.37	18	−0.32
6	−0.65	19	−0.12
7	−0.55	20	−0.39
8	−0.21	21	−0.81
9	−0.11	22	−0.61
10	−0.35	23	−0.33
11	−0.88	24	−0.14
12	−0.51	25	−0.42
13	−0.27	26	−0.91

Personnel:

1. adequacy of the number of personnel
2. competency of personnel to implement security programmes
3. clarity of organizational structure
4. appropriateness of salary levels paid to security personnel
5. qualifications of personnel employed are suitable for the job.

Policy and planning:

1. adequacy of security plans
2. necessity of approval by an independent authority
3. need for a mandatory appointment of a security officer
4. understanding of responsibilities and liabilities by employees
5. employee guidelines for rewards and punishment for security awareness.

Drills and training:

1. general accessibility of security plans
2. professionalism in personnel training on security matters
3. necessity of certification of training programmes
4. periodic reviews of security policies.

Security audit:

1. length of the audit period
2. security audits are carried out objectively by independent auditors
3. audit findings are accepted without prejudice
4. mandatory action is necessary for implementing security audit guidelines
5. adequacy of procedures for the appointment of auditors.

13.7 CLASSIFICATION OF RESEARCH FINDINGS

Our research reveals that the container security failures may be broadly classified under three types.

13.7.1 Type I

This risk signifies minor non-matching of containerized cargo and those declared in the manifest by quantity, quality and value. The reason for this risk could be human error/theft/pilferage either by accident or by design. This risk has economic implications only and as such is the sole responsibility of Customs authorities.

13.7.2 Type II

This risk signifies the entire container contents do not match with those declared in the manifest. This is obviously an attempt to defraud and may or may not have criminal third-party implications in addition to economic ones. As such, the DPO could assist Customs in detecting and minimizing the risk.

13.7.3 Type III

This risk involves undeclared dangerous goods of any kind being transported with a criminal content to cause third-party damage to property or person or both. Customs is the authority responsible for collecting revenues and does not bear or accept any responsibility for third-party damage nor is liable to pay compensation. As such, it would be reasonable to expect the DPO to exercise due diligence in minimizing this type of risk and should be held liable for third-party damage if found wanting in discharging his duty to exercise due diligence.

Table 13.4   Break-up of container security failures at dry ports in the period 2008–11

Dry port	Type I		Type II		Type III	
	Exports	Imports	Exports	Imports	Exports	Imports
1	45	32		2		
2	68	44				
3	17	19	7			
4	62	37				
5	33	28				
6	29	36	11	1		1
7	16	21				
8	19	19				
9	21	8		1		
10	37	22				
11	45	65				
12	63	154	4			1
13	114	81				1
14	89	67				
15	76	32				
16	39	21		5		
17	54	34				
18	88	54	2			
19	98	45				
20	65	32				
21	32	19				
22	39	22		6		
23	36	37				
24	42	54	8			
25	19	29				
26	37	19				

13.8   A BREAK-UP OF SECURITY FAILURES

Our research of container security failures at dry ports (as shown in Table 13.4) revealed that a majority of the failures were of Type 1 class. Furthermore, a larger proportion of the security failures occurred at North Indian public sector dry ports with regards to import containers. The obvious reason for such failures appeared to be the intention to evade Customs duty on the part of the consignee. However, a significant portion of such failures have also occurred with respect to export containers also for obvious intention of tax evasion on the part of the shipper. Customs have in respect of both types of failures held the shipper and the consignee responsible and have penalized them. However, it is important to note that in no single instance have they held the shipping line or DPOs responsible for such failures.

With regards to Type II and Type III classes of failures, Customs have conducted investigations and again held the consignee/shipper responsible while absolving both the shipping line and the DPO. In several of such cases, the decisions of Customs have been judicially challenged and are *sub judice*.

13.9 MINIMIZATION OF CONTAINER SECURITY FAILURES

As discussed above, the DPO could play a major role in minimizing Type III risk and could at best play a supporting role in minimizing the other two types of risks. Considering the fact that the gateway sea ports along with Customs also play a big part in minimizing container security risks, it would be beneficial to analyse risk by studying the container movement flows between the dry port and sea ports.

It is imperative to use one or more types of non-intrusive scanners that are available commercially at both the dry ports as well as the sea ports. The DPO should manage and operate the scanners as he is responsible not only for stuffing/de-stuffing of containers at the dry port but also inland transportation between the dry port and seaport. At present, the DPO accepts responsibility for loss of revenue vis-à-vis Customs but refuses to do so for third-party damage as he is not legally liable to do so.

13.9.1 Cost of Minimizing Security Risks

The capital and revenue costs of installing and operating non-intrusive scanners are quite small (US$2 million). The cost could be further minimized if it is spread over a long time period as well as the annual throughput. However, it is not being done for the simple reason that the current legal regime does not give the DPO any responsibility for nor does the DPO wish to accept any liability for container security failures. It should be noted that the cost of security failure in terms of human life and property could be massive. At the same time, it is also imperative to reiterate that the cost of minimizing such a huge risk is insignificant if due processes/procedures are adopted by the DPO.

13.9.2 Automatic Targeting System

It is fairly obvious that in the interest of competitive advantage and efficiency it is neither pragmatic nor feasible to inspect each and every container. On the other hand, the risks of container security failure are too big to ignore. In such circumstances, it is imperative to arrive at equilibrium. The solution to this conundrum is to develop a targeting system (ATS) that will automatically identify the high-risk container, which could then be segregated from the rest and the risk neutralized. The flowchart in Figure 13.1 explains how the ATS could work.

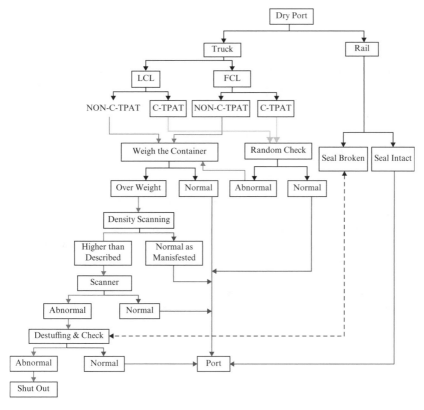

Notes: FCL = Full Container Load; LCL = Less than Container Load.

Figure 13.1 Flowchart for risk minimization

13.9.3 Usage of Radio Frequency Identity Device Technology

It has been noted that there have been numerous instances of cargo pilferages/shortages in spite of the One Time Lock (OTL) or bottle seals found intact. This is because the integrity of the container can easily be breached through its sides, bottom or roof. This problem can be solved by use of a Radio Frequency Identity Device (RFID), which records all activity taking place inside a container.

13.9.4 Customs-Trade Partnership Programme

Barring a few notable exceptions of international logistics service providers such as Maersk, the majority of the dry ports do not participate in the CT-PAT programme initiated by the US CBP. This is despite the obvious benefits for participants in terms of transit time and convenience, especially when one is exporting to the USA. The reason for such apathy appears to be ignorance on the part of the DPOs and lack of encouragement on the part of the government.

13.10   CONCLUSION

The majority of the container security failures detected at the dry ports could be classified as Type I failures and have economic/commercial implications only. The neutralization of such security failures is solely within the purview of Customs. Perhaps not surprisingly, a larger proportion of the failures have occurred at the public sector dry ports situated in the northern region of the country, which are situated farther away from the gateway sea ports.

The Government of India is yet to prescribe the required minimum security standards for a DPO. Lack of a visible and certified security system in India is resulting in increased instances of security failures at the dry ports. This may also result in higher risk premiums paid to insurance companies; especially so if a dry port is allowed to absolve itself of almost entire liability (including third party) for ensuring the correctness of the cargo particulars declared by the consignor. Such lacunae could be rectified as and when the Government of India ratifies the Rotterdam Rules applied in Europe and gives the DPO the responsibilities and liabilities of a 'performing party'.

The provisions and requirements of the European Union Authorized Economic Operator (AEO) regulations are stricter than the ones of the ISPS regime. Some dry ports in Europe have been 'encouraged' to voluntarily comply with the ISPS regulations and have been granted AEO status. This also enhances the competitive advantage of the dry ports. The Government of India too should adopt such practices. Installation of non-intrusive scanners, RFID and ATS systems, both at the sea ports and the dry ports, would go a long way to enhance container security without a commensurate increase in associated costs. However, building up a security conscious culture is the paramount need of the day.

REFERENCES

Benacchio, M., H.E. Haralambides and E. Musso (2000), 'On the economic impact of ports: national vs. local costs and benefits', NAV 2000: International Conference on Ship and Shipping Research, Venice, September.

Claims Procedure of CONCOR (n.d.), http://www.concorindia.com (accessed March 2012).

Customs Act of India (1962), http:// www.customsindiaonline.com (accessed February 2012).

CBP (US Customs and Border Patrol) (2012), http://www.cbp.gov/ (accessed April 2012).

Customs Circular (2008), F. No. 450/105/2008-Cus.IV, 25 July.

Customs Circular (2012), No. 2011/37, 23 August.

Dryport (2009), Workshop on ICT and Security, Emmen Dryport, European Comission.

General Clauses Act (1897), http://lawcommissionofindia.nic.in/51-100/Report60. pdf (accessed January 2012).

Haralambides, H.E. (2007), 'Structure and operations in the liner shipping industry', in K.J. Button and D.A. Hensher (eds), *Handbook of Transport Modelling*, Amsterdam, Pergamon-Elsevier Science.

Juhel, M. (2011), 'Supply chain security', Presentation, World Bank.

Levinson, M. (2006), *The Box: How the Shipping Container Made the World Smaller and the World Economy Bigger*, Princeton, NJ: Princeton University Press.

Monios, J. (2011), 'The role of inland terminal development in the hinterland access strategies', *Research in Transportation Economics*, 59–66.

Nozick, L. and M. Turnquist (2000), 'A two-echelon inventory allocation and distribution centre location analysis', *Transportation Research Part E: Logistics and Transportation Review*, **37** (6), 425–41.

Paul, J. (2005), 'India and the global container ports', *Maritime Economics and Logistics*, **7** (2), 189–92.

RMG (Rotterdam Maritime Group) (2004), *Study on Maritime Security Financing*, Rotterdam: DG Tren.

Stopford, M. (2000), 'Defining the future of shipping markets', Presentation on global shipping trends. ITIC Forum.

Woxenius, J., V. Roso and K. Lumsden (2004), 'The dry port concept – connecting seaports with their hinterland by rail', in *Proceedings of the First International Conference on Logistics Strategy for Ports*, Dalian, China, 22–26 September.

14. Security in the Straits of Malacca in recent years

Nazery Khalid

There has not been much news about the security situation in the Straits of Malacca in recent years. Underscoring this is the sharp decline of piracy cases in the Straits from the 38 attacks in 2004 as reported by the International Maritime Bureau (IMB). In 2006, 2007 and 2008, there were six, four and two cases, respectively, and there have been no piracy cases for three consecutive years from 2009 (New Strait Times, 2012).

The decline in piracy cases in the Straits can be largely attributed to efforts of the littoral states to enhance security in the Straits such as the MALSINDO-coordinated patrol by the navies of the littoral states, the Eye in the Sky air patrol, the formation of the Malaysian Maritime Enforcement Agency (MMEA) and increased unilateral and bilateral patrols by the enforcement agencies. There has also been no recorded attempted, much less actual, terrorist attack in the Straits thanks to the efforts taken by the littoral states to protect the Straits from this particularly dangerous threat.

Despite this, it is important to discuss two major developments that pose a real threat to lives and assets in this busy shipping lane. In recent years piracy and terrorism warrant close attention by the stakeholders of the Straits to ensure safety from these menacing threats.

14.1 A 'WAR-RISK ZONE'?

The declaration of the Straits of Malacca as a 'war risk area' by the Joint War Committee (JWC) of Lloyd's Market Association (LMA)[1] in 2005 spurred the littoral states into action. Due to the measures they took as mentioned earlier, the number of piracy cases in the Straits declined sharply from the highs of 2005.

The declaration was made after the JWC issued a list on 20 June 2005 detailing procedures for amending the war risk areas used on marine hull war risk contracts. The list was a sweeping overhaul of its listed war-risk areas, provided new guidelines to underwriters listing a total of 21 areas worldwide in jeopardy of 'war, strike, terrorism and related perils'. The areas specified included the Straits of Malacca and adjacent ports in Indonesia. Other countries on the list include Iraq, Somalia and Lebanon.

The decision by the LMA to add the Straits to its list of high-risk areas was taken following recommendations by a private defence consultant, Aegis Defence Services, which carried out risk assessments on the Straits and suggested that it was a potential site for a terrorist attack. It was anybody's guess how they arrived at this conclusion but there was a tendency at the time to find a nexus between piracy and terrorism, which has since shown to be incorrect and debunked by many analysts.

The governments of Malaysia, Singapore and Indonesia were vocal in calling on the JWC to review its position on the Straits of Malacca. In an August 2005 joint statement, the foreign ministers of the littoral states urged the JWC to 'review its risk assessment accordingly'. The ministers expressed their regret that the decision was taken without their consultation and failed to take into account their existing efforts to deal with the threats to safety and security in the Straits.

The Federation of ASEAN Shipowners' Association declared that the decision was 'misguided'. Similar strong protestations have been registered by shipping industry associations in the region against the assessment.

Despite strong protestation by the littoral states over the declaration, the LMA stoutly defended its classification of the Straits of Malacca as a war-risk zone, citing that its decision was made based on a rational and reasoned analysis by professional intelligence specialists (Aegis). During a private briefing given by the JWC and Aegis at the International Chamber of Shipping in London in August 2005, the committee affirmed that the Straits would remain on the list 'until it was clear that the measures planned by government and other agencies in the area had been implemented and were effective'.

The JWC declaration resulted in higher insurance costs for ships transiting the Straits. An increasing number of insurers started to charge additional war-risk premiums for vessels using the Straits of Malacca. The Lloyd's of London underwriting market quoted additional premiums at that time, calculated as a percentage of the value of a ship's hull and machinery, of 0.05 per cent for base war-risk cover and 0.01 per cent for each transit of the Straits. This translated into around US$12,500 for the base war-risk premium for a small 1100 Twenty-foot Equivalent Unit (TEU) container feeder vessel and US$2500 for each passage through the Straits. In the case of a very large crude carrier (VLCC) or 'supertanker', this would rise to about US$63,000 for the base premium and US$12,600 for each transit.

After the JWC declaration, several top non-life insurers in Japan such as Tokio Marine Insurance and Mitsui Sumitomo Insurance levied additional premiums for Japanese-insured ships transiting the Straits. With the declaration, terrorism had been added to the definition of war-risk insurance in a scenario where a vessel is damaged from what appears to be a pirate attack. It would now be possible for an underwriter to refuse to entertain the claim as it could interpret it to be a terrorist act.

The risk of normal accidents at sea is already covered in the hull and machinery insurance, which mainly encompasses coverage of such tangible assets. The risks are placed directly by underwriters in the insurance market. It is up to shipping lines and shippers to take extra coverage for terrorism-related risks.

It is interesting to note that underwriters based in the littoral states do not impose additional premiums on vessels plying the Straits but regional insurers such as in Japan are more keen to do so. This could be based on differing perceptions of the security risk in the Straits.

Stung by the declaration of the Straits as a 'war-risk zone', the littoral states quickly took measures to enhance security in the Straits. Increased patrols by maritime security agencies resulted in a sharp decline of piracy cases following the declaration. This led to the JWC removing the 'war-risk' rating for merchant ships transiting the Straits based on its assessment that there had been an improvement in security in the sea lane. Following this, however, ships calling at ports in northeast Sumatra were still subject to war-risk charges. This decision seems to have taken into account three back-to-back incidents of piracy attacks in July 2006 in the waters off northern Sumatra. In actual fact, these and another incidents in January 2006 at Dumai Port involving a chemical tanker should have been viewed as a mere act of crime on an anchored vessel, not an act of piracy occurring at high sea. Arguably, the fact that such incidents were too quickly labelled as 'pirate attacks' contributed to the high number of cases reported during that period.

The littoral states are steadfast in their commitment to maintaining security in the Straits, as evidenced by the many initiatives undertaken at the national, bilateral and multilateral levels. The drop in piracy cases in recent years is testimony to their commitment and efforts to provide security to shipping in this important sea lane.

14.2 SECURITY ALARM IN THE STRAITS IN 2010

It is a measure of the initiatives by the littoral states and their vigilance in providing security in the Straits of Malacca that no single terrorist attack has been recorded here thus far. However, there is room for complacency when it comes to safeguarding the Straits from the threats it faces.

This is especially so when it comes to the threat of terror, especially post-9/11. While it is a matter of debate if South East Asia is the 'second front' in the so-called 'global war against terror', as declared by former US President George W. Bush in 2003, the possibility of a terror attack in the region and particularly in the Straits can never be dismissed.

The importance of being vigilant against the threat of terror was underscored in 2010 with the raising of the security alarm in the Straits from an unspecified threat but was believed by many analysts to be a potential threat of terrorist attack. After enjoying a period of 'no news is good news' after the revocation of the 'war-risk tag' by the LMA, the issuance of a security alert in the Straits of Malacca in March 2010 put the strategic waterway back in the international spotlight.

A report by French international news agency AFP emerged in March 2010 cautioning that an 'unidentified terrorist group' was planning to 'mount attacks against oil tankers in the Straits', quoting the Singapore Navy (Teh, 2010). The Singapore Shipping Association (SSA) then announced that it received an advisory from the Singapore Navy Information Fusion Centre about 'an indication that a terrorist group is planning attacks on oil tankers in the Malacca Straits' (Teh, 2010).

According to the Singapore Navy, the indication did not preclude 'possible attacks on other large vessels with dangerous cargo' (CBS News, 2010). It warned that the 'terrorists' may probably intend to achieve widespread publicity and to demonstrate that theirs was a 'viable group' (CBS News, 2010). In a chilling reminder of the boldness of the terrorists in carrying out attacks on maritime targets, the Singapore Navy told shipping operators that the militants could use small vessels including 'dinghies, sampans and speedboats' to mount attacks on oil tankers and urged them to be cautious towards such a possibility (CNN, 2010).

Subsequently, the IMB piracy reporting centre in Kuala Lumpur was alerted to a security threat and passed on the alert to the relevant regional authorities in Malaysia, Singapore and Indonesia (The Straits Times, 2010a). The Singapore Navy then issued a warning that oil tankers transiting the Straits could be targeted and asked shipowners to increase vigilance while transiting the sea lane.[2]

In response to the raising of the alarm, Malaysia, Indonesia and Singapore increased patrols in the Straits. The Royal Malaysian Navy said it was 'prepared to handle this threat' (Kennedy, 2010), while the MMEA, Malaysia's coast guards, increased patrols in the waterway (Reuters Online, 2010a). Indonesia's Defense Minister also announced that his country's maritime security agencies had stepped up patrols in the sea lane in reaction to the warning (Bernama Online, 2010).

A week after the alert was issued, Indonesia made an announcement that Aceh police had shot dead one suspect and arrested four more men in two raids in the previously restive region where a bloody insurgency had been carried out by Gerakan Aceh Merdeka (Arnaz and Hasan, 2010). This was followed by another announcement in April 2010 of the arrest of six militants in Medan, Sumatra while undergoing militant training at a camp (The Straits Times, 2010b). This prompted several security analysts to link the security alert in the Straits with the raids, but there was no confirmation forthcoming from any side of the connection between them.

Some rather confusing media reporting ensued as attempts were made to trace the origin and nature of the threat. A Singapore-based Thai naval attaché was quoted as saying that the original warning could be traced to Japan, which informed the IMB that vessels traversing the Straits could be targeted. This suggested the involvement of pirates who were active in the Straits and had in the past hijacked oil tankers (Bernama Online, 2010). The IMB, in turn, said it had received information from a 'foreign government agency' of a possible 'terror threat' (Reuters Online, 2010b).

The situation understandably caused anxiety to the littoral states and international community. Singapore was especially concerned; being one of the world's key maritime, trade and financial hubs, it was a target for attacks by militant groups based on the revelation by Singaporean security agencies of several plots to attack selected targets in the city state. One of the plots thwarted by the authorities was an attempt by militants to hijack an airliner in Bangkok in 2001 and crash it into Singapore's Changi Airport, not long after the 9/11 attacks in the USA. Singapore also arrested several militants believed to be affiliated to Jemaah Islamiyah who were allegedly planning to bomb the US Embassy in Singapore and other targets in the island nation.[3]

Several analysts called on stakeholders of the Straits to take seriously the information provided by the Singapore Navy. John Harrison, a maritime security expert at the S. Rajaratnam School of International Studies in Singapore, said that on the threat level scale, an 'indication' is lower than a 'warning' but nonetheless requires precautions to be taken. According to him, a 'warning' refers to a credible threat that an attack is likely to be carried out against a target over a specific timeframe, while an 'indication' is used to describe a threat arising from information gathered from a series of suspicious activities in a certain area (CNN, 2010).

Thankfully, nothing untoward happened during and after the security alert was raised. In all likelihood, actions must have been taken by security enforcement agencies behind the scene to thwart the threat. There was no announcement of how this was done, presumably due to the sensitive nature of the security threat.

There are several lessons that can be drawn from the episode. To attain a level of optimal alert and readiness to respond to security threats in the Straits requires significant investment in resources and capacity building. The funds needed to procure security systems, equipment and services, and to equip personnel with the necessary skills to use them effectively can be prohibitive. For shipping lines, any extra costs incurred in the name of increasing security would be treated with disdain even in the best of times. Particularly at a time when shipping companies and many others along the maritime supply chain are reeling from the global recession and credit crunch. Boosting security means additional costs, more stringent checks, frequent delays and reduced efficiency along the maritime supply chain. However, in the midst of looming security threats from terrorists, stakeholders along the chain must be extra vigilant and extremely cautious. The price of ignoring security alerts in a key trade lane and strategic waterway like the Straits of Malacca could be very high for businesses, coastal communities, security agencies, littoral states and ultimately global trade and security.

14.3   SEPARATING PIRACY FROM TERRORISM

Post 9/11, the maritime industry has found itself in the spotlight of great concern as authorities initiate moves to shore up defences against the menace of terrorist onslaught. Much of their focus has been trained on merchant ships, deemed to be among the components of the maritime supply chain that are most vulnerable to terrorism. Attacks on ocean-going vessels can result in huge financial losses, casualties and environmental damage. Not to mention crippling maritime trade waterways and delivering a severe psychological blow to a world already edgy after 9/11.

The fact remains that there has not been a single terrorist attack, or even an attempted assault, on vessels traversing the Straits. Yet, the doomsayers are almost wishing for one to happen, perhaps to eventually vindicate their skewed belief that the littoral states are not capable of maintaining security in the waterway. Already saddled with the threat of piracy, a threat that has existed for centuries along the Straits, fears over potential acts of terror have added an extra burden to the littoral states in maintaining security in the waterway.

It is crucial at this juncture to separate piracy from terrorism. Pirates commit their deeds for monetary and commercial reasons, while terrorists want to score political points and make ideological statements more than make commercial gains. Although many pseudo-analysts have made a dubious name for themselves in the media for speaking about the perceived link between piracy and terrorism, they are distinctly separate from one another as defined by international law. Thus far, a definitive link between the two has yet to be established, although security analysts have warned of the possibility of terrorists 'subcontracting' their dirty deeds to pirates. But since this anxiety is based on mere opinions inclined towards worst-case scenarios, the discussion on the possible threat to vessels in the Straits of Malacca should be focused more on the issue of piracy, which can be substantiated by available and reliable statistics, instead of terrorism, which has yet to occur in the waterway.

One good thing coming out of the Straits being viewed as a war-risk zone is an increasingly widespread appreciation that the threats of piracy and terror know no boundary. Virtually every nation now realizes that such threats must be fought off resolutely, sometimes ruthlessly, on all fronts. It is comforting to note that security planners and enforcers and the maritime industry have become appreciative of this reality and taken many efforts to mitigate the risks of such threats. Governments, enforcement agencies and industry players have also pulled their individual and collective weights to improve maritime security in the Straits.

While piracy has proved to be a bigger and more common threat in the Straits than terrorism thus far, many measures have been taken to neutralize the scourge of terror in the area. These involve the introduction of counter-terrorism laws, frequent patrolling of the seas, tighter border controls and aggressive sanctioning of activities that may lead to terrorism activities. All these, taken unilaterally by the littoral governments or in cooperation with one another and with other states, are laudable steps in the right direction in fighting the threat of terror.

The maritime community has no doubt benefited tremendously from the many initiatives, on top of its own efforts, to beef up security. The revocation of the JWC listing is testimony to the effectiveness of the measures implemented and their diligent efforts, especially since 9/11, to create a better security environment in the maritime sector.

The responsibility of ensuring the security of ships in the Straits should not only be confined to governments, as the ultimate custodians of the waterway. A systemic and holistic view should be taken to ensure that safety of ships is ensured from the point of departure to the point of arrival. There must be coordination amongst all the entities in the entire maritime supply chain – shippers, shipping companies, ports, insurers, freight forwarders, security enforcement and intelligence agencies, among others – to create a security-conscious culture in the maritime industry.

Given the changed maritime security matrix post-9/11 and the emerging unconventional threats of terrorism, it is crucial that such a culture be nurtured and the need to maintain security constantly stressed in the maritime industry. A safety ethos that focuses on security management systems and practices, and a proactive, anticipative approach towards security can complement the work of enforcement and intelligence agencies and buttress the security shield they provide.

A sense of perspective should be exercized to frame the discourse of security in the Straits of Malacca in a realistic context. Merchant shipping, by nature of their operations, features and load, can be inviting to potential evil-doers. But a few isolated incidents in a few known hotspots should not taint the threat perception of security in the Straits.

The gravity of incidents involving ships in the Straits should be seen in the context of their low frequency and be assessed in proportion to the traffic volume it hosts. Just as we have not stopped flying or taking the train despite the persistent terror threat faced by these transport modes, we should not allow the perception of shipping in the Straits as being risky to hold sway based on a few recorded incidents of piracy, or worse, based on questionable terror threat perception. That said, everyone involved in the maritime sector must retain vigilance to ensure safety and security of passage while traversing the Straits.

In the final analysis, it is important that a comprehensive and multidimensional approach is taken to combat the scourge of piracy and terrorism, and to understand the dynamics and complexities of both issues. This would help effective pre-emptive and reactive measures to address their root causes and to ensure security in the Straits.

The transnational, fluid nature of piracy and terrorism demands a comprehensive and sustained multinational effort in countering their threats. This is especially so in a strategically sensitive waterway like the Straits that can easily be tainted by bad public relations and the distorted perception of the influential few.

NOTES

1. LMA is an insurance trade association based in London acting for its members in the Lloyd's underwriting market. Lloyd's is the world's leading insurance market providing specialist insurance services. LMA acts as an advisory body to marine insurers based in London. JWC represents the interests of the London marine insurance community and comprises members of the LMA and the International Underwriting Association (IUA).
2. The Singapore Shipowners' Association (SSA) was quoted as saying that the Singapore Navy in its advisory recommended shipowners to 'strengthen their onboard security measures and to adopt community reporting to increase awareness and strengthen the safety of all seafarers'. See 'Malacca Strait – possible security threat', *International*

Chamber of Shipping Circular MC, **10** (32), 4 March 2010, available at http:// (accessed 29 April 2010).
3. For succinct discussions on this, see Tan (2002) and Acharya (2004).

REFERENCES

Acharya, A. (2004), 'Defending Singapore's vital infrastructures against terrorism', *ISDS Commentaries*, **37**, 2 September.

Arnaz, F. and M. Hasan (2010), 'Two more suspected terrorists killed in Aceh as hunt for militants goes on', *The Jakarta Globe*, 12 March, available at http://www.thejakartaglobe.com/home/two-more-suspected-terrorists-killed-in-aceh-as-hunt-for-militants-goes-on/363624 (accessed 30 April 2010).

Bernama Online (2010), 'Singapore raises security alert after Malacca threat', 6 February, available at http://web10.bernama.com/apmm/news.php?id=926434&lang=.

CBS News (2010), 'Singapore Navy: oil route a terror target', 4 March, available at http://www.cbsnews.com/stories/2010/03/04/world/main6265613.shtml (accessed 27 April 2010).

CNN (2010), 'Terror threat in Malacca, Singapore Straits', 4 March, available at http://edition.cnn.com/2010/WORLD/asiapcf/03/04/singapore.malacca.terror.threat/index.html (accessed 27 April 2010).

Kennedy, A. (2010), 'Tankers warned of terror threat in Malacca Strait'. *The Daily Caller*, 4 March, available at http://dailycaller.com/2010/03/04/singapore-warns-of-terror-threat-in-malacca-strait/ (accessed 28 April 2010).

New Straits Times (2012), 'Number of piracy cases down', 7 November, available at http://www.nst.com.my/nation/general/number-of-piracy-cases-in-malacca-straits-down-167670#ixzz2U71CmL00 (accessed 22 May 2013).

Reuters Online (2010a), 'Malaysia boosts Malacca Strait security over threat', 4 March, available at http://www.alertnet.org/thenews/newsdesk/SGE6230DW.htm (accessed 28 April 2010).

Reuters Online (2010b), 'Security raised in Malacca Strait after terror warning', 4 March, available at http://www.reuters.com/article/idUSTRE62335120100304 (accessed 30 April 2010).

Tan, W. (2002), 'Terrorism in Singapore: threats and implications', *Contemporary Security Policy*, **23** (3), December, 1–18.

Teh, E.H. (2010), 'Terror threat in Malacca, Singapore Straits (update)', *The Star Online*, 4 March, available at http://thestar.com.my/news/story.asp?file=/2010/3/4/nation/20100304181347&sec=nation accessed 29 April 2010.

The Straits Times (2010a), 'Straits terror attack alert', 4 March, available at http://www.straitstimes.com/BreakingNews/SEAsia/Story/STIStory_497928.html (accessed 29 April 2010).

The Straits Times (2010b), '6 terror suspects nabbed',13 April, available at http://www.straitstimes.com/BreakingNews/SEAsia/Story/STIStory_513911.html (accessed 30 April 2010).

15. Maritime security regulations and policies in Hong Kong: a critical review and the development of a risk-based security assessment model

Adolf K.Y. Ng and Zaili Yang

15.1 INTRODUCTION

The 9/11 terrorist attacks exposed the brittleness of the international transportation system, including shipping and ports. A terrorist event involving the system could lead to unprecedented disruption of global trade (Flynn, 2006) that would not only lead to human casualties but also significant economic impacts like the breakdown of supply chains and potentially global economic recessions (Greenberg et al., 2006). Being nodal points, security of ports is pivotal to ensure the smoothness and efficiency of an increasingly complex logistical supply chain (Robinson, 2002; Ng, 2007). It covers all security- and counter-terrorist-related activities, including the protection of critical infrastructures, as well as the protection and coordination of security activities when ships and ports interact.

Although many studies on maritime security have been conducted (for example, Hesse, 2003; OECD, 2003; Roach, 2003; Bichou, 2004; Kumar and Vellenga, 2004; King, 2005; Greenberg et al., 2006; Zhu, 2006; Bichou et al., 2007; Yang et al., 2013), a comprehensive review of how international guidelines, notably the International Convention for the Safety of Life at Sea (SOLAS, chapter XI-2) and the International Ship and Port Facility Security (ISPS) code promulgated by the International Maritime Organization (IMO, 2002a, 2002b), could be applied to enhance maritime security, notably the problems and possible solutions, was found wanting. Understanding such deficiency, using Hong Kong as the case study, the chapter analyses how international regulations and guidelines on maritime security, as laid down in the aforementioned IMO documents, were implemented in ports. Being one of the world's leading container ports,

Hong Kong serves as an excellent case to illustrate how countries, regions and their respective ports developed security capacity and capability when such requirements were still developing at an embryonic stage. Much of the analysis in the chapter is based on documental reviews, including the minutes of various official security-related meetings, and information obtained conducting informal discussions with relevant personnel from the Hong Kong Marine Department (HKMD), public agencies and designated facility operators on the past, current and future development of maritime security in Hong Kong port.[1] We believe that the chapter will offer substantial constructive insight to public agents and other maritime stakeholders in sustaining the security of the port in a cost-effective manner.

The chapter is structured as follows. Section 15.2 describes the port security regulations and policies in Hong Kong port, while Section 15.3 discusses the major strengths and weaknesses of the current system. Based on the identified shortcoming, a quantitative, security risk-based assessment model is introduced in Section 15.4. Finally, the conclusion, including the contribution of this study, is in Section 15.5.

15.2 MARITIME REGULATIONS AND POLICIES IN HONG KONG PORT

15.2.1 Administrative Framework

The HKMD[2] is the designated authority responsible for all port security affairs in Hong Kong. Since 2004, the major legal framework in tackling port security issues in Hong Kong is

> An Ordinance to implement the December 2002 amendments to the International Convention for the Safety of Life at Sea (SOLAS), 1974 and the International Ship and Port Facility Security (ISPS) Code and related provisions in the Convention to enhance security of ships and port facilities, and to provide for incidental or related matters, or usually known as Merchant Shipping (Security of Ships and Port Facilities) Ordinance. (CAP582, Ordinance No. 13 of 2004, hereinafter called the 'Ordinance')

In Section 6 of the Ordinance, security is complemented by empowering rules, known as the Merchant Shipping (Security of Ships and Port Facilities) Rules (CAP582A, hereinafter called the 'Rules').

To fulfil the objective of port security, the Ordinance and Rules largely made reference to IMO documents.[3] For instance, the Rules clearly required designated port facilities to comply with Chapter XI-2 of the

SOLAS Convention (see Section 23 of the Convention). Simultaneously, issues related to port security, as laid down in the ISPS code (Part A), were cited four times (Sections 24, 25, 28 and 29).[4] Nevertheless, the major diversification was in that they explained in more detail how the international guidelines, as indicated in the stated IMO documents, should be practised within the port, such as penalties for failure of compliance, power and responsibilities of the designated authority, that is, the HKMD and its Director, as well as the process of appeal against any decisions of the designated authority. The Director of the HKMD was empowered to specify how the stated international regulations and guidelines should be implemented at any designated port facility, including the granting of exemptions from the Ordinance. He or she was also empowered to designate any relevant organizations and personnel (with appropriate expertise knowledge) as having security-related responsibilities.

15.2.2   Implementation

The security level system in Hong Kong port largely referred to the ISPS code: L1, L2 and L3. The port security level, supported by intelligence provided by the Hong Kong Police Force, was frequently updated and accessible from HKMD's website (HKMD, 2012) 24 hours a day, seven days a week.[5] In general, the HKMD was expected to closely follow the mandatory requirements laid down by IMO documents in governing any vessels staying or intending to enter Hong Kong via Port State Control. In accordance with the Rules, all related sections (like sections 11 and 12 of CAP582A) had cited the contents of SOLAS chapter XI-2, but with additional (optional) requirements nearly completely overlooked. In terms of personnel, all the port facility security officers (PFSOs) must receive full training and certification from a port security programme accredited by the designated authority (HKMD, 2007a). In most cases, these programmes were offered by recognized security organizations. For an organization to be recognized (and thus qualified) to offer such programmes, they must strictly comply with the conditions laid down by IMO's Maritime Safety Committee (MSC) Circular No. 1188 (IMO, 2006) and HKMD's document, entitled *Guidelines for Approving Port Facility Security Officer Training Course* (HKMD, 2007b; PASAC, 2007).[6]

Audits on Port Facility Security Plans (PFSPs) took place via regular, notified, in advance site visits to the designated facilities. In most cases, the schedule and management of audit would be led by a relevant personnel appointed by the HKMD, and included officers from different public agencies (notably the Hong Kong Police Force, Customs & Excise and Immigration Departments) depending on the nature of the facility concerned. Generally speaking, the auditing team would focus on whether the facility had complied with the security requirements on documentation, cargo and passenger-handling, ship–port interface, access and control of restricted area, general awareness of facility employees and security infrastructure. The auditing team would then prepare a confidential report to the designated authority about the findings, suggestions and required actions from the facility operator concerned. However, one should note that neither the HKMD nor the government of the Hong Kong Special Administrative Region (HKSAR) of the People's Republic of China (hereinafter called the 'HKSAR government') possessed budgets of any significance dedicated to port security (and related affairs). Indeed, according to the minutes of the second meeting of the Port Area Security Advisory Committee (PASAC), all the designated facility operators were required to bear all the financial costs in undertaking Port Facility Security Assessments (PFSAs), preparing PFSPs[7] as well as implementing them (PASAC, 2003b). The lack of financial obligation by the HKMD and the HKSAR government was closely associated with the laissez-faire approach that characterized Hong Kong's traditional economic policy. Nevertheless, occasional drills were undertaken by designated facility operators in cooperation with the designated authority and other public agencies, such as the joint exercise in October 2008 at the Hong Kong International Terminals' (HIT) Terminal 9 (North), with HIT (the facility operator), HKMD, the Hong Kong Police Force, Customs & Excise and Immigration Departments being involved (PASAC, 2009).

15.2.3 Advisories and Industrial Inputs

Under the designated authority, the port was supported by an advisory committee dedicated to security affairs, the PASAC, chaired by the deputy director of the HKMD. The major function and objective of the committee was to advise the designated authority and the HKSAR government on all the affairs (including ship–port interface) related to the imposition of the IMO documents and guidelines to Hong Kong port, as well as providing feedback from industrial stakeholders (PASAC, 2003a, 2004). PASAC consisted of the chairman, representatives from HKMD, public agencies with direct interests in port security (like the Hong Kong Police Force) and other (non-governmental) designated port facilities. At the same time, a working group was established to implement the required duties in Hong Kong port called the Port Facility Security Working Group (PFSWG). Chaired by HKMD, PFSWG included representatives from the Hong Kong Police Force, Customs & Excise and the Immigration Departments. PFSWG was also the main organization to assess the quality and competency of PFSAs, and the subsequent PFSPs, undertaken and prepared by designated facility operators, respectively, forwarding them to the HKMD for its final endorsement. Within this system, any upcoming affairs would first be discussed within PFSWG, usually focusing on their potential impacts and practicality in Hong Kong port. If further works were needed, it would recommend the issue to the forthcoming PASAC meeting for further discussions. Based on anecdotal information, any new issues, including all amendments to current regulations and practices, must first be discussed and agreed within PASAC before forwarding to HKMD for consideration.

15.3   STRENGTHS AND WEAKNESSES: A CRITICAL ASSESSMENT

There were few doubts that Hong Kong had, in general, largely complied with the international regulations and guidelines, as laid down mainly by the IMO documents. All the core elements of the international mandatory requirements had been cited, while considerable information related to security was readily available to industrial stakeholders and the public. Despite the lack of financial backing from the public sector, a reasonably well-supported administrative structure in facilitating the international guidelines and requirements in Hong Kong seemed to be in place.

The current system was not without its shortcomings though. A major problem was that innovation in the implementation process was limited. The legal documents were made as simple as possible, and just endorsing the necessity of complying with the international guidelines and regulations, as reflected by the Ordinances and Rules. Additional commitments (and thus measures) were often deemed unnecessary, and this was not helped by the city's local circumstances that, in practice, often distanced itself from active innovation. Except in extraordinary circumstances the designated authority was not empowered to close down (or suspend operation of) any designated facilities. Instead, they were mainly empowered through the provision of directions to non-complying facilities to rectify deficiencies. Even under extraordinary circumstances (like L3), the designated authority withdrew security certification from the facilities and reported them to the IMO (PASAC, 2006). Despite the existence of occasional initiatives, like hosting a pilot programme to develop a new technological process in the scanning of containers, the International Container Inspection System (ICIS) (Mitchell, 2008), under the aforementioned policy and regulatory system, there were still questions whether Hong Kong port would be able to provide quick reactions in tackling the challenges posed by the occurrence of extraordinary security-related incidents where immediate, but appropriate, actions were critical. As such 'extraordinary' incidents have yet to exist, and the port generally considered to be of 'low risk' by government officials and industrial stakeholders with few chances to be targeted by terrorists (PASAC, 2003b), it was not surprising that the so-called 'extraordinary security incidents' was rather ambiguous and mainly determined on ad hoc basis. In other words, the efficiency of the whole system was reliant on the extent of the 'professionalism' of the relevant personnel, where the acid test had yet to be seriously undertaken. The chairman of one of the PASAC meetings warned that, as in time gone by, port security had been such a 'daily routine' that the general awareness or interest might dissipate gradually (PASAC, 2009).

As mentioned earlier, the HKSAR government attempted, as much as possible, to stick to its traditional laissez-faire policy that was included in port (security) operations. Hence, it was found that while complying with virtually all of the mandatory requirements, the optional requirements, like PFSAs (section 15.2), the preparation of PFSPs (section 16.1.1) and the training and certification of PFSOs (Sections 17.1 and 18) were mostly outsourced, and this was not helped by its unwillingness to recommend recognized security organizations. In practice, this implied that facility operators were virtually given a freehand to identify and choose any recognized security organizations (PASAC, 2003a). As a result, what and how security measures should be implemented in the designated port facilities actually depended on the preferences of the operators as they deemed fit. There still seemed to be inadequate enthusiasm among port-related stakeholders, public or private, about massively investing in security infrastructure and measures other than fulfilling the basic mandatory requirements as laid down by the international regulations and guidelines. This was perhaps exemplified by the fact that the designated authority, HKMD, did not even have the required resources to undertake un-notified facility inspections apart from routine audits (Ng and Vaggelas, 2012). This seemed to (partially) contradict the claim by Mitchell (2008) that Hong Kong is always situated at the forefront of advances in port security.

Furthermore, the auditing process was, to say the least, rather vague and ambiguous. During a meeting with HKMD officials, when being queried about the criteria and benchmarks in assessing the quality of the security infrastructures, as well as under what circumstances the operators would be deemed as not complying with the stated requirements, the response was rather simple. Quoting a senior official from the designated authority:

We do not have any kinds of scoring or benchmarking. Assessments were mainly based on the experiences and professional judgments of our appointed team and personnel . . .

Hence, while the necessary framework had already been established, the implementation of the security assessment process was still, as stated, rather ambiguous and vague. It is very clear that the port is in urgent need of prescribing a generally accepted methodology (by any IMO document) to carry out desirable security assessments in a quantitative manner for a benchmarking purpose. As discussed above, such a deficiency posed significant consequences, implying that the returns from security-related investments were largely implicit or hypothetical by nature. Quoting the speech of an expert during the Total Port Security Forum (TPSF) 2012:[8]

So far, no security-related incidents of any significance have taken place within the maritime sector . . . but does it imply that the heavily-invested security tools and measures are working? Or does it simply mean that we have overly exaggerated the risks of terrorist attacks on the maritime sector and such investments should be reduced? This is subject to discussions . . .

If the existing security management system could not be assessed quantitatively in a state-of-the-art approach, it was unlikely to encourage industrial stakeholders to seriously comply with it, as indicated from the above discussions and the rather passive approach by other Asian ports in implementing it (Ng and Gujar, 2008). Recognizing such a deficiency, in the next section, the advances in technology for quantitative port security assessment and management, including the introduction of a risk-based analytical model, is presented to offer an effective tool to enhance the best practice of port security in Hong Kong and other ports. This initiative also serves as a response to Yang's (2010) call for the design of security-related infrastructure, both hardware and software, in enhancing maritime security as a whole.

15.4 A RISK-BASED MODEL FOR PORT SECURITY ASSESSMENT AND MANAGEMENT

From the above analysis, it is not difficult to see that the implementation of port security is gradually moving towards a 'goal-setting' risk-based regime, in which decision makers explore and exploit flexible and advanced risk modelling and decision-making approaches to ensure the high security level of their own properties to be achieved. This is complicated by the fact that the responsibilities of port security mainly lie with the contracted governments, who have the final power in making all decisions. Such authority includes the approval of PFSAs and PFSPs, the appointment of PFSOs, reviewing (parts of) the vessel security plan in outstanding circumstances, as well as other related responsibilities. Although there exists various works on port security from political, economic, social and technological perspectives, little has been done to develop a generic methodology and supporting approaches to address all aspects of port security in an integrated and quantitative way as well as provide a rational basis that security policy and regulatory requirements are in proportion to the severity of the risks. In this section, after a brief discussion of the development of a generic port security assessment methodology, three novel risk modelling and decision-making approaches are outlined with illustrative examples to demonstrate their use. Such approaches may be used as alternatives to facilitate port security management in general and port security regulations and policies implementation in Hong Kong in specific in situations where conventional techniques cannot be appropriately applied.

The problem of developing and sustaining a highly capable port security assessment methodology to meet the diverse needs of sophisticated port security systems is extremely onerous and arduous, particularly in view of the plethora of challenges and uncertainties posed by the unavailability and incompleteness of historical data and the relatively modest level of funding available. One realistic and reliable way to deal with such a situation is to quantitatively assess risk priorities to ensure that the limited resources and assets are capable of cooperating cohesively together and being used for those key risk factors for security improvement. This goal may be fostered through a novel port security assessment framework, which is formulated by taking into account appropriate elements such as threats, vulnerabilities, risks and costs in the following three integrated steps.

Step 1 is the identification of the pairs of vulnerabilities and threats (V-T). Security vulnerabilities in port need to be identified through a pairwise analysis because the criticality of the vulnerabilities varies when facing different threats. Vulnerabilities are identified from the multiple levels of assets, infrastructures and systems analysed in port. The relevant threats of the identified vulnerability will be analysed and its criticality will be prioritized with regard to these threats.

Step 2 is the risk estimation and synthesis of the vulnerabilities identified in Step 1. The V-T pairs of high criticalities from Step 1 will be further investigated in a bidirectional (upward and downward) analysis. First, the criticalities of a specific vulnerability under different threats are synthesized using a bottom-up method in order to obtain the overall security level of a port facility. Similarly, the security estimate of the facility (as a component of a port system) will be combined with the estimates of the other critical components in the system. On the other hand, a top-down approach will be used to analyse the root causes leading to the high criticality of a particular V-T pair. By doing this, appropriate risk control options (RCOs) can be developed.

Step 3 is the selection of RCOs for controlling the high-risk vulnerabilities estimated in Step 2. In order to achieve risk reduction, a list of countermeasures based on human, procedural or equipment solutions can be applied to reduce the likelihood of occurrence or severity of the consequences of the high criticalities. RCOs can be developed to improve the security levels of the high-risk vulnerabilities with reference to the root causes from Step 2. Effective security management often requires identifying the 'optimal' RCO by taking into account multiple attributes with uncertainty such as risk, cost, technical difficulties, time and so on. The effectiveness of the RCOs will be analysed with respect to cost and benefit attributes in an uncertain environment where they are often ill-defined and interdependent.

15.4.1 Port Vulnerability Prioritization Model to Identify the V-T Pairs

A new port vulnerability prioritization model is developed through the combination of fuzzy logic and Bayesian reasoning in a complementary way to facilitate the treatment of uncertainty in data and realize effective quantitative analysis of the vulnerabilities under different threat modes in a port. The core of the model relies on a Fuzzy Rule Based Bayesian Reasoning (FuRBaR) risk inference system (Yang et al., 2009a).

The security criticality of each V-T pair in a port can be analysed through defining detailed risk parameters such as 'Will' (W), 'Damage capability' (D), 'Recovery difficulty' (R) and 'Damage probability' (P) (Yang et al., 2009b). W is the likelihood of a threat-based risk, which directly represents the lengths one goes through in taking a certain action. The combination of D and R responds to the consequence severity of the threat-based risk. Specifically, D indicates the destructive force/execution of a certain action and R hints at the resilience of the system after the occurrence of a failure or disaster. P means the probability of the occurrence of consequences and can be defined as the probability that damaging consequences happen given the occurrence of the event. It is often difficult, if not impossible, to use objective data to estimate each parameter.

One realistic way to analyse vulnerability criticality with incomplete objective data is to employ fuzzy *IF-THEN* rules where conditional parts and conclusions contain the linguistic variables used to describe the

Table 15.1   Linguistic variables of risk parameters and their fuzzy memberships

Risk parameters	Linguistic variables	Fuzzy memberships
'*Will*' (*W*)	Very weak (*W1*)	(0,0,0.3)
	Weak (*W2*)	(0.1,0.3,0.5)
	Average (*W3*)	(0.3,0.5,0.7)
	Strong (*W4*)	(0.5,0.7,0.9)
	Very strong (*W5*)	(0.7,1,1)
'*Damage capability*' (*D*)	Negligible (*D1*)	(0,0,0.1,0.3)
	Moderate (*D2*)	(0.1,0.3,0.4,0.6)
	Critical (*D3*)	(0.4,0.6,0.7,0.9)
	Catastrophic (*D4*)	(0.7,0.9,1,1)
'*Recovery difficulty*' (*R*)	Easy (*R1*)	(0,0,0.2,0.4)
	Average (*R2*)	(0.3,0.5,0.7)
	Difficult (*R3*)	(0.5,0.7,0.9)
	Extremely Difficult (*R4*)	(0.8,0.9,1,1)
'*Damage probability*' (*P*)	Unlikely (*P1*)	(0,0,0.2,0.3)
	Average (*P2*)	(0.2,0.4,0.5,0.7)
	Likely (*P3*)	(0.5,0.7,0.8,1)
	Definite (*P4*)	(0.9,1,1)
'*Security level of vulnerabilities*' (*S*)	Poor (*S1*)	(0,0,0.1,0.2)
	Fair (*S2*)	(0.2,0.3,0.4,0.5)
	Average (*S3*)	(0.5,0.6,0.7,0.8)
	Good (*S4*)	(0.8,0.9,1,1)

Source: Yang et al. (2009b).

criticality parameters. The linguistic variables defined using fuzzy membership functions are found in Table 15.1.

For example, a belief *IF-THEN* rule can be developed as follows:

IF W is 'Very strong (*W5*)' AND *D* is 'Catastrophic (*D4*)' AND *R* is 'Extremely difficult (*R4*)' AND *P* is 'Likely (*P3*)', *THEN S* is 'Good (*S1*)' with a belief degree of 0, 'Average (*S2*)' with a belief degree of 0, 'Fair (*S3*)' with a belief degree of 0.1 and 'Poor (*S4*)' with a belief degree of 0.9.

Such a rule can be simplified and expressed as follows:

IF W5 AND *D4* AND *R4* AND *P3, THEN* (0, *S1*), (0, *S2*), (0.1, *S3*), (0.9, *S4*).

It can be further converted and represented in the form of conditional probabilities as follows:

Given *W5* AND *D4* AND *R4* AND *P3*, the probability of *Sh* (h = 1,. . .,4) is (0.9, 0.1, 0, 0). Or $p(Sh|\ W5,D4,R4,P3) = (0.9, 0.1, 0, 0)$,

where '|' symbolizes 'conditional probability'. Using a Bayesian network (BN) technique, the rule base can be modelled and converted into a five-node converging connection. It includes four parent nodes, N_W, N_D, N_R and N_P (Nodes *W, D, R* and *P*), and one child node N_S (Node *S*). Having transferred the rule base into a BN framework, the rule-based risk inference for the security analysis will be simplified as the calculation of the marginal probability of the node N_S as shown in Equation 15.1:

$$p(Sh) = \sum_{i=1}^{5}\sum_{j=1}^{4}\sum_{k=1}^{4}\sum_{l=1}^{4} p(Sh|Wi, Dj, Rk, Pl)p(Wi)p(Dj)p(Rk)p(Pl) \quad (15.1)$$

To marginalize *S*, the required conditional probability table of N_S, $p(S|W, D, R, P)$ can be obtained by converting the rule base into a conditional probability format. The prior probabilities of the four parent nodes, which are symbolized as $p(Wi)$, $p(Dj)$, $p(Rk)$ and $p(Pl)$, respectively, can be obtained from real observations by domain experts directly using linguistics variables as the grades of the criticality parameters, which assists in raw data collection. To prioritize security, *Sh* (h = 1, . . ., 4) requires the assignment of appropriate utility values U_{Sh} that can be calculated by defuzzifying the memberships of *Sh* (Table 15.1) using the centroid method. Consequently, *S1* = 0.923, *S2* = 0.65, *S3* = 0.35 and *S4* = 0.077 (Yang et al, 2009b). After this, a new vulnerability criticality ranking index can be developed as shown in Equation 15.2:

$$RI = \sum_{h=1}^{4} p(Sh) U_{Sh} \quad (15.2)$$

The model has been computerized using Hugin software to realize a visualized tool for decision makers to prioritize vulnerabilities under various threats in a port by directly using linguistics variables (Figure 15.1). In Yang et al. (2011), an illustrative example has been given to demonstrate its application to a container terminal. The outcomes can be used either as a stand-alone technique for prioritizing critical systems such as port facilitates with high values and significant functions or as part of an integrated decision-making method for evaluating the security level of the whole port system or the effectiveness of security control options in sections 4.2 and 4.3, respectively.

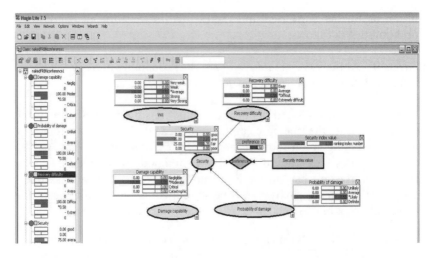

Figure 15.1 *The computerized FuRBaR approach to estimate
vulnerability criticality values*

15.4.2 Risk Estimation and Synthesis Using Evidential Reasoning

From the perspective of security analysis, a port can be treated as a complex system constructed by some sub-systems with the support of different components. Under such a hierarchical structure, security analysis at a higher level usually makes use of the information produced at lower levels. Therefore, it is very important to synthesize the risk evaluations of the components in a rational way to obtain the risk evaluations of the sub-systems and the whole system. The importance of such a synthesis is further reinforced by the requirements of combining the evaluations of all the V-T pairs associated with a particular vulnerability to obtain the overall security estimate of a port facility/activity.

Unlike the risk evaluations in traditional quantitative risk analysis (QRA), which are precisely expressed by numerical values, the risk evaluations obtained from the FuRBaR method in Equation 15.1 using linguistic variables and fuzzy sets are not possibly synthesized using normal mathematic logical operations. An Evidential Reasoning (ER) approach is well suited to modelling subjective credibility induced by partial evidence. The kernel of this approach is an ER algorithm developed on the basis of the Dempster-Shafer (D-S) theory, which requires modelling the narrowing of the hypothesis set with the requirements of the accumulation of evidence (Yang and Xu, 2002). Consequently, the ER approach and its attached IDS calculation software (Yang and Xu, 2002) can be used to combine the relevant V-T pairs and generate security assessment results at any level of the port system hierarchy, of which it will also provide a panoramic view on the security critical vulnerabilities, facilities and various sub-systems in a port for the development of appropriate RCOs.

The approach and its associated IDS software have been applied to analyse a security scenario of terrorists attacking container cranes in three ways: container bombs (bombs hidden inside containers); bomb/ missile attacks; and vessel 'suicide' attacks. Three V-T pairs (defined as Crane-Container (CC), Crane-Person (CP) and Crane-Vessel (CV), respectively) are estimated using a top-down approach in which the major generic key security performance indicators (KSPIs) used by the designated authority in PFSPs are identified in a hierarchy (Table 15.2). Figures 15.2 illustrates the security inputs to CC, while Figure 15.3 reveals the overall security estimation of the crane under the three threats by combining security outputs of CC, CP and CV. The advantage of the ER approach lies in the flexibility of analysing the security estimate of any level within the hierarchy (Table 15.2). This enables RCOs to be effectively developed with respect to the KSPIs of the highest risk contribution when the security level of a particular V-T pair is estimated to be critical.

15.4.3 A Dynamic Security-based Decision-making Tool Using Bayesian TOPSIS and Entropy

The purpose of conducting security risk estimation is to ensure that RCOs are in proportion to the severity of the risks to provide a rational basis for optimal security resource allocation. Effective security management requires identifying the 'optimal' RCO based on multiple uncertain attributes such as risk reduction and costs incurred. While traditional utility theory-based techniques, such as the multiple attribute utility technique (MAUT), have been generated to deal with the 'multiplicity' of the attributes, many problems regarding their uncertainty are observed, but not well-addressed. In this subsection, a new hybrid method is developed to explain the role of BNs and entropy theory in MAUT in a complementary way, in which all relevant decisional attributes in the form of the nodes in BNs will produce certain associated attribute values expressed by posterior probabilities, which can first be used in entropy calculations to figure out the objective importance of each attribute and then combined in a traditional MAUT framework, that is, TOPSIS, as a parameter to rank a set of RCOs in a cost-effective way. Once applied to a security risk area, the methodologies of BNs and MAUT have many common characteristics. Both studies start with the identification of research objectives and

Table 15.2   The hierarchy of KSPIs

Code	Key Security Performance Indicators (KSPIs)
S	PORT FACILITY SECURITY LEVEL
S-P1	*ACCESS CONTROL*
S-P1-I1	Identify and prevent unauthorized substances introduced into ship/port facility and its restricted areas
S-P1-I2	Identify and prevent unauthorized entry to ship/restricted areas of port facility and its restricted areas
S-P1-I3	Control activities within the restricted areas
S-P1-I4	Clearly identify the restricted areas within port facility
S-P1-I5	Identification of port personnel, transport workers and visitors
S-P2	*AWARENESS*
S-P2-I1	Professional training of security personnel
S-P2-I2	Periodic drills and exercises
S-P2-I3	Periodic review of security responsibilities and procedures
S-P2-I4	Periodic inspection to facility to ensure that security equipment is properly operated, tested, calibrated and maintained
S-P3	*DOCUMENTATION*
S-P3-I1	Periodic review and update of PFSP and other security-related documents
S-P3-I2	Prevent unauthorized access, disclosure, amendment and destruction of PFSP and other security-related documents
S-P3-I3	Report and maintain records of occurrences that threaten the security of port facility
S-P4	*HANDLING OF CARGOES*
S-P4-I1	Supervision of the secure handling of cargoes/baggage
S-P4-I2	Prevent tampering of cargoes
S-P4-I3	Prevent non-carriage entering and storing within storage areas
S-P4-I4	Routine inspection of cargoes, transport units and storage areas
S-P4-I5	Supervision of the secure handling of unaccompanied baggage
S-P5	*INFORMATION AND COMMUNICATION*
S-P5-I1	Gather and assess information related to security threats
S-P5-I2	Communicate and exchange of information between contracting governments (including share of best practices)
S-P5-I3	Communicate and exchange of information between designated authorities, facility operators and other security-related institutions
S-P6	*SHIP–PORT INTERFACE*
S-P6-I1	Respond to security threats/breaches of security of port facility or ship–port interface
S-P6-I2	Maintain critical operations of port facility or ship–port interface
S-P6-I3	Interface with ship security initiatives
S-P6-I4	Facilitate shore leave for ship personnel
S-P6-I5	Facilitate access of visitors to ship, including their identities

Notes: S – Security level; P – Parameter level; I – Indicator level.

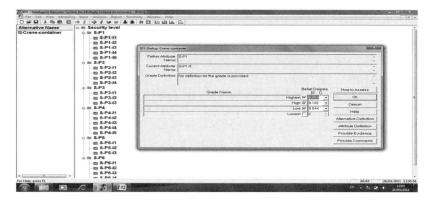

Figure 15.2   The use of IDS in port security estimation

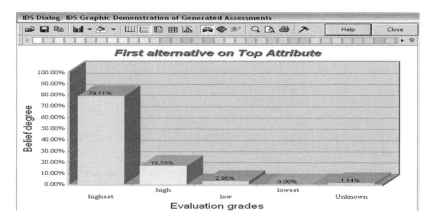

Figure 15.3   The security level of the CC pair

then analyse the attributes/factors influencing the objectives. Next, they both measure these attributes and calculate the analysis results using the measures when actions are taken. Such commonalities provide the basis of combining them. The interaction between BNs and MAUT are investigated to deal with complex security risk decision-making problems (Yang et al., 2009a). By doing this, the misunderstandings of the important concepts in making multiple uncertain attribute decisions (that is, randomness, dependency, unpredictability and fuzziness) can be clarified and the limitation of the single risk attribute consideration of BNs can also be avoided. More elements of the new hybrid method and their relationships are presented in a graphical flowchart (Figure 15.4). The explanation for each component is given below.

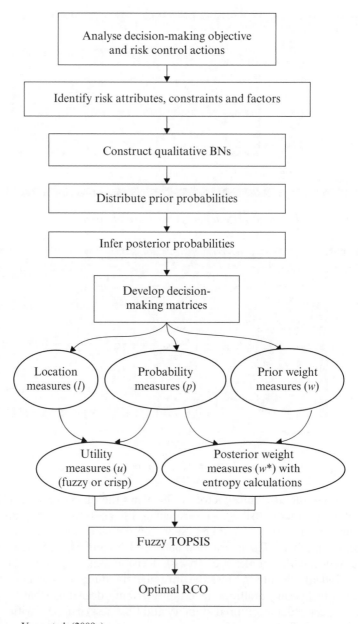

Source:　Yang et al. (2009a).

Figure 15.4　The method of combining MAUT, BNs, fuzzy logic and entropy measures

1. Identify risk-based decision problems (objectives) and RCOs (actions/functions). Obviously, the objectives of dealing with security risk-based decision-making problems are to determine the optimal RCO from multiple potential actions or their combinations. Technically, RCOs can be obtained using methods such as the chain rule (PVA, 1997) with reference to the KSPIs.

2. Identify decision attributes and constraints and analyse risk factors and their causal relationship with the attributes and constraints. Although with the identification of the objective and perspective, risk-based decision problems can be expressed using a kind of summary prose, they will not be truly well defined until the following are completely identified and developed:

   ● The set of possible RCOs, which may be identified after appropriate risk analysis.
   ● The set of decision attributes, which function to distinguish the options.
   ● The set of constraints, which are usually considered as some realistic conditions and requirements and enter the analysis networks as evidence.
   ● The set of risk factors, which can connect decision attributes as their media.
   ● The set of directed acyclic arrows, which represent the causal relationships between the risk factors, attributes and constraints.

3. Connect all risk factors and attributes to form qualitative BNs. After identifying all risk factors and decision attributes, one can start to confirm the relationship between them and construct a qualitative BN to represent their interactive dependencies. The knowledge about the decision problem and intuitive understanding of the various dependencies are then used to construct the causal structure. Here the graphical representation becomes very handy and permits the decision makers to express the fundamental relationships of direct or indirect influence between decisional attributes. The influence relationships expressed in BNs have a feature with causality. The concept of d-separation can be used to ensure that the BN models correspond with a real-world situation (Yang et al., 2007).

4. Distribute prior probabilities to model the uncertainties of decision attributes/criteria. When the qualitative BNs have been built, the prior probabilities of all nodes in the networks are distributed to model the uncertainties of the decision attributes and quantify the BNs.

5. Infer the uncertainties given actions and constraints and obtain the posterior probabilities of the decision attributes. Once the qualitative

and quantitative BNs are appropriately constructed, the next task is to analyse the networks to obtain the posterior probabilities of the decision attributes given risk control actions and constraints from a realistic situation. The objective of using BNs in a risk-based decision-making model is to predict and infer the unobservable situations (uncertainties) related to the decision attributes using the posterior probabilities when observable evidence (alternative risk control actions and constraints) is provided. Such posterior probabilities can be obtained using the Bayes' rule and the Chain rule (Jenson, 2001) with the assistance of computing software such as Hugin (Andersen et al., 1990).

6. Select the best security RCOs by constructing decision-making alternative matrices based on the posterior probabilities. The posterior probabilities associated with the decision attributes will be used, together with the location measurement of each grade of the decision attribute nodes, to calculate the utility (performance) measures of each security RCO alternative with respect to different decision attributes and combined with prior subjective weight assignment of the decision attributes in the entropy algorithm to compute the adjusted importance of each attribute. With both performance measures of each security RCO and the importance of each attribute as the inputs in a TOPSIS matrix, the best RCO can be eventually selected cost-effectively.

15.5 CONCLUSION

The 9/11 terrorist attacks exposed the brittleness of the transportation system leading to unprecedented disruption of global trade and the economy. Responding to such challenges, various security enhancement measures were introduced by the IMO and the international community. Although research on maritime security has been carried out throughout the past decade, those dedicated to port security have remained scarce, and reviews on how such guidelines, usually rather 'bare bone' in nature, could be effectively applied locally were found wanting.

Hence, using Hong Kong as the case study, the chapter has described how international guidelines and regulations on maritime security have been applied in a local perspective, and critically discussed the strengths and weaknesses of Hong Kong's maritime security regulations and policies. Based on the analysis, we argue that Hong Kong port is a rather passive follower in dealing with security issues. This is not helped by the relatively low priority of security-related affairs on the political agenda, especially being largely perceived as a low-risk port with few chances of being targeted by terrorists. Another problem is the rather vague and ambiguous security assessment process, with a generally accepted methodology in assessing and implementing port security found wanting.

To address this deficiency, we have introduced a risk-based decision-making model and three supporting methods as to help maritime stakeholders design rational port security regulations and policies. They are used to discuss various steps that should be in place to develop security measures to sustain and improve Hong Kong port's security in a cost-effective manner. Investigating the above methodology was largely motivated by the need to rationalize the development of cost-effective security measures, thus facilitating the implementation of Hong Kong port security regulations and policies, and ensuring the port's leading world position. However, the presentation of the framework together with novel supporting models have been kept as generic as possible, so that the associated technique advances, as well as the best practices based on the Hong Kong port experience, can be disseminated in a wide port security context.

As a pioneering work, we have investigated how the innovative theoretical research on risk-based security management can best fit in shipping and port facility security regulations at both national and international levels by acting as a bridge to fulfil the gaps between legal requirements and practical operations in terms of enhancing port security. This is far from adequate and further research on this area is an absolute necessity. Indeed, the attack during the Boston Marathon in April 2013 illustrates that the threats of terrorists still exist, and that security-related issues will remain a high priority in the research and policy agendas for years to come. To conclude, this chapter serves as a very timely reminder to scholars and policy makers of the criticality of security issues in the maritime and transport sectors.

ACKNOWLEDGMENTS

Adolf K.Y. Ng is supported by the University of Manitoba's VPRI and the I.H. Asper School of Business Research Funds (314942), while Zaili Yang is supported by the European Union FP7 Marie Curie project (REFERENCE). An earlier version, entitled 'Port security regulations and policies in Hong Kong: a risk-based analysis', was presented during the Annual Conference of the Association of Transport, Trade and Service Studies (ATTSS), held in Hong Kong, China, 18–20 June 2012, and was included in the conference proceedings. The usual disclaimers apply.

NOTES

1. The discussions took place between the fall of 2010 and early 2012.
2. HKMD was subordinated to the Transport and Housing Bureau of the Hong Kong Special Administrative Region government. See Ng and Vaggelas (2012) for a detailed description on the reasons and background of HKMD's appointment as the designated authority for Hong Kong port.
3. See Ng and Gujar (2008) for a detailed elaboration on the IMO documents.
4. By May 2013, there were 33 designated facilities (with port facility security plan being approved) within Hong Kong port. For further details, see the HKMD website.
5. There is a continuous debate on under what circumstances should the designated authority be empowered to order the closure/suspension of operation to a particular designated port facility. According to PASAC minutes (PASAC, 2003b) and other anecdotal information, one of the conditions to allow the designated authority to do so should be under the circumstance that the L3 security level had been launched.
6. The qualification would be valid for five years. After then, the person concerned must have served as PFSO or Deputy PFSO for at least 12 months (not necessarily consecutive though) during this preceding period before he or she could renew the qualification (PASAC, 2007).
7. For a detailed description on PFSA and PFSP, see IMO (2002a, 2002b).
8. TPSF was held in Kuala Lumpur, Malaysia, on 20–21 February 2012.

REFERENCES

Andersen, S.K., K.G. Olesen, F.V. Jensen and F. Jensen (1990), 'Hugin – a shell for building belief universes for expert systems', in G. Shafer and J. Pearl (eds), *Reading in Uncertainty*, London: Morgan Kaufman, pp. 332–7.

Bichou, K. (2004), 'The ISPS code and the cost of port compliance: an initial logistics and supply chain framework for port security assessment and management', *Maritime Economics and Logistics*, **6**, 322–48.

Bichou, K., M.G.H. Bell and A. Evans (eds) (2007), *Risk Management in Port Operations, Logistics and Supply Chain Security*, London: LLP.

Flynn, S.E. (2006), 'Port security is still a house of cards', *Far East Economic Review*, **196** (1), January/February, 5–11.

Greenberg, M.D., P. Chalk, H.H. Willis, I. Khiko and D.S. Ortiz (2006), *Maritime Terrorism: Risk and Liability*, Santa Monica: RAND.

Hesse, H.G. (2003), 'Maritime security in a multilateral context: IMO activities to enhance maritime security', *International Journal of Marine and Coastal Law*, **18** (3), 327–40.

HKMD (n.d.), http://www.mardep.gov.hk (accessed May 2013).

HKMD (2007a), *Guidelines for Application of Qualification Recognition as Port Facility Security Officer*, available at http://marsec.mardep.gov.hk/pfso_train ing.html (accessed October 2013).

HKMD (2007b), *Guidelines for Approving Port Facility Security Officer Training Course*, available at http://marsec.mardep.gov.hk/pfso_training.html (accessed April 2009).

IMO (2002a), *Amendments to the Annex to the International Convention for the Safety of Life at Sea, 1974 as Amended*, London: International Maritime Organization, SOLAS/CONF.5/32, December.

IMO (2002b), *International Code for the Security of Ships and Port Facilities*, London: International Maritime Organization, SOLAS/CONF.5/34, December.

IMO (2006), *Guidelines on Training and Certification for Port Facility Security Officers*, MSC.1/Circular 1188, Maritime Safety Committee, International Maritime Organization (IMO), London, available at http://www.marad.dot. gov/documents/MSC_1_Circ_1188.pdf (accessed October 2013).

Jenson, F.V. (2001), *Bayesian Network and Decision Graphs*, New York: Springer-Verlag.

King, J. (2005), 'The security of merchant shipping', *Marine Policy*, **29**, 235–45.

Kumar, S.H. and D. Vellenga (2004), 'Port security costs in the US: a public policy dilemma', in *Proceedings of the Annual Conference of the International Association of Maritime Economists 2004 (IAME 2004)*, Izmir, Turkey, July.

Mitchell, D. (2008), 'On the front lines: Hong Kong's role in international security', in C. McGiffert and J.T.H. Tang (eds), *Hong Kong on the Move: 10 Years as the HKSAR*, Washington, DC: Center for Strategic and International Studies, pp. 111–13.

Ng, A.K.Y. (2007), 'Port security and the competitiveness of short sea shipping in Europe: implications and challenges', in K. Bichou, M. Bell and A. Evans (eds), *Risk Management in Port Operations, Logistics and Supply Chain Security*, London: LLP, pp. 347–66.

Ng, A.K.Y. and G.C. Gujar (2008), 'Port security in Asia', in W.K. Talley (ed.), *Maritime Safety, Security and Piracy*, London: LLP, pp. 257–78.

Ng, A.K.Y. and G.K. Vaggelas (2012), 'Port security: the ISPS code', in W.K. Talley (ed.), *The Blackwell Companion to Maritime Economics*, Hoboken, NJ: Blackwell, pp. 674–700.

OECD (2003), *Security in Maritime Transport: Risk Factors and Economic Impact*, Paris: OECD.

PASAC (2003a), Minutes of the 1st Meeting of the Port Area Security Advisory Committee, HKMD, Hong Kong, July.

PASAC (2003b), Minutes of the 2nd Meeting of the Port Area Security Advisory Committee, HKMD, Hong Kong, September.

PASAC (2004), Minutes of the 4th Meeting of the Port Area Security Advisory Committee, HKMD, Hong Kong, May.

PASAC (2006), Minutes of the 8th Meeting of the Port Area Security Advisory Committee, HKMD, Hong Kong, October.

PASAC (2007), Minutes of the 9th Meeting of the Port Area Security Advisory Committee, HKMD, Hong Kong, June.

PASAC (2009), Minutes of the 11th Meeting of the Port Area Security Advisory Committee, HKMD, Hong Kong, August.

PVA (1997), *PVA Risk Guide: A Guide to Improving the Safety of Passenger Vessel Operations by Addressing Risk*, Arlington, VA: PVA.

Roach, A. (2003), 'Container and port security: a bilateral perspective', *International Journal of Marine and Coastal Law*, **18** (3), 341–61.

Robinson, R. (2002), 'Ports as elements in value-driven chain systems: the new paradigm', *Maritime Policy and Management*, **29** (3), 241–55.

Yang, J.B. and D.L. Xu (2002), 'On the evidential reasoning algorithm for multiple attribute decision analysis under uncertainty', *IEEE Transactions on Systems, Man and Cybernetics – Part A: Systems and Humans*, **32** (3), 289–304.

Yang, Y.C. (2010), 'Impact of the container security initiative on Taiwan's shipping industry', *Maritime Policy and Management*, **37** (7), 699–722.

Yang, Z.L. and J. Wang (2009), 'Quantitative analysis of maritime security assessment in ISPS', Paper presented at the European Safety and Reliability Association Conference (ESREL09), Prague, Czech Republic, September.

Yang, Z.L., S. Bonsall, J. Wang and S. Wong (2007), 'Risk management with multiple uncertain decision making attributes', Paper presented at the European Safety and Reliability Association Conference 2007 (ESREL07), Stavanger, Norway, June.

Yang, Z.L., S. Bonsall and J. Wang (2009a), 'Use of hybrid multiple uncertain attribute decision-making techniques in safety management', *Expert System with Applications*, **36** (2), 1569–86.

Yang, Z.L., S. Bonsall and J. Wang (2009b), 'Use of fuzzy evidential reasoning in maritime security assessment', *Risk Analysis*, **29** (1), 95–120.

Yang, Z.L., A.K.Y. Ng and J. Wang (2013), 'Prioritizing security vulnerabilities in ports', *International Journal of Shipping and Transport Logistics*, **5** (6), 622–36.

Zhu, J. (2006), 'Asia and IMO technical cooperation', *Ocean and Coastal Management*, **49**, 627–36.

16. Maritime security and piracy in Mauritius

Shakeel B. Burthoo-Barah and
Verena Tandrayen-Raghoobur

16.1 INTRODUCTION

An expansion in the level of international trade over the last few decades has highlighted the importance of the maritime sector to the global economy. Estimates suggest that more than 90 per cent of global trade is transported by sea (IMO, 2009). Maritime activity extends beyond the international transport of goods to national revenue-generating activities that include fishing and aquaculture, recreation and tourism, as well as extraction of non-renewable marine-based resources, and can be a critical source of income and food for populations at the community level.

The maritime realm, defined as encompassing oceans, seas, lakes, rivers, coastlines and harbours, is vulnerable to a wide array of threats, including illegal, unreported and unregulated fishing; environmental degradation; smuggling; trafficking in persons; narcotics trafficking; piracy; proliferation of weapons of mass destruction; and aggressive actions, including terrorism. These maritime threats all have significant land-based dimensions, whether related to the origin of the threat, the locus of its effects or the land-based capabilities required for preventive or enforcement interventions. As a result, land-based actors and capabilities are as important to maritime security as the specialized maritime capabilities usually associated with maritime activities and institutions.

Small Island Developing States (SIDS), in particular, are heavily dependent on their marine resources, for the sustainable livelihoods of coastal communities. Thus, the management of coastal and marine resources has become integrated into broader ocean management strategies since the entry into force of the United Nations (UN) Convention for the Safety of Life at Sea (SOLAS). Security for SIDS is a multidimensional concept. Specific challenges for them include, inter alia, environmental degradation, natural disasters, food security, water scarcity, HIV/AIDS, narco trafficking, small arms trafficking and the impact of terrorism on the economic sectors and tourism in particular. Mauritius is no exception to this threat.

Although Mauritius is a small island, it is highly dependent on trade and it has an Exclusive Economic Zone (EEZ) of nearly 2 million square kilometres, that is, an area a thousand times larger than the island itself. This maritime territory holds huge economic potential for the nation and can play a vital role in its development. However, maritime security remains a major threat for the island. There is deep concern from the authorities over the persistent scourge of piracy, particularly its impact on peace, security, stability and maritime security, its links to transnational organized crime, as well as its possible links to terrorist activities and the challenges it poses to private sector development, regional and international trade, economic integration and development.

Despite its small size and limited resources, Mauritius has been showing high commitment to combat maritime piracy via a number of concrete initiatives. Mauritius is positioning itself as an example for other countries in the region and other small island states around the globe in the domain of combating maritime piracy to promote regional and international peace and security. The objective of this chapter is to investigate the maritime security system in Mauritius and the appropriate maritime security policies adopted in relation to maritime defence, safety and governance issues. Relevant policies and an adequate policy plan for maritime security are recommended in line with the idiosyncrasies of the small island economy of Mauritius.

The chapter is structured as follows. Section 16.2 briefly reviews the concept of maritime security and the International Ship and Port Facility Security (ISPS) code as well as non-ISPS security initiatives. Section 16.3 analyses the evolution of the Mauritian maritime sector and its development over the years. Section 16.4 presents the various maritime security initiatives and policies adopted by the Mauritian authorities. Section 16.5 concludes with policy recommendations.

16.2 THE MARITIME SECTOR AND MARITIME SECURITY

16.2.1 The Global Maritime Sector

The maritime sector is of crucial importance to modern societies as it is an essential element in terms of social and economic development, and as a potential source of excellent employment and career opportunities, with several million people currently working in activities and companies directly and indirectly related to oceans and seas worldwide. Historically, the shipping and fishing industries have experienced a continuous trend of increases both to their fleets and total trade volume and fishing capacity, respectively. Thus, shipping has long been the major form of transport, as well as an essential communication link connecting coastal cities, countries and continents. Water transportation is economically and environmentally the most efficient way to travel or transport merchandise; and, to date, around 90 per cent of world trade is carried by the international shipping industry.

In parallel to the significant increase of traditional sea-related activities, the maritime sector has experienced a significant qualitative and quantitative expansion with the appearance and development of two new industrial growth poles: the offshore oil exploration and production industry and the cruise sector. Around 50,000 merchant ships, registered in over 150 nations and manned by over a million seafarers of nearly all nationalities, transport every kind of cargo internationally[1]. Several thousand oil rigs and support and supply offshore vessels are engaged in the exploration and drilling for oil and gas in almost every corner of the globe. Nearly four million commercial fishing vessels ply the seas and oceans at any given moment. And a myriad of recreational ships, including several hundred large and mega cruise ships, offer the most diversified leisure and tourism services to an expanding market.

The maritime sector is composed of organizations and activities such as maritime transportation, the naval industry (naval engineering and shipbuilding companies, and the component supply sector), commercial fishing and aquaculture industry, the cruise and recreational sector, sport and commercial ports and marinas, marine energy sources, navies, marine and ocean research and sciences, maritime training academies and training centres, a wide range of professional services around the maritime activities and professional associations, trade unions and organizations supporting the rights and interests of seafarers and maritime professionals. This global sector has shown strong growth over the last four decades from just over 8000 billion tonne-miles in 1968 to over 32,000 billion tonne-miles in 2007;[2] and it is expected to witness a further growth in the coming decades by the demands of China's and India's emerging economies, with a subsequent rise in the level of maritime activities and the economic value and impact they represent.

It is difficult to quantify the total value of the world maritime industry, and the economic relevance of a sector that affects a wide range of aspects of modern societies and their development. The maritime industry is of huge importance in terms of natural resources and energy, trade and industry, sciences and leisure activities. An essential part of our trade and prosperity, which demands innovative solutions and careful management systems to ensure its long-term sustainability, as well as the implementation of national and international regulations and instruments to address some still unsolved issues and new problems are expected to emerge in the near future (social and labour rights, international registration of ships, taxes, maritime environmental protection and so on). The maritime sector is fundamental, directly or indirectly, to national defence, law enforcement, social and economic goals and objectives of nearly every country. It is a crucial source of livelihood for many in developing nations, a platform for trade (including for landlocked countries) and a theatre for potential conflict or crime.

Given the transnational aspect of oceans, as well as many rivers, coastlines and estuaries, governments do not operate, regulate and police the maritime domain alone. For example, most ports are public–private partnerships and in some jurisdictions, coastal lands may be privately owned. Shipping and transport companies play major roles in maritime commerce, and maritime law enforcement can be a cooperative endeavour between national, regional, sub-national and private agencies and actors (Figure 16.1).

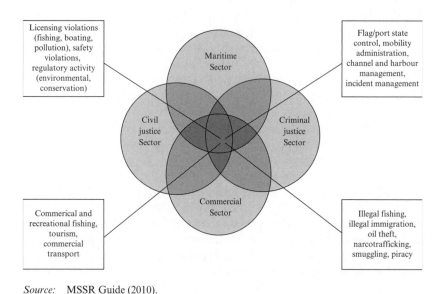

Source: MSSR Guide (2010).

Figure 16.1   Linkages between the maritime sector and other sectors

Maritime security is thus a key component of collective security and thus forms part of the foundation for economic development.

16.2.2   Maritime Security

Maritime security through improvements to maritime governance, law enforcement and safety may have a positive impact on citizens far beyond the maritime sector, by enhanced livelihoods and food security, improved access to goods and services or freedom from fear. A systemic overview of maritime security includes regulatory, operational, institutional policy, and human resource components. The six key areas of maritime security involve maritime governance, a maritime civil and criminal authority, maritime defence, maritime safety, maritime response and recovery and maritime economy (MSSR Guide, 2010), summarized in Table 16.1.

In 2002, the International Maritime Organization (IMO) addressed security threats to maritime transportation systems essentially by: (a) dividing the 1974 International Convention SOLAS chapter XI into two parts, chapter XI-1 'Special measures to enhance maritime safety' and a new chapter XI-2 'Special measures to enhance maritime security', and (b) establishing a ISPS code to support the security regulations incorporated in the SOLAS XI-2 regulations. In addition, SOLAS XI-1 introduces the new regulation XI-1/5 requiring ships to be issued with a Continuous Synopsis Record (CSR), and modifies regulation XI-1/3 for ships' identification numbers to be permanently visibly marked (UN, 2006).

The ISPS code is a comprehensive set of measures to enhance the security of ships and port facilities, developed in response to the perceived threats to them. It is the most important global security initiative, with impacts affecting the entire international shipping industry and beyond. The implementation of the code tests the ability, reliability and liability of active members across the logistics and supply chain system (shippers, carriers, ports, freight forwarders, logistics providers and so on), but also external members such as governments, insurance companies and maritime education and training institutions to meet security requirements while ensuring efficient and cost-effective movements of goods, cargo and other associated flows and processes (Bichou, 2004).

The ISPS code is divided into two parts: part A is a mandatory section, while part B is a non-compulsory guidance detailing procedures. The code sets three maritime security (MARSEC) levels ranging from low/ normal (1) to high (3) in proportion to the nature/scope of the incident or the perceived security threat. MARSEC level 1 is compulsory. Level 2 indicates a heightened threat of a security incident, while level 3 refers to a probable or imminent threat of a security incident. Other statutory

Table 16.1   Six key areas of maritime security

Functions	Maritime governance	Maritime civil and criminal authority	Maritime defence	Maritime safety	Maritime response and recovery	Maritime economy
Sub-functions	Maritime Mission Maritime Agency Organization Maritime Law and Policy Diplomatic and Foreign Affairs Support Maritime Programmes Maritime Professionals Maritime Agency Outreach and Stakeholder Coordination Maritime Accountability and Oversight	Enforcement of Civil and Criminal Laws Integrated Border Management Judicial Sector Support Port Security Vessel Security Supply Chain Security Maritime Environmental Enforcement	Maritime Defence Administration Maritime Defence Forces Maritime Situational Awareness/ Maritime Domain Awareness	Maritime Safety Administration Flag State Control Port State Control Fishing and Small Vessel Safety and Operations Management Maritime Facility Safety Management Mariner Licensing Administration Aids to Navigation Infrastructure, Equipment and Maintenance Channel and Harbour Management Maritime Safety Interagency Coordination	Emergency Response Administration Incident Management Search and Rescue Fire Environmental Maritime Defence Assistance to Civil Authorities Investigation and After-action Analysis	Economic Activity Regulation and Management Commercial Ports Transport Market Conditions

Source: MSSR Guide (2010).

instruments have been developed and implemented at various national and regional levels. The most significant initiatives include the US Maritime Transportation Security Act (MTSA) of 2002, which incorporates mandatory and voluntary ISPS provisions, the Container Security Initiative (CSI), the Customs-Trade Partnership Against Terrorism (C-TPAT) and the 24-hour advance vessel manifest rule, commonly known as the '24-hour rule'. The CSI requires ports to purchase scanning devices that cost millions of dollars. C-TPAT in turn requires firms to undergo costly security self-assessments and improvements, while the 24-hour rule requires that carriers and shippers purchase information technology (IT) systems for their entire operations.

As far as ports are concerned, the ISPS code is applicable to port facilities serving 500+ gross tonnes ships engaged in international voyages, but contracting governments are given the option to extend the application of the code to other types of ports and terminals. The code sets three security levels ranging from low to high in proportion to the nature and scope of the incident or the perceived security threat. Ports and port authorities are required to develop and implement enhanced port facility security plans (PFSP) for each level as set and approved by the governmental authority within whose territory the port is located. They accordingly need to provide the necessary financial, human and information resources, including the designation of a port facility security officer(s) (PFSO), and also the appropriate training drills and exercises for the PFSO and other security personnel. PFSP are based on the outcome of the port facility security assessment (PFSA), a 'risk-analysis' scheme undertaken by contracting governments, or authorized security organizations, in order to assess the vulnerability of port facilities against security threats and the consequences of potential incidents. Unlike ships and shipping companies, ports do not require international certification apart from a statement of compliance delivered and regularly reviewed by contracting governments.

The immediate challenge to the shipping community is, however, how to finance the costs of the ISPS implementation, incorporate and adjust them to pricing and marketing strategies while maintaining their market shares and achieving reasonable profit margins. Based on a global survey undertaken by the United Nations Conference on Trade and Development (UNCTAD) in 2007, to establish the range and order of magnitude of ISPS code-related expenditures, the initial reported cost figures for respondent ports range between a low US$3000 to a high of US$35.5 million with reported annual costs ranging between US$1000 to US$19 million. These costs include respondent ports' annual revenues, cargo throughput, ship calls and number of ISPS port facilities. There were important cost differentials between respondent ports and especially between larger and smaller ports. In fact, relative costs appear to be much higher for smaller respondent ports.

The long-term challenge involves adjusting relations with suppliers and customers to ensure agile and competitive supply chains capable of overcoming risk and vulnerability threats while still delivering value to customers and users. Ports are complex and multipart organizations in which institutions and functions often intersect at various levels. It is very important to recognize this strategic role of ports because although security measures have targeted a variety of entities and facilities across the international shipping and logistics community, ports stand as the only node/link that can bring together all these institutions, functions, assets, processes and flow-type elements. Thus, the scope and dimensions of port security go beyond the IMO agenda of facility security to include the wider framework of logistics and supply chain security.

16.3   THE MAURITIAN MARITIME SECTOR

16.3.1   An Overview of the Mauritian Maritime Sector

Situated on the north-west coast of Mauritius, Port-Louis is the capital city and the only commercial port of the island. Port-Louis harbour is the principal gateway of Mauritius and plays a vital role in the national economy, handling about 99 per cent of the total volume of the country's external trade. Over the past two decades, the port has been transformed into an economic nerve centre, with modern port facilities, a dynamic Freeport and excellent port-based facilities together with impressive waterfront developments. With its strategic location in the Indian Ocean, Port-Louis harbour is an excellent interface between Africa, Asia and Europe. In this context, the port has been transformed from an old light-erage port into a modern facility. Thus, Port-Louis has been developed into a regional maritime and business hub, with a modern container terminal spanning over 26 hectares and equipped with five rail-mounted post panama gantry cranes and state of art terminal management IT system. Facilities for the handling of a wide range of cargo are also available.

The Mauritius Ports Authority (MPA) is the sole national port authority set up by the Ports Act 1988 to regulate and control the port sector. The MPA is a landlord port authority, providing the main port infrastructure and superstructure together with related facilities. It also provides maritime services and navigational aids, and regulates and controls all port activities as well as environmental issues within the port area. The MPA has focused on the execution of key development projects, with massive investments in building new and modern infrastructures, trans-shipment of containers, the seafood hub, cruise tourism, ships' bunkering and the development of the 'Front de Mer' project. As a shipping hub, Mauritius aims to increase the current contribution of the shipping and maritime sector from 2.4 per cent to 3.5 per cent of gross domestic product (GDP) by 2015. This can be achieved by attracting additional shipping lines to register in Mauritius, increasing investment in ship bunkering facilities, establishing ship brokerage and ship financing companies and developing maritime training institutions.

16.3.2   The Mauritian Maritime Sector and Economic Development

Through its membership of the Common Market for Eastern and Southern African (COMESA) countries, the Southern African Development Community (SADC) and the Indian Ocean Commission (IOC), Mauritius offers access to a regional market of around 425 million consumers and with an import market currently valued at over US$35 billion. More importantly, some of Africa's leading ports are only a few days sailing from Mauritius, making it an ideal regional logistics platform for leading shipping companies using Port-Louis harbour as a regional hub. The port sector has been leading the way in the area of private sector involvement. This is confirmed by the concessioning of port terminals of Maputo, Beira and Nacala in Mozambique, Dar es Salaam in Tanzania and Luanda in Angola.

In addition, the Mauritius Freeport is the main trading hub of the Eastern and Southern African region. It boasts excellent warehousing, logistics and trans-shipment facilities to investors in order to access Asia, Africa and Europe. The Freeport is built around ten storage areas, with a 120,000 square metres capacity; 370 companies are operating in the Freeport (75 per cent are foreign-owned companies) and employ around 1500 workers. The Freeport infrastructures include dry warehouses, cold rooms, processing units and integrated office facilities. Thus, through the strategic location of Mauritius, the Mauritius Freeport aids in developing a competitive logistics and distribution platform for international trade between Mauritius and other trading partners.

Port trade performance has in fact witnessed a significant growth over the years. Total cargo traffic is on the rise and this trend is also reflected in total container traffic, which is depicted in Figure 16.2 from 1979 to 2011. Since 2002, trans-shipment activities have given a significant boost to container traffic at Port-Louis.

Further, during the period from January to December 2011, total cargo

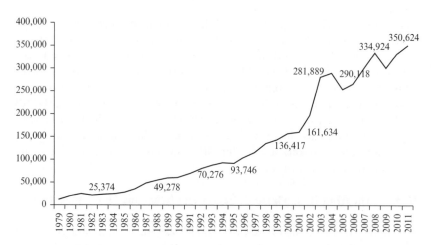

Source: Mauritius Ports Authority (2011).

Figure 16.2   Total container traffic, 1979–2011

Table 16.2   Total cargo traffic, 2010–11

	2010	2011	Difference	Percentage change
Total imports	4,190,635	4,323,251	132,616	3.1
Total exports	1,130,049	1,090,655	−39,394	−3.5
Total containerized trans-shipment inwards	908,993	1,063,314	154,321	17
Total	6,229,677	6,477,220	247,543	3.9

Source: Mauritius Ports Authority (2011).

traffic stood at around 6.4 million tonnes compared to 6.2 million tonnes recorded for 2010, representing a rise of 3 per cent (Table 16.2).

Total imports expanded by 3.1 per cent to reach 4,323,251 tonnes in 2011 as there were nominal increases recorded for some items such as animal feed (+8.7 per cent) and cements (+1.3 per cent), petroleum products (+8 per cent) and containerized imports (+3.8 per cent). Other items like fish traffic, wheat edible oil and maize registered declines. Total exports in turn experienced a decline of 3.5 per cent. In fact, two major export components, namely, sugar and molasses, saw drastic falls of 79 per cent and 42 per cent, respectively, in 2011. Total container traffic went up by 4.5 per cent in 2011, with captive container traffic increasing by 5.6 per cent and trans-shipment container traffic also registering a rise of 5.1 per cent in the same year.

Today, Mauritius stands at the crossroads of its future development. The main engines of growth in the Mauritian economy, namely, the sugar and textile industries, have faced the erosion of preferential trade arrangements stemming from the reforms of the European Union sugar regime, the phasing out of the Multi Fiber Agreement and the increasing trend towards the globalization of world trade. Sugar, which was the main export commodity, for a long time benefited from guaranteed prices and preferential access into the European markets under the Sugar Protocol and the Lomé Convention, and now the Cotonou Agreement. These preferences are no more and a 36 per cent fall in the price of sugar has greatly affected the sugar industry. As regards the textile sector, the prospects of intensified global competition from low-wage countries (particularly China and India) and limited future opportunities for preferential trade arrangements represent serious constraints on future growth. Hence, Mauritius has been exploring new economic activities in order to sustain economic growth in the country. The government is actively promoting the seafood hub, which has become one of the main pillars of the economy. In an increasingly liberalized world, the importance of port in economic development is gaining prominence. Port-Louis has become an important trans-shipment hub after Durban. This trans-shipment business has improved connectivity and enabled Mauritius us to compete for global markets. With the erosion of trade preferences, the traditional sectors are facing many difficulties to remain viable. Today, high connectivity has enabled the ailing sugar sector to move to higher-value addition activities, that is, refinery.

The Mauritius EEZ extends widely over a surface area of 1.9 million square kilometres and provides the right business environment to position itself as a vibrant seafood hub in the region. In fact, it has been noted that over 23 per cent of the global tuna catch comes from the Indian Ocean. In this respect, the Mauritian government is promoting the seafood industry and transforming Mauritius into a world-class seafood hub for trading, warehousing, processing, distribution and re-export of fresh, chilled and frozen raw or value added seafood products. The domestic seafood industry has attracted international seafood players from countries like Spain, Malaysia, Japan, USA, Sri Lanka and France. The contribution of both the Freeport sector and the seafood industry to GDP between 2007 and 2011 is shown in Table 16.3. The seafood hub is gradually showing higher value added and a positive contribution to the economy. However, it registered a negative growth rate of 1.3 per cent

Table 16.3   GDP contribution of seafood hub and the Freeport sector (2007–11)

Sectors	2007	2008	2009	2010	2011
Value added (Rs million)					
Seafood	2691	3293	3050	3367	3434
Freeport	1648	1422	1314	1350	1450
Share in the economy (%)					
Seafood	1.2	1.4	1.2	1.3	1.2
Freeport	0.8	0.6	0.5	0.5	0.5
Growth rate (%)					
Seafood	2.2	7.3	12.1	10.4	−1.3
Freeport	−30	−18	−11	3.3	3.1

Source: Statistics Mauritius (2011).

in 2011 while the Freeport recorded a growth rate of 3.1 per cent in the same year.

16.4   THE MARITIME SECURITY INITIATIVES AND POLICIES IN MAURITIUS

16.4.1   The Maritime Security System in Mauritius

Since 2004, the Port-Louis harbour has been ISPS compliant. To comply with the ISPS code, the MPA has implemented various measures such as the erection of 6 kilometres of high security fencing to secure the port and the construction of six new gate posts to control access to the port. The port area is a restricted area with all accesses into and exits from the port controlled. While land side access to the port is controlled by the police, the national Coast Guards control access on the water plan. Further, all stakeholders within the port area operate their own security service on a 24-hour basis to prevent unauthorized access or exit within their premises. In addition, to enhance maritime security and tighten control on the movement of all vessels in the port, a harbour radio station equipped with state of art communications equipment has been constructed. With a view to further exercise control on the movement of vessels in Mauritian waters an Automatic Identification System (AIS) has been installed. Furthermore since 2008, the port has been covered by CCTV system of more than 100 cameras to detect suspicious activities or movement. A Port Security Unit has also been set up to enhance security on a 24-hour basis and monitors the CCTV cameras, issues access passes, performs sentry duties at key installations of the port and effects regular patrols in the port area.

The response to the security threat of the international customs community was to implement measures to secure a trade policy chain. Spearheaded by the USA, the main initiatives included C-TPAT, CSI and the 24-hour rule. Mauritius is not a CSI-compliant port, although initial discussion has taken place between Customs and US CSI resident officers in Durban to provide assistance to start the project. Given that all containers destined for the USA have to trans-ship through Durban, a CSI protocol potentially boosting trade in the region, Mauritius is keen to adopt the CSI certification. Two companies have been granted C-TPAT status, namely, MAZAVA Limited and Esquel Limited. However, the security initiative implemented by Customs in Mauritius is the SAFE Framework. From a Customs perspective, the World Customs Organization (WCO) developed the SAFE Framework of Standards to Secure and Facilitate Global Trade including the Authorized Economic Operator (AEO) concept, which to a large extent can be considered an alternative to C-TPAT. Compared to C-TPAT, the SAFE Framework is less stringent and based on risk management and operator compliance principles. The SAFE Security instrument emphasizes submission of advance electronic data, the use of common risk management principles to assess riskiness of cargo based upon the use of Non-Intrusive Inspection (NII) such as scanners to examine high-risk cargo and the introduction of AEO for low-risk-compliant stakeholders.

According to the SAFE Framework of Standards, the eight security elements that a trading company must address are:

1. premise security and access controls
2. personnel security
3. business partner security
4. cargo security
5. conveyance security
6. information and IT security
7. incident management and investigations
8. crisis management and incident recovery.

Mauritius has domesticated the provisions of the SAFE Framework by enacting the Customs (Cargo Community Systems) Regulations 2008, setting up the Mauritius Cargo Community System (MACCS), a public-private partnership (PPP) project to give effect to the regulation. The

MACCS is an IT platform that networks all economic operators and is designed to capture all logistics data elements in the supply chain as soon as an exporter orders a container. It is also capable of capturing import advance manifest data. MACCS has a modular configuration for each Customs procedures; some modules are at an advanced stage of development. It has also put in place scanners to assess risk, set up a dedicated Risk Management Section since 2009 and introduced a simpler version of the AEO on a pilot basis since January 2012.

With a view to mitigating the impact of the various measures on cost and dwell time, the government has decided not to charge any fees on scanning, although MACCS does charge US$10 per declaration. Compensating trade facilitation measures such as paperless Customs, e-payment and reduced inspections have contributed to reduce clearance requirements, decrease dwell time of import, export and transit and ultimately reduce overall cost. Both the Mauritius Export Association and the Mauritius Chamber of Commerce share the fact that implementation of the above security measures coupled with compensating trade facilitation measures have not increased business costs.

Although Mauritius has not enacted the 24-hour rule and is not CSI compliant, it has the capability with the MACCS system to submit advance cargo and logistics information in case these are required by any importing country. With a view to assisting small and medium-sized enterprises (SMEs) to boost exports, ships and aircrafts allowed consignments to be loaded even during the last hour before departure. Given there is no duty and taxes on exports, Customs normally acceded to last hour requests for export, unless it had information otherwise. This practice, however, stopped once the export module in MACCS was implemented in October 2013. All cargo now have to be manifested and sent to Customs at the latest 24 hours before loading.

16.4.2 Maritime Piracy and Security Measures Adopted by the Mauritian Government

SOLAS chapter XI-2 and the ISPS code have been the major focus of maritime security during their adoption and early implementation (2004–07). In 2007–08, the focus shifted to other pressing issues, including piracy and armed robbery, specifically Somalia-based piracy. Maritime piracy, which includes hijacking for ransom, robbery and criminal violence, is very prevalent in the Indian Ocean. Though incidents of piracy seem to have decreased in the wider Indian Ocean since 2003, it increased along the east coast of Africa owing to increasing activity linked to Somalia. Statistics of the International Maritime Bureau (IMB) indicate that of the 406 reported pirate attacks around the world in 2009, 297 occurred in the Indian Ocean region. In 2010, piracy attacks in the same area increased to 311. The large number of pirate attacks and hijackings off the Horn of Africa, specifically around Somalia and in the Gulf of Aden, is of great public concern, often making international headlines, and has resulted in considerable international reaction.

Piracy around Somalia is different from other parts of the world as the pirates are well armed and use a range of weapons, including automatic weapons, handguns and rocket-propelled grenades. Attacks take place while ships are underway, mostly but not exclusively in the Gulf of Aden or off the coast of Somalia. Pirates often use mother ships to enable them to conduct operations far from their bases and such attacks have even taken place off the coasts of Kenya, Tanzania and the Seychelles. Ships are boarded or the pirates induce the ships to slow down by firing at them. If a vessel is boarded and captured, it is sailed to the Somali coast and the pirates then demand a ransom for the ship and its crew.

The lack of maritime security around the Horn of Africa causes a great deal of international concern as it not only threatens commerce but also peace and regional stability, international trade and international energy flows. The pirates often operate from Somalia's semi-autonomous Puntland province and specific parts of southern Somalia where there is no government authority and no law enforcement. The hijacking of ships for ransom is most common and such activities clearly have an economic motive. Piracy around the Horn of Africa has increased alarmingly since the late 1990s. By 2005, Somalia was a piracy hotspot with 35 recorded attacks and 15 hijackings, a figure that increased to 45 attempted and 19 successful hijackings by April 2006. During 2007, pirate attacks off Somalia more than doubled to 31, but this paled in significance to the 111 reported attacks and 42 successful hijackings in 2008, which constituted nearly 40 per cent of the 293 attacks reported internationally in that year (Potgieter, 2009).

Notwithstanding the international naval presence around the Horn of Africa in 2009, 217 incidents were attributed to the Somali pirates, who managed to hijack 47 vessels and took 867 crew members hostage. Somalia accounted for more than half of the 406 reported international incidents of piracy and armed robbery in 2009. In 2010, Somalia pirates were responsible for 48 of the 53 vessels hijacked internationally. The pirates continued to intensify their activities beyond Somalia's coast, operating as far south as the Mozambique Channel. By the end of 2010, Somali pirates still held 28 ships and 638 hostages. In November 2010, they received US$9.5 million for the release of the *Samho Dream*, a South Korean tanker hijacked in April 2010. Since then, other high ransoms have been collected, notably US$2 million for the Kuwaiti-owned tanker *Zirki* and US$13 million for the tanker *Irene* in April 2011, the highest-known ransom paid to pirates. Piracy in the Indian Ocean is not abating – quite the opposite: 266 pirate attacks occurred in the first six months of 2011. Attacks ascribed to Somali pirates were up from 100 for the comparable period in 2010, but fewer vessels were hijacked (21 compared to 27) because of more effective anti-piracy measures (Potgieter, 2009).

The cost of international piracy today is estimated at around US$5 to 7 billion excluding the additional costs associated with the naval operations and the loss of revenue to states from national and international trade. The average ransom paid increased from around US$150,000 in 2005 to US$5.4 million by the end of 2010. Since January 2010, Somali pirates received approximately US$75–85 million in the form of ransom payments. Concrete steps are being taken in Mauritius for the prosecution of pirates operating off the coast of Somalia. In spite of all efforts by the US and European navies to patrol shipping lanes off the Somali coast, there has been no letup in pirate attacks, and in the face of such threats, it is imperative that anti-piracy efforts be broadened to allow every country to contribute to that effort.

Despite being a small island economy with limited resources and capacity, Mauritius has reacted to the piracy threat by taking a wide range of measures in the field of maritime security to ensure safety at sea. Safety and security are treated under the aegis of a single ministry, the Prime Minister's Office. So an integrated approach is adopted to enhance the safety and security of citizens, tourists, seafarers and the general fishing/boating community through effective community policing and to promote awareness and sensitivity on safety at sea. The enforcement of any law relating to the security of the country and protection of the EEZ and marine resources is crucial as well as for the detection, prevention and suppression of any illegal activity, including any act of piracy or maritime attack referred to in the Piracy and Maritime Violence Act 2011 within the maritime zones.

In fact, in 2011, Mauritius enacted the Piracy and Maritime Violence Act to make provision for the prosecution of pirates and became operational from June 2012. A National Piracy Contingency Plan setting out a national framework to tackle piracy-related incidents within the local area has been formulated. In addition, a National Plan to combat maritime piracy has been adopted since 2010 and a National Coast Guard Commando team has been set up for anti-piracy operations since 2009. Increased surveillance operations have been carried out by national

Coast Guard vessels and the Dornier aircraft in the EEZ. Joint operations have also been carried out with the assistance of India. In 2009, an AIS was installed in the port to enable the detection of vessels above 300 tonnes navigating in the international shipping lanes of Mauritian waters and a Vessel Monitoring System was installed to track the positioning of all Mauritian vessels. Private armed security guards have further been authorized onboard merchant ships and fishing vessels proceeding through high-risk areas.

From a regional and international perspective, Mauritius is collaborating with international organizations to tackle piracy in the Indian Ocean. Mauritius fully supports all regional and multilateral efforts undertaken by the international communities to find a solution to the piracy problem. In 2010, Mauritius signed the Djibouti Code of Conduct (DCoC) concerning the repression of piracy and armed robbery against ships in the Western Indian Ocean and the Gulf of Aden. The DCoC is based on four main pillars, namely, regional training, national legislation, information sharing and operational capacity building. In 2010, Mauritius in collaboration with the European Union, COMESA and the Indian Ocean Commission, hosted the Second Regional Ministerial Conference on Maritime Piracy where a regional strategy and an Action Plan were adopted to fight piracy and promote maritime security in the Eastern Africa and Indian Ocean region.

Moreover, a programme for the implementation of a Regional Maritime Security Strategy (MASE) for the Eastern and Southern African-Indian Ocean region has been developed. The estimated cost of the project is around 25 million euros and will be implemented over a period of 15 years. Mauritius also signed an agreement with the European Union in 2011 for the transfer of suspected pirates for investigation, prosecution, trial and detention in Mauritius. In this respect, the European Union is providing financial and technical support for the implementation of the Transfer Agreement and funding to finance the construction of a new prison to detain pirates. In 2012, Mauritius signed an agreement with the Transitional Federal Government (TFG) of the Republic of Somalia and a Memorandum of Understanding (MoU) with the Puntland State of Somalia for the transfer of convicted Somali pirates to their homeland. Mauritius also signed a MoU with the UK on the conditions of transfer of suspected pirates and seized property to Mauritius. Additionally, owing to lack of required resources for the surveillance of its territorial waters, especially given its huge EEZ, Mauritius is also working with the Indian and French authorities for joint surveillance as well as training and capacity building.

Though various policies have been established to deal with piracy and it has been seen that Somalian piracy is not as widespread as it was a few years ago, we cannot assess the effectiveness of Mauritian policies with regards to security. Data is not available and to the best of our knowledge no previous study has been undertaken on this issue.

16.5 CONCLUSION

As a small island economy, highly dependent on international trade, Mauritius needs to have a strong maritime sector where maritime security is the prime objective. Mauritius is keen to facilitate vibrant maritime commerce and economic activities at sea since these strengthen economic security. At the same time, the island economy endeavours to protect its maritime domains against ocean-related threats such as piracy and criminal activities, among others. These objectives can best be achieved by blending public and private maritime security activities, and by tackling maritime threats by integrating efforts with other countries ideally within a specific legal framework. Regional and international cooperation on maritime security is essential, as virtually all nations benefit from maritime activity. It must be emphasized that trans-oceanic security cooperation in the region is very important. Regional, sub-regional and international organizations can contribute much in this regard. India is considered a leader in the Indian Ocean and the Indian Navy's Indian Ocean Naval Symposium (IONS) initiative is welcomed in many circles because of its potential to improve maritime security cooperation. Greater collaboration with India may promote maritime security in the Mauritian seas and also in the Indian Ocean.

Further, Indian Ocean countries have a long history of trade, culture and military interaction with the rest of the world. Today, the Indian Ocean's traditional status as an international trade highway is more significant than ever before. Although the Indian Ocean region is experiencing marked development and economic growth, security concerns often dominate the agendas of its states. As many extra-regional powers have a stake in the Indian Ocean security, these powers can assist with regional maritime security and capacity building. Though each sub-region has its own unique challenges, the capabilities required to deal with maritime security are often the same. The need to have a structure that addresses maritime security capacity building and involves both regional and extra-regional countries is evident. Great potential exists for the international community and regional organizations to improve international cooperation, to strengthen security in the region and to create a broad-based Indian Ocean security strategy that is acceptable to all.

NOTES

1. http://www.windrosenetwork.com/Maritime-Sector.html (accessed 30 May 2013).
2. http://www.windrosenetwork.com/Maritime-Sector.html (accessed 30 May 2013).

REFERENCES

Bichou, K. (2004), 'The ISPS code and the cost of port compliance: an initial logistics and supply chain framework for port security assessment and management', *Maritime Economics and Logistics*, **6**, 322–48.

IMO (International Maritime Organization) (2009), *Maritime Knowledge Centre: International Shipping and World Trade, Facts and Figures*, London: IMO.

Mauritius Ports Authority (2011), *Trade Statistics*, Mauritius.

MSSR (2010), *Maritime Security Sector Reform Guide*, Washington, DC: US Bureau of Political-Military Affairs.

Potgieter, T. (2009), 'The lack of maritime security in the Horn of Africa region: scope and effect', *Strategic Review for Southern Africa*, **18**, 70–2.

Statistics Mauritius (2011), *National Accounts Aggregates*, Mauritius.

UN (2006), *Maritime Security: Elements of an Analytical Framework for Compliance Measurement and Risk Assessment*, New York: United Nations.

17. Conclusions: comparative analysis of transport policies and relevant benchmarks and best practices

Khalid Bichou, Joseph S. Szyliowicz and Luca Zamparini

On the basis of a structured and peer-reviewed selection of contributions from both academia and industry, this book has aimed at providing a coherent framework associating the risks and impacts of maritime security to their policy frameworks and applications within and across a wide range of countries and maritime regions. Moreover, this book has also served to show that further, deeper and somehow distinctive research is needed on the subject. The specific issues worthy of additional research were highlighted in each part of the book as follows:

1. The wider scope and themes of maritime security are still evolving in view of the existing and emerging challenges in regional and global security and the operational shifts and market trends in international shipping and ports (Chapters 2–7).
2. The policy options and applications of maritime security have not been researched in the depth and breadth required to analyse country- or region-specific needs or derive global maritime security frameworks and comparative benchmarks (Chapters 8–16).

The chapters have used a mix of empirical and conceptual frameworks in order to address several major themes related to these issues and examined their policy principles and applications in national, regional and international contexts. While authors have converged on certain aspects and recommendations, it is obvious that many fundamental issues still remain contentious.

The first of these is the lack of agreement on the main drivers and objectives of maritime security. Some countries, such as the USA and members of the European Union (EU), have focused their attention on terrorist attacks that could result in mass casualties or cripple global supply chains.

Here, the scope of maritime security goes beyond international shipping and ports to include land-based facilities, for example, when ships were used to launch attacks against land-based facilities in the Mumbai terrorist attacks in 2008, and international trading and supply systems, for example, when port security threats have resulted in wider disruptions of regional and global supply chains. Other countries, such as some African, Middle Eastern, Asian and small island states are more concerned with the risks posed by piracy; a phenomenon that has in some cases thrived due to weak governments, often plagued by corruption. Chapter 4 highlights the difficulties involved in dealing with piracy and suggested various approaches and policies to deal with it. It should be noted though that despite the prominence of piracy threats and incidents in recent years, researchers are yet to agree on the scope and categorization of piracy – is it simply a criminal activity implemented by gangs concerned with monetary rewards and should therefore be treated as such (Chapter 14) or should it be viewed within a terrorism activity including the risk of terrorist groups using piracy as a fundraising strategy (Chapter 2).

Thus, while there is agreement that maritime security entails political, economic, social, environmental and cultural dimensions, little or no consensus exists on how to conceptualize and assess maritime security risks and vulnerabilities. Not surprisingly, therefore, there is also no agreement on which tools within the wide range of available policy options and mechanisms can best promote maritime security. On the one hand, for smaller countries, such as Oman (Chapter 12), and countries whose economies rely on exports to neighbouring countries, such as Canada (Chapter 9), the desire to foster international cooperation and coordination appears to be the main driver to enhance maritime security. On the other hand, countries such as the USA (Chapter 8) appear to develop initiatives on their own and then work to gain international support for these measures.

Achieving the necessary cooperation for such initiatives is, however, a difficult matter and often complicates the efforts to achieve national maritime security. This issue has been highlighted in several country case studies, most notably in Chapter 11 related to Nigeria, Chapter 12 related to Oman and Chapter 13 related to Indian dry ports. The Indian case also brings to our attention the rich variety of port facilities that serve global supply chains, each with distinctive security concerns.

Cooperation is also difficult to achieve when both private and public interest are involved. A case in point is the reluctance of countries bordering the Straits of Malacca to accept the declaration of the Straits as a war-risk zone by Lloyd's Market Association, a major insurance group (Chapter 14). This case reflects the ways in which external actors often influence national and regional decisions regarding maritime security.

International bodies such as the International Maritime Organization (IMO) have obviously played a prominent role in this regard through the adoption of various rules and regulations, but so have individual states. The USA, as argued in Chapter 8, has clearly played a leading role in this regard as evidenced by Canada's willingness to accommodate its powerful neighbour. Chapter 9 goes further by suggesting that the USA, through the nature and structure of its Department of Homeland Security (DHS), can even influence Canada's decisions indirectly. As noted above, many other countries also seek to enhance their maritime interests through diplomacy as shown by the case of Oman in Chapter 12 as well as seeking to reach formal agreements regionally. This proves a challenging task, however, as the case of the countries around the Malacca Straits indicates (Chapter 14).

Moreover, the role of the various tools and mechanisms that are available to decision makers remains controversial. Nations disagree, for example, on the need for and relevance of legislation to reduce maritime security risks, on the adequacy, and efficiency, of a multi-layer and multi-level regulatory framework and on the requirement for and functioning of a standardized global regulatory framework.

Even where a wider agreement on such issues is reached, several operational issues must be addressed prior to achieving secure maritime and trading systems. Chapter 10 highlights some of the failings of the current maritime security system with a focus on real cases from the EU. Examples include failures in cargo reporting procedures in the Entry Summary Declaration (ENS), problems with the Authorized Economic Operator (AEO) and issues with container and cargo scanning.

Another area that deserves equal importance is the interplay and the difference between maritime safety and maritime security. The essence of safety risk models is a probabilistic approach based on the assumption of unintentional human and system behaviours to cause harm. This is not the case for security incidents stemming from terrorism, piracy and other criminal and malicious acts. Chapter 5 examines these issues thoroughly and crucially criticizes the current risk approach to maritime security. A major shortcoming of the current regulatory framework is its conceptualization of maritime security as a sub-system of maritime safety. On the one hand, much of the assessment of security threats is based on intelligence work, which does not always follow the scrutiny of statistical reasoning. On the other hand, conventional risk models may not be appropriate for assessing and managing maritime security given the complexities of the maritime networks, the rarity of occurrence of large-scale maritime security incidents and the lack of historical data thereof. Even though maritime safety and maritime security differ in both risks and impacts, they also concur and overlap at several management and operational levels. The objective is therefore to adequately conceptualize and assess differently the risks stemming from each system while pooling the resources of both systems to address their operational and management implications. From the empirical viewpoint, some policies and practices that aim at enhancing safety (that is, labour, health and safety) can also have positive externalities on security.

At the implementation phase, any effort to enhance maritime security will necessarily involve the search and allocation of appropriate financial resources. However, it is not at all clear which countries or stakeholders should bear the responsibility for providing these resources. The list of stakeholders is indeed a long one and includes both private and public actors. The former includes shipping companies, terminal operators, multimodal transport providers, labour unions and a range of maritime agents and intermediaries. The latter includes maritime and trade regulators, maritime and port authorities, customs agencies and the many security- and safety-related agencies, be they national or international. Recent years have clearly witnessed a great emphasis on maritime security as countries, regional and international organizations have all adopted and implemented policies and projects designed to safeguard maritime, port and supply chain interests. These measures have certainly enhanced the security of maritime and port operations but it is not at all obvious that their cost, which runs into billions of dollars, have been spent most effectively (see Chapter 4). What is clear though is that it is essential to involve all the stakeholders in attempting to enhance security at any port. The case of Hong Kong (Chapter 15) illustrates how such involvement can take place.

The extent of any particular stakeholder's interests in, and responsibility for, financing maritime security is difficult to assess. Complicating this problem is the problem of costing maritime security and assessing the risk reward ratios of different levels of security investments. Chapters 3 and 5 tackle this problem. They examine the economic valuation of maritime security and highlight the methodological and practical difficulties in quantifying and assigning monetary values to the costs and benefits of security. The chapters also discuss the limits and extents to which the policy maker can externalize the costs of maritime security against the willingness to pay of users and what the market can bear. On the other hand, there seems to be a need but also a growing trend from several market players towards internalizing the costs and benefits of security.

Financial considerations are of particular concern especially to many small islands and developing countries. Small islands such as Mauritius (Chapter 16) essentially lack the required resources to fully protect their maritime interests. On the other hand, large developing countries such as Nigeria (Chapter 11) confront different problems revolving around the structure and the organization of the political system and the policy-making process, both of which do not facilitate the development and implementation of effective maritime security policies. Regrettably, this problem extends to several other African countries, most notably Somalia whose piracy problem has required the deployment of external naval forces and the use of private security guards onboard commercial ships.

While it is clear that our understanding of maritime security, though certainly enhanced, has by no means reached a stage where additional research will yield diminishing returns. On the contrary, the contents of this book reveal how much remains to be done. Essentially, this book has served to illustrate that while there exist various methods, frameworks and policy options for maritime security, no generic framework can be selected and replicated globally.

Clearly, countries, regions, market players and industry stakeholders all face a wide range of maritime security threats and vulnerabilities, but each of them may have a different perspective on (1) the identification and prioritization of those threats and vulnerabilities; (2) the perception and assessment of the risks associated with them; and (3) the tools and measures (regulatory or otherwise) that best reduce the probability of occurrence and severity of impacts of security incidents. Even where policy and industry stakeholders both concur on an agreed set of international measures, procedures and benchmarks for maritime security, they may diverge in the way such measures are designed, interpreted and implemented for reasons related to operational and safety standards, policy guidelines and principles, market forces and dynamics, cultural and social differences, implementation costs and financing, and regulatory enforcement and compliance.

We believe failure to provide a comprehensive and global framework may not be attributable to the difficulty on reaching a consensus between the various maritime stakeholders, including trading nations, but could be simply related to the inherent fallacy that a global and homogeneous strategy is needed and desirable. Maritime systems and operations are by definition complex and dynamic. They often involve a wide range of stakeholders with different, overlapping and sometimes conflicting interests. They also evolve in different spatial, economic, political and social ways. If it is assumed that international shipping and ports involve a large number of stakeholders and interest that do not always operate under similar political, economic, social and operational environments, then it would be understandable, and to some extent predictable, that maritime security would be, and should be, conceptualized accordingly.

At the same time, we stress that maritime security should not be the responsibility of policy makers and regulators alone. For many years, the international maritime community has responded solely to the crude influence of internal commercial pressures, whereas security was considered only during times of huge claims and insurance premiums, or as a result of wars and political conflicts. Now, however, there is a need for a more preventative and proactive approach to maritime security. Aside from the need for regulatory compliance, increased awareness of the role and impact of maritime security in international trading and supply chain systems has led market players to fully integrate the maritime security element into their strategic plans and operational procedures. Several industry players have indeed adopted and implemented a range of security programmes and initiatives that go beyond regulatory requirements, thus indicating a shift towards internalizing the costs and benefits of security. Furthermore, there already exists evidence of a positive correlation between best-compliance practices for maritime security and long-term commercial rewards.

With the above in mind, we call for a wide and flexible policy framework allowing various maritime interests to develop by selecting and implementing programmes and initiatives that best respond to their particular needs and policy objectives. However, a general warning should be given against any suggestion that consensus building and cooperation among nations working together to improve the security of international shipping and ports should now be abandoned, or that studies and research works aiming at achieving a global framework on maritime security would be considered inappropriate and their results not used and accepted. On the contrary, both the authors and editors of this book converge on the need for further collaboration between nations towards a more collective and multilateral approach following the way by which the international maritime community has traditionally been structured and regulated.

In a similar vein, we advocate that policy making in the field of maritime security should work towards a balanced approach between the security requirements from a regulated environment and the efficiency benefits from a deregulated environment. Such an approach could take the form of cooperative arrangements between private operators and public regulators in developing, financing and implementing targeted maritime security programmes and initiatives. In this context, we emphasize the efficiency and equity objectives for financing and implementing maritime security programmes and regulations. The objective of efficiency implies the absence of distortion on competition and that there is an incentive to contribute to the production of security. The objective of equity implies that the contributive capacity of the different nations be taken into consideration.

Index